DEATH ROW WOMEN

Recent Titles in
Crime, Media, and Popular Culture

Media Representations of September 11
Steven Chermak, Frankie Y. Bailey, and Michelle Brown, editors

Black Demons: The Media's Depiction of the African American Male Criminal Stereotype
Dennis Rome

Famous American Crimes and Trials, Volumes 1–5
Frankie Y. Bailey and Steven Chermak, editors

Killer Priest: The Crimes, Trial, and Execution of Father Hans Schmidt
Mark Gado

Public Executions: The Media, the Death Penalty, and American Culture
Christopher S. Kudlac

DEATH ROW WOMEN

Murder, Justice, and the New York Press

Mark Gado

Crime, Media, and Popular Culture
Frankie Y. Bailey and Steven Chermak,
Series Editors

Westport, Connecticut
London

HV6517
.G33
2008
0 156902269

Library of Congress Cataloging-in-Publication Data

Gado, Mark, 1948–
    Death row women : murder, justice, and the New York press / Mark Gado.
        p. cm. — (Crime, media, and popular culture, ISSN 1549-196X)
    Includes bibliographical references and index.
    ISBN 978-0-275-99361-0 (alk. paper)
    1. Women murderers—New York (State)—Case studies. 2. Death row inmates—New York (State)—Case studies. 3. Electrocution—New York (State)—History. 4. Women murderers—Press coverage—New York (State) 5. Sing Sing Prison. I. Title.
    HV6517.G33   2008
    364.66092'2747—dc22   2007029126

British Library Cataloguing in Publication Data is available.

Library of Congress Catalog Card Number: 2007029126
ISBN: 978-0-275-99361-0
ISSN: 1549-196X

First published in 2008

Praeger Publishers, 88 Post Road West, Westport, CT 06881
An imprint of Greenwood Publishing Group, Inc.
www.praeger.com

Printed in the United States of America

The paper used in this book complies with the
Permanent Paper Standard issued by the National
Information Standards Organization (Z39.48-1984).

10   9   8   7   6   5   4   3   2   1

"Because I could not stop for Death,
He kindly stopped for me."

from *The Chariot* by Emily Dickinson (1830–1889).

For Alanna and Ryan, the future.

Contents

Series Foreword

This volume is part of an interdisciplinary series on Crime, Media, and Popular Culture from Praeger Publishers. Because of the pervasiveness of media in our lives and the salience of crime and criminal justice issues, we feel it is especially important to provide a home for scholars who are engaged in innovative and thoughtful research on important crime and mass media issues. The books in the series touch on many broad themes in the study of crime and mass media, including process issues such as the social construction of crime and moral panics; presentation issues such as the images of victims, offenders, and criminal justice figures in the news and popular culture; and effects such as the influence of the media on criminal behavior and criminal justice administration.

As this foreword was being written, two events illustrative of the interaction of media, popular culture, and crime occurred. First, the critically acclaimed and immensely popular HBO series, *The Sopranos*, broadcast its last first-run episode. The event was covered by the media with interviews of the cast and creators of the show and with discussion of the series as a cultural phenomenon. Why were so many people so intrigued by a show about mobsters living in New Jersey? Why did so many people care if Tony Soprano and his family survived the end of the show or were wiped out in one final, devastating act of violence? The second event involved the Church of England and Sony, the manufacturer of the PlayStation video game, "Resistance: Fall of Man." BBC News reported that the Church is considering legal action against Sony because the company did not obtain permission to use the interior of the Manchester Cathedral as the scene for a violent confrontation in which hundreds of combatants in the game are killed. The Church and concerned citizens of Manchester assert that the company has been irresponsible in setting the game in a city that has been plagued by real-life gun violence and has been struggling to deal with the problem.

These two events, the end of a television crime drama about mobsters that have become a part of American culture and the response of the Church and citizens of a city to the use of a real setting in a violent fantasy game illustrate the various ways in which the media are involved in the social construction of images of crime, criminals, and the criminal justice system. In this series, scholars engage in research on issues that examine the complex nature of our relationship with media. Peter Berger and Thomas Luckman coined the phrase "the social construction of reality" to describe the process by which we acquire knowledge about our environment. They and others have argued that reality is a mediated experience. We acquire what Emile Durkheim described as "social facts" through a several-pronged process of personal experience, interaction with others, academic education, and, yes, the mass media. With regard to crime and the criminal justice system, many people acquire much of their information from the news and from entertainment media. The issues raised by *The Sopranos* phenomenon and the use of the Manchester Cathedral by Sony in a violent fantasy video game concern not only the blurring of the line between make-believe and reality but more generally the impact of what we consume—what we read, watch, see, play, and hear—on our lives.

What we do know is that we experience this mediated reality as individuals. We are not all affected in the same way by our interactions with the media. Each of us engages in interactions with mass media and popular culture that are shaped by factors such as our social environment, interests, needs, and opportunities for exposure. We do not come to the experience of mass media and popular culture as blank slates waiting to be written upon or voids waiting to be filled.

However, it is also true that the interactions of crime and mass media/popular culture that we now observe have evolved over a period of time. In fact, print media in the nineteenth century assumed its modern form at the same historical moment when criminal justice agencies were being created. With the birth of the "penny press," newspapers became inexpensive enough for the working man. The editors of these newspapers quickly realized that they could sell more papers by not only introducing regular "police beats" in their pages, but by reporting on sensational crimes. In New York City, the birth place of the penny press, two such crimes in 1836 and 1841, respectively, the murder trial of a young clerk for the murder of a stylish brothel prostitute named Helen Jewett and the mysterious death of Mary Rogers, "the beautiful cigar girl" who was found floating in the Hudson River, increased circulation.

By the end of the nineteenth century, the idea of journalistic professionalism had emerged. At the same time, the newspaper wars between the Pulitzer and Hearst newspapers had given rise to the sensational reporting that came to be called "yellow journalism." This was followed by the "jazz age" reporting of the 1920s, which focused on the kind of story that a journalist character in *Chicago*, the play by journalist Maurine Watkins, describes as one with all "the makin's: wine, woman, jazz, a lover." The presence of women reporters in the late nineteenth century covering such cases as the Lizzie Borden double-homicide trial and thereafter at many of the more sensational trials of the early twentieth century gave rise to the derisive term "sob-sister journalism." But these women were making their way into the newsroom and into the courtroom.

In this volume, Mark Gado examines the media coverage of the trials and the deaths of six women who spent their last days on death row in Sing Sing Prison. His book is an exciting addition to the series for several reasons. First, the reader is provided an intriguing look into one of America's oldest and well-known prisons. Second, although several important exceptions exist, there is very little research examining the presentation of female offenders in the news generally. Finally, although the focus here is on New York State, the issues Gado discusses concerning the depiction of female offenders by the media are not unique to this state. In fact, the issues that Gado uncovers in his analysis of the coverage of the executions of these women in the early decades of the twentieth century are still relevant today.

Frankie Y. Bailey and Steven Chermak, Series Editors

Preface

A diversified number of sources were used in the preparation of this book. They include a voluminous array of newspaper articles from the *New York Times*, the *Herald-Tribune*, *The Sun*, the *Daily News*, the *Daily Mirror*, the *New York Post*, Albany's *Times-Union*, Oneonta's *Daily Star* and Ossining's *Citizen Register*, to name a few. Though newspapers are, in general, a notoriously inaccurate medium and the author found many discrepancies in reporting, nothing so captures the atmosphere, emotions, and anxieties of an era like newspaper stories. They are written coetaneous with events, frequently within the same twenty-four hour period, and reveal—sometimes with startling clarity—the passions and prejudices of the day. Even advertisements can furnish background information on contemporary society and provide valuable insight into ordinary, everyday life. News reports, as imperfect as they may be, also serve as a type of blueprint for the researcher and furnish vital clues to other sources whose inaccuracies are less of a problem.

Official transcripts and police reports were used as sources whenever possible. For example, the police file on Mary Frances Creighton consists of over six hundred typewritten pages and became a priceless tool in the recreation of that case. When compared to newspaper reports, even just a cursory review reveals gross exaggerations and misstatements by the print media when they reported on the same event. The Creighton-Appelgate trial was one of the most lurid, sensational crimes of 1935. It became the subject of many rumors and false reporting by the New York tabloids, which were eager to outdo each other in the battle for circulation dominance. The case file describes the progress and frustrations during that murder investigation with unforgiving veracity, and was utilized prodigiously in the *Rough on Rats* chapter.

The prison files of the condemned, which include personal correspondence, legal letters, and other official documents, provide a new perspective on the final months of life for Helen Fowler and Martha Beck during their stay on the nation's most populated Death Row. Beck was a neurotic letter writer. Her file is crammed with handwritten communications to her lawyer, family, and friends. They tell her side of the story in emotional, admittedly biased tones. Though her crimes were many and media criticism relentless, her letters reveal a sensitive and hopelessly immature woman who certainly didn't start out life as a killer. Prison records such as these were utilized when available to help reconstruct the Death Row scenarios throughout the text. In addition to sworn testimony, which must carry more weight than newspaper stories, eyewitness accounts were given priority over media reporting. That is, when both sources were available for a particular event, eyewitness reports took precedence, even if it was contradictory with tabloid descriptions.

Some very important texts were consulted in order to guide the narrative through its chronological order and confirm certain details that could only have been known by people who were there. Warden Lewis Lawes' *20,000 Years at Sing Sing*[1] (published in 1932) helped to accurately portray prison life and the procedures used in the death house during the 1920s and 1930s. As one of the country's most famous penal reformers and an articulate spokesman against the death penalty, Lawes had a special understanding and compassion for the condemned. His perceptions, though influenced by his responsibilities as Sing Sing's warden and witness to one hundred and fifty executions, were invaluable for their insight, logic, and intelligence. "There is no place for sentiment either of hate or sympathy in dealing with capital punishment," Lawes wrote. "What is needed is common sense and understanding."[2]

Dr. Amos Squire's *Sing Sing Doctor*[3] (published in 1935) contains many thoughtful observations on the lives and habits of inmates as well as some compelling accounts of his time as the prison physician. Like Lawes, Squire was an opponent of the death penalty. The obvious conflict between Squire's role as a man of healing and his demanding role as execution attendant inspired a great deal of personal introspection and doubt. Both were abundantly clear in *Sing Sing Doctor.* "We cling to the principle of capital punishment as a stern ideal," he once wrote. "But through our sentimentality and our tenderness, we do all that we can do to aid murderers in their fight to escape execution."[4]

Robert Greene Elliott's stunning *Agent of Death*[5] was published in 1940. It is one of the most extraordinary books in the history of criminal justice. Elliott's story provided a glimpse into the mind and emotions of the person who executed three hundred eighty-seven men and women during his unpar-alleled career as America's premier executioner. There will probably never be another like him. But *Agent of Death* is more than just an executioner's diary. It offers a certain level of understanding and some insight into the soul of a man who could kill six people in one day—as he did on January 6, 1927—then return home to sit down at the dinner table with his family and show no signs of the dreadful work he performed only hours before. "Am I a mur-derer?" he wrote. "A great many people are convinced I am . . . but my responsibility is no greater than that of any member of society that demanded this person's life."[6] Elliott was single-minded in his purpose and convinced that he was simply a tool of the state, a paid and necessary imple-ment of death. In his unprecedented narrative, Elliott allowed himself no opportunity for doubt and sought to explain, perhaps to himself, how he was able to perform successfully in his rather unique profession.

On the other hand, *Death Row Women* offers much doubt, though that is not its intention. In any thoughtful discussion of the death penalty in America, doubt comes with the territory. That ambiguity extends to the verdict, the methods used to convict, and the irreversible punishment meted out to defen-dants who, in some cases, deserved better, despite their crimes. The facts here speak for themselves. Final judgment rests with the reader.

Acknowledgments

There are many people I'd like to thank for their help in this project. The staff of the Niagara Falls Public Library in Niagara Falls, New York, provided an assortment of material for the Helen Fowler chapter. Detective Raymond Olsen of the Records Unit of the Nassau County Police Department in New York contributed hundreds of pages of police reports from 1935 that proved to be invaluable for the Mary Frances Creighton story. The New York State Historical Association at Cooperstown, New York, and the Huntington Library in Oneonta, New York, provided a great deal of information and local historical details on the Eva Coo case. Former Chief of Police of South Nyack/Grand View and now M.B.A. Director at St. Thomas Aquinas College in New York, Alan B. Colsey, supplied editorial assistance. Roberta Arminio of the Ossining Historical Society in New York is everyone's favorite source of information on the history of Sing Sing prison. Mitchell Librett, PhD, formerly of the New Rochelle Police Department in New York, now Professor of Criminal Justice at Bridgewater State University in Massachusetts, contributed editorial suggestions and comments for some of the conclusions in the final chapter. Additional support was received from the Municipal Archives of New York City; the patient staff of the New York State Archives and the State Library in Albany, New York; the Vassar College Library in Poughkeepsie; the Main Branch of the New York City Library; and the New York City Police Department Office of Personnel. Professor Frankie Bailey of the University at Albany and Professor Steve Chermak of Michigan State University sponsored this project to Praeger Publishing and contributed editorial comments to the manuscript as well. I would also like to thank my editor at Praeger, Suzanne Staszak-Silva, for her professional advice during this long project.

And finally, I thank my wife, Jill, who provided editorial assistance, a great deal of patience, and a valued woman's perspective on the subject matter in *Death Row Women*.

Introduction:
Blonde Fiends and
Giggling Grandmas

*I have been directed to kill lawfully one hundred and fifty men and one
woman . . . but actually I have never seen an execution . . .*
—Warden Lewis Lawes of Sing Sing (1932)

"I am almost dead now. I feel at times, I am not breathing," said Anna
Antonio in 1934, as she waited for her inevitable death in the nation's most
prolific and feared electric chair. During one of her three postponements
from execution—which arrived just minutes before she was scheduled to
die—Anna, mother of three small children, collapsed to the concrete floor
unable to withstand the terrible pressures. "I've been through enough to kill
a million men," she told the prison staff. As her excruciating ordeal continued
for a period of sixteen months, every detail of her torture was faithfully
described in the New York tabloids. In a sense, the public became unwilling
but helpless onlookers to her death. Day by day, hour by hour, readers "witnessed" the deterioration of this pathetic figure who begged for life and spiritual salvation, right up until the moment she was placed in the electric chair.
"He has three children himself," Anna said of Governor Herbert Lehman.
"He won't do this to me! God won't let him do it!"

In some ways, Mrs. Antonio's march to death resembled that of Karla Faye
Tucker in Texas in 1998, when an outpouring of public sympathy threatened
to stop her execution. Tucker was convicted of a vicious double murder while
she was under the influence of drugs. Like Antonio, Tucker had a great deal
of support from a variety of sources, including several religious organizations,

who claimed her life was one worth saving because she had expressed remorse and converted to Christianity. But Tucker and Antonio (who was a Catholic) were unsuccessful in their campaigns for mercy. The political consequences for a governor who halted an execution could be enormous, especially in a pro-capital punishment environment, as New York was during the era covered in this book. Historically, commutations of sentences were rarely given and the evidence to support that decision had to be well-publicized in order to minimize the political fallout.

The death penalty and the execution process utilized during the first half of the twentieth century in America are so unlike the ones in use today, that it sometimes seems as if those events took place on another planet rather than in another era. The electric chair was invented in 1890. It was the brainchild of an eccentric New York dentist named Dr. Alfred Southwick. With the adoption of the electric chair capital punishment entered the Industrial Age. There were lofty expectations and unrestrained excitement, even though the first electrocution was a public relations nightmare. "Far Worse Than Hanging," said a *New York Times* headline on August 7, 1890. The story, which encompassed eight page-length columns of print, went on to say that the electric chair was "a sacrifice to the whims and theories of the coterie of cranks and politicians . . . a discredit to the State of New York and a disgrace to civilization." But hanging, which had been the accepted method of execution for centuries in America, was seen as even more barbaric and very difficult to control. Most authorities wanted to abolish hanging but were unsure what method to use in its place. Once an expeditious method could be found for executions, juries, and the society from which they sprung, could be confident they were compassionate people when they sentenced someone to death.

Death Row Women describes the crimes and trials of the six women who were executed at Sing Sing prison during the twentieth century. It also details the press coverage of each case, how it differed from the others and what effect, if any, that coverage had on their prosecution. Only female executions at Sing Sing were chosen for this book because it was once the most notorious penal institution in the country and, for generations, the standard by which all other prisons were judged. Its reputation reached beyond America's shores, to Europe, Asia, and across the world. During the period 1900–1963, Sing Sing executed more inmates than any other facility in the United States and still holds claim to that somewhat dubious achievement. And up until 1972, when the Supreme Court decided that the death penalty was unconstitutional in *Furman v. Georgia,* New York had already executed more prisoners than any other state in America and, as such, was the undisputed leader of capital punishment in the Western world.

During one twelve-month period in the 1930s, twenty-one men died in Sing Sing's electric chair, an average of one prisoner every eighteen days. If someone committed murder in New York, he or she was more likely to receive a death sentence than anywhere else in America, including Texas or Georgia. And yet, it has never been conclusively proven, and there is no credible research anywhere, that the death penalty is—or ever was—an effective deterrent to criminal behavior. If that were true, then it would stand to reason that the crime rate during the 1920s and 1930s, when executions were at their most frequent, should be low as opposed to the crime rate after 1972 when the death penalty was temporarily abolished. Of course, it was not.

Despite what proponents on both sides of the issue claim, the frequency of crime and the implementation of the death penalty are probably unrelated to each other, and always have been. As every researcher knows, data can be manipulated to support different conclusions with little effort. To use the concept of deterrence as a justification for the use of capital punishment, without a firm factual basis, is both illogical and deceptive.

In today's world, it is not uncommon for an inmate to linger on death row for more than ten years waiting for his execution. One study discovered that, since 1972, the average stay on death row for a typical male prisoner is ten years and one month. And as of 2007, there are some female prisoners who have been on death row for more than twenty years. Whether a punishment administered so many years after a crime can act as a deterrent for others is a question that can have no definitive answer. This book is not a condemnation of the death penalty, nor is it a defense of the nation's troubled use of capital punishment. The author strives for a sense of balance between those opposing viewpoints.

Death Row Women is not simply a litany of facts and names. Nor does it seek to break new academic ground in the cyclical debate on capital punishment. Rather, it is a somewhat unusual journey through another time and place whose boundaries are marked by much more than the decades that have transpired since then. *Death Row Women* describes an age when the electric chair was a very real threat to criminals and some trials evolved into extended soap operas in which defendants were perceived as doomed players in a modern-day Greek tragedy. Tabloid reporters wrote on every minutiae of a death process, which was supervised by prison wardens who behaved as if they were autonomous kings in their own private realm. Like celebrities, the condemned were quoted from inside their cells, during their walk to the death chamber, and sometimes at the moment they sat in the electric chair. Executioners were peculiar figures, sinister men to be feared and despised. "I think you are the worst specimen of a man," said one letter to Sing Sing's executioner, "you are not fit to live with human beings." Their homes were sometimes bombed and their photographs were highly sought after by the press who displayed an ongoing obsession with their lives and habits.

As the reader will discover, the emphasis on criminal prosecutions during this era was speed. Justice—at least the way it was defined then—often became secondary to that end. Penologists felt that in order for the death penalty to be effective as a deterrent to crime, it had to be quick and final. Deterrence was a concept that was embedded in the criminal justice system as one of its fundamental building blocks; it was embraced by judges, district attorneys, police, and the prison system. However, in some instances, vengeance and retribution were surely hidden under the cloak of deterrence. The swiftness of the criminal justice system was truly remarkable, for it was not unusual for death penalty trials to begin and end the same day. That one-day period would sometimes include jury selection and verdict as well. Reformers were convinced that speedy justice was a necessary ingredient of the deterrence formula and should be the goal of the nation's courts. One of the most famous examples of this method was the prosecution of would-be assassin Giuseppe Zangara in 1933.

Zangara was a thirty-one-year-old Italian bricklayer who harbored an irrational grudge against President Franklin D. Roosevelt. In Miami, on February 15, 1933, he fired a handgun at the President and Chicago Mayor Anton J. Cermak. The shots missed Roosevelt but struck Cermak, seriously wounding him. Zangara was arrested at the scene and had to be quickly removed from the street where an angry mob threatened to lynch the would-be assassin. Mayor Cermak survived for a few days but died on March 6. *Just fifteen days later*, on March 21, 1933, Zangara was already indicted, tried, convicted for murder, and executed in Florida's electric chair.

Though *Death Row Women* profiles six death penalty cases, seven females were put to death at Sing Sing during the period 1900–2000. Ethel Rosenberg, though executed at that facility with her husband in 1953, was prosecuted and sentenced under Federal authority and not as a prisoner of the State of New York. Rosenberg, unlike the six defendants profiled in this book, was convicted of espionage, not murder. The circumstances of her crimes and prosecution were unique; her case does not fit into the same category as the others. Ethel Rosenberg, along with Mary Surratt, an alleged conspirator in President Lincoln's assassination in 1865, and Bonnie Brown Heady, Chicago's most famous female child killer in 1953, are the only three women in American history to receive a death sentence under federal authority.

Female executions in America have always been controversial and the abundant historical data on the subject supports that notion. Of the approximately eight thousand executions that took place in the United States during the twentieth century, forty-seven have been of females, a number which represents only 0.6 percent of the total. Sixteen states have never executed a female and in the entire American Northwest (also including Alaska and Hawaii)—a region that comprises more than a quarter of our country—not one single female has ever been executed. The disparity becomes even more dramatic in Texas where four hundred and forty-one executions were carried out between 1930 and 1977, but not one was of a female. Ohio Northern University Law Professor Victor Streib, one of the nation's foremost experts on the history of the death penalty, attributes that reluctance to a gender bias in death sentences that benefits female defendants. Supreme Court Justice Thurgood Marshall once said, "It is difficult to understand why women have received such favored treatment since the purposes allegedly served by capital punishment seemingly are applied to both sexes."[1]

America harbors a strong cultural objection to female executions which extends back to Colonial times. That may help explain why press coverage of female killers, and especially those who are sentenced to death, can be extremely intense and analytical to a fault. It may be that society has to see these women as evil, beyond redemption, and unworthy of compassion. On occasion, that pattern can be broken, as it was during the Karla Fay Tucker case in 1998 when the nation's press rallied in a futile attempt to prevent her execution in Texas. Similar confusion can be found in the press coverage of Anna Antonio's heartbreaking path to the execution chamber in 1934. Compassion for Antonio was abundant, but public sympathy was always intermingled with the caveat that justice had to be served.

In the overwhelming majority of cases, media coverage has been consistently negative, thoroughly hostile and, at times, hateful toward women accused of murder. Barbara Graham, convicted in California of murder in 1953, was called "a rattlesnake" and part of an "unholy trio" by the Los Angeles tabloids. Outlaw Irene Schroeder, executed in Pennsylvania in 1931, was most often referred to as the "animal woman" after she survived several bloody gun battles with police. Aileen Wournos, convicted of murder and executed in Florida in 2002, was vilified by the press in a way few male killers experience. Interestingly, Wournos was frequently described as the nation's first female serial killer. In fact, there have been dozens of female serial murderers before Wournos. As recently as 1984, North Carolina executed Velma Barfield who murdered at least five people. In her book on female killers, *When She Was Bad*, Patricia Pearson writes, "about 17 per cent of known American serial killers are women and at least twenty-five of them have been arrested and convicted since 1972."[2] That should have been a simple fact for the Florida press to research and verify and just one example of the many inaccuracies to be found in the media's coverage of female prosecutions.[3]

Like their male counterparts, condemned female killers are frequently given derogatory labels, not only to promote reader interest, but perhaps to reinforce preconceived beliefs held by reporters and editors as well. "Tiger Woman," "Sugar Woman," "Black-Eyed Borgia," "Granite Woman," "Blonde Fiend," "Giggling Grandma" and "Vampire," are examples of this trend, a trend that apparently began when Martha Place, the first woman to die in the electric chair, was convicted of the murder of her stepdaughter in 1898. In a lengthy article published on July 9, 1898, the *New York Times* described her as having "a pale, sharp face. Her nose is long and pointed, her chin sharp and prominent, her lips thin and her forehead retreating. There is something about her face that reminds one of a rat's." Follow-up articles in the same newspaper, published on July 13, 1898, and March 16 and 20, 1899, displayed similar antagonism toward the defendant.

Women are frequently ridiculed for their behavior in media stories while their physical appearance is almost always scrutinized by reporters. A review of the newspaper clippings on the six women profiled in this book also shows an amazing compulsion to report on the style of their dress. In all cases, the press included a description of the clothes the defendant wore to the execution. As Helen Benedict points out in her study of how the media covers sex crimes, *Virgin or Vamp,* that a condescending attitude extends to women when they are victims as well. Benedict found that the most likely characterization of a female in the press is that of a sex object, even if she had done nothing except become the victim of a crime. "Obviously, women fare badly at the hands of the press," Benedict writes. "Pushed into subordinate roles of sex objects, wives, mothers, or crime victims . . . not only are the conventional images of women so limited, but our very language promotes those images."[4]

Though Benedict studied the treatment of women as victims by the press, her observations seem equally valid when women are charged with crimes. Martha Beck, the female half of the "Lonely Hearts Killers," convicted of murder in 1949 in Bronx Criminal Court, was usually characterized as "a fat mistress," "plump," "obese," and worse. Beck was ridiculed on the subject of her weight right up until she was executed on March 8, 1951. It is important to note that these negative perceptions appeared in hard news stories, not opinion columns or editorials. It is a pattern that became a type of journalistic pandemic that has transcended generations; its origins seem entrenched in the early circulation wars between the powerful New York City tabloids. And nowhere was that tendency revealed so blatantly—and with such passion—as it was when a young, sexy housewife by the name of Ruth Snyder was arrested for murdering her husband in New York City in 1927.

A Morality Play:
Ruth Snyder and Judd Gray

This woman, this peculiar venomous species of humanity was abnormal;
possessed of an all-consuming, all-absorbing sexual passion, animal lust,
which seemingly was never satisfied!
> —Attorney William J. Millard describing the defendant,
> Ruth Snyder, during his closing statement, May 9, 1927.

The story of Ruth Brown-Snyder and her corset-salesman lover, who killed
her husband for money in 1927, is one of the landmark murder cases of
the twentieth century. Like other trials which took on symbolic issues that
transcended crime, her prosecution became epic theater which contained
powerful, yet unspoken themes that reflected the cultural, social, and sexual
mores of the era. Her case generated the sort of newspaper headlines that
were usually reserved for only the most catastrophic of events, such as an
earthquake or a war. A virtual army of reporters attended her trial each day
and recorded every excruciating detail of the drama that held New York City
spellbound during the spring of 1927. Even the *New York Times*, not known
for its crime coverage, frequently reported the case on its front page and
published a verbatim transcript of court testimony for readers, who followed the
trial much like movie fans would follow their favorite serials in later generations.
"Newspapers were the main source for information, and somewhat for entertainment before television . . . the present day equivalent of television soap
operas ran in many newspapers . . . and some news stories fitted the serial
presentation, especially a crime that was sensational enough to merit almost day-
to-day coverage."[1] Such an event was the Snyder-Gray murder case.

Thousands of people packed into and around the Queens County courtroom where Snyder and her codefendant Henry Judd Gray stood trial for the killing of her clueless husband, Albert Snyder. In the streets near the courthouse, dozens of vendors sold souvenirs and memorabilia, while radio hosts described in breathless tones the carnival-like atmosphere; it seemed as if the very fate of American womanhood depended on the outcome of the trial. Ruth Snyder became a genuine celebrity and, in some ways, coverage of her trial even surpassed the media hysteria over O. J. Simpson in 1994. But unlike Simpson, who had a certain appeal to some of the nation's media, Snyder evoked only deep resentment from the press. The saga ended abruptly on January 12, 1928 when Ruth was executed in Sing Sing's electric chair, a moment that was immortalized in one of the most notorious photographs in the history of journalism.

Ruth Brown was of Swedish-Norwegian descent. She had an unblemished complexion and facial features that were balanced and nicely defined. She also had striking blue eyes that contributed to her sometimes sensual appearance. "Each man admitted that his appraisal of her was governed by the impact of her sex appeal . . . she unquestionably possessed a full measure . . . a shapely body . . . her best features seem to have been her eyes . . . they held the deep intensity of blue ice."[2] Her accomplice in murder, Henry Judd Gray, later told police that Ruth was "a woman of great charm. I probably don't have to tell you that, and I did like her very much and she was good company and apparently a good pal to spend an evening with."[3] Ruth was born in upper Manhattan on W. 125th Street, the daughter of a carpenter. She was raised in modest circumstances and attended a local public school. After working as a secretary, telephone operator, and salesgirl, she landed a job as a stenographer with *Cosmopolitan* magazine in 1914. A few months later, as a result of a misdialed phone number, she reached the art editor of *Motor Boating* magazine.[4] His name was Albert Snyder.

They spoke on the phone daily for a week until they finally agreed to meet. When they met, the impressionable Ruth may have seen her opportunity to escape from the drudgery of the "working girl's life," a role to which she never aspired. Albert was a successful businessman with a fine future. He was making $5,000 a year, a princely sum in 1914. Tanned, trim, and at ease around the upscale yachting community in Long Island, Albert represented everything that Ruth wanted in life. But at first, she was not totally happy with his demeanor. "He took me out dining and dancing," she said later, "then got real angry when I wouldn't come across and get into the sack with him."[5] But they continued dating until Albert decided to wed her, despite his previous relationship with a woman named Jessie Geshard. That romance ended when Jessie died suddenly from pneumonia. Though Ruth knew about the relationship, Albert did not tell her that he was grief-stricken over her loss and still in love with his dead fiancée.

In late 1914, Ruth and Albert married. They settled into a comfortable multilevel home in Queens where Ruth became a housewife and Albert commuted to his editing job in Manhattan. Within the first few months of their marriage, trouble began. "I was apparently too giddy for his years," she said, "while he was only thirty-three at the time, he was like a man of fifty to me."[6] Another source of trouble was Albert's boat which he had named the *Jessie G* after his deceased lover. The name was still on the vessel when he married Ruth. Though Albert changed it, it took a lot of convincing on her part to get it done. However, Albert insisted that a photo of Jessie, which hung on the wall of their family room, stay where it was. He once told his friends that she was the finest woman he ever met. Ruth was just nineteen at the time of her marriage and because Albert was twelve years older, he was more mature and serious-minded. He did not share her fun-loving personality or her yearnings for the Manhattan night life. Much to his disapproval, Ruth loved to dance, stay out late, and have a good time. But it wasn't only Ruth who was feeling a new sense of independence and empowerment. American women were changing as the results of a slow, yet powerful cultural revolution that began shortly after World War I.

The decade beginning in 1920 was a time in which prosperity seemed to be everywhere and opportunities were limitless. "We in America today are nearer to the final triumph over poverty than ever before in the history of our land," said President Herbert Hoover. "The poor-house is vanishing from among us."[7] When World War I ended, there was a general sense that America was destined to do better, that the quality of life had to improve, and the future would be brighter, especially for the younger generation. By the early 1920s, a spirit of boundless optimism, fueled by technological advancements, swept over the country.

For the first time, motion pictures became an integral part of American culture and those who worked in film became known as "movie stars." They were worshiped by an adoring public who saw actors as larger than life, as almost mythic figures who were as close to true royalty as any American could ever hope to be. An Italian national, a former street beggar and ex-con named Rodolfo Guglielmi, better known as Rudolph Valentino, was one of the most popular and sought-after actors in the world. His exotic appearances in films such as *The Sheik* (1920) and *The Four Horsemen of the Apocalypse* (1921) caused legions of women to swoon and faint in the aisles. "Within a couple of years, he was a national phenomenon, a male star of unprecedented sensual appeal to women."[8]

Music also underwent a dramatic and historic change when jazz finally emerged from the cramped saloons of Bourbon Street in New Orleans and exploded across the national landscape, thanks to the magic of radio. Born in that city's French Quarter and exported to Chicago's south side and Harlem nightclubs in New York, jazz's liberating, free-flowing style, led by musicians like King Oliver and the soaring horn of Louis Armstrong, had teenagers dancing in the streets. Jazz became the perfect compliment to a frantic age. Young people quickly embraced this new music and reveled in the anger and disgust that the older generation displayed towards the sound. No aspect of American life so defined the 1920s era as did jazz music.

In 1920, a local radio station in Pittsburgh broadcast the returns of the Warren G. Harding presidential election. Soon, the same station began to broadcast weather, news and sports. Within a few years, hundreds of radio stations appeared in communities across the nation, broadcasting everything from comedy shows to political discussions and serial dramas. The invention and widespread acceptance of radio transformed America from a disconnected, fragmented society into an electric village where, for the first time in history, information could be disseminated to the masses instantaneously. In very real ways, radio reduced America to smaller dimensions and it involved people in national issues and events as never before.[9] Radio educated the public, occupied their free time, and made the audience eyewitness to current events as if they were there themselves.[10] Radio also brought the suspense and drama of the era's most famous criminal trials into the nation's living rooms for the first time.

The ongoing saga of the Bartolomeo Sacco and Nicola Vanzetti murder case, which began with a robbery in Braintree, Massachusetts in April 1920, received unprecedented media coverage and split the nation into various political camps. Though the subject of anarchy was never a part of their trial, the anarchist movement in the United States, promoted by the charismatic Emma Goldman, became the focal point of the case in the years that followed.[11] Debates over the guilt or innocence of Sacco and Vanzetti helped keep the case alive in the pubic mind for six years. The defendants were supported by many celebrities such as H. G. Wells, Felix Frankfurter, Dorothy Parker, and Albert Einstein. Even the Vatican appealed for mercy in their case. Despite worldwide controversy, and persistent doubts about their guilt, Sacco and Vanzetti were executed in Massachusetts on August 22, 1927.

In May 1924, college students Nathan Leopold and Richard Loeb murdered fourteen-year-old Bobby Franks simply for the sake of committing what they imagined to be the perfect crime. It became one of the most infamous bizarre murders of the age and underscored controversial themes of privilege and class in American society. Their crime amplified fears of a younger generation that seemed out of control. "The Leopold and Loeb case forever altered perceptions of youth . . . young people were becoming uncontrollable, a result of the new parenting culture that allowed too much freedom."[12] This growing sense that the younger generation, and especially women, was vastly different from the previous generation was a common theme of the era.

In the midst of the cultural changes that were taking place during the 1920s, women occupied center stage, both figuratively and in reality. Fashions began to evolve dramatically during the early part of the decade. Gone were the Victorian dresses and elaborate hairstyles of the nineteenth century. They were replaced by knee-length skirts and short hair, rolled stockings and men's pants, all of which were considered shocking and rebellious. It was a trend that began, at least symbolically, in 1920 when the Nineteenth Amendment was passed. For the first time in American history, women were guaranteed the constitutional right to vote. Emboldened by newly discovered freedoms, women began to feel a sense of independence which they had never experienced before. They smoked cigarettes, drank illegal booze, and wore bathing suits that exposed their knees and shoulders at the nation's beaches. The modern woman was called a "flapper." Her idols were film stars like Clara Bow, Greta Garbo, and the mysterious Pola Negri.[13] She read F. Scott Fitzgerald and Sinclair Lewis whose novels lambasted the provincial middle class with unbridled fervor and exposed—at least to some—the hypocrisy of class structure in America.

The ascent of the modern woman did not come without a price. Her independence represented a threat to the traditional image held by many men of what a woman, and especially a wife, should be. The sexually dominant male had a vital stake in the continued subjugation of women. Rejection of that role, symbolized by the Jazz Age flapper, directly threatened the established order so cherished by the average man. That may help explain why the Ruth Snyder case took on a hidden meaning and why the sexual mores of the era became the underlying theme of her prosecution. "Conflict over modernity came into sharp focus in the Snyder case, particularly as Ruth came to represent for many, the dire outcome of modernization . . . people perceived an enormous rise in crime . . . and saw Ruth as symptomatic of a modern society out of control."[14] According to the tabloids, she was "a bad woman, a bad wife, a bad mother, and at the same time an utterly cold, inhuman vampire completely unlike those good, warm, self-sacrificing wives and mothers who represented the best of American womanhood."[15] The subtle message was written between thousands of lines of newsprint and made abundantly clear by the endless stream of hatred exhibited toward Ruth Snyder that appeared in many editions of the city's tabloids.

The New York City tabloids were unlike the more traditional newspapers such as the *Times* or the *Herald-Tribune*. Those publications reported the news in a more sedate and conservative style, a style which editors insisted had to be accurate and straightforward. Traditional newspapers subscribed to an ethos that had been carried over from the previous century when a certain segment of the press believed that news should be reported truthfully. Tabloids, however, saw truth as a concept that could be manipulated for the sake of entertainment and profit. In 1924, one tabloid editor explained his philosophy of news reporting for readers. "We intend to interest you mightily. We intend to dramatize and sensationalize the news and some stories that are not news."[16]

In all probability, Ruth should not have married so young, but the promise of security in an anxious age may have been too much for her to resist. "I was only a child at the time," she said later. "I didn't know my own mind then. He [Albert] was good to me and I fell for it."[17] But it didn't take long for Ruth to become bored with married life and disillusioned with her role as the dutiful, obedient housewife. She cut her hair in the contemporary style, took up playing cards, and learned how to do the Charleston, the frenzied dance step that swept over the nation during the years after the First World War. Despite her growing unrest, Ruth eventually had a daughter, Lorraine, an event which upset Albert because he had wanted a boy. But even motherhood didn't slow Ruth down. She frequently disappeared from their Queens Village home to take the subway over to Manhattan where she drank bootleg gin with friends and partied all night. She had a succession of boyfriends while Lorraine was still an infant. But, according to Ruth, Albert never suspected the truth. "He did not know," she said later. "He thought I was with my girlfriend."[18] Though it seems unlikely that he never suspected his wife's infidelity, Albert appeared content that he had his own life and Ruth had hers. He was condescending toward her and tolerated her desire to be with friends. However, no evidence was ever presented that Albert had a girlfriend of his own.

In June 1925, Albert planned a summer vacation on Shelter Island with business associates. At the same time, Ruth decided to go shopping in Manhattan with a neighbor, Karen Kaufmann. When it came time for lunch, they dined at Henry's, a popular Swedish restaurant in midtown. There, through a mutual friend, Ruth met thirty-two-year-old Henry Judd Gray. Gray was a slightly built young man with dark hair who wore thick glasses. He also had a square chin, good looks, and a friendly, courteous manner in conversation. He was a corset salesman who traveled a great deal in his job. But he never called the articles he sold "corsets." He always referred to them as "intimate garments." Gray was born in Westchester County, the son of a businessman who made a sizable fortune selling jewelry. As a young boy, he was groomed to enter the business world when the time was right. Gray was an obedient and mindful child who usually conformed to family wishes and had a somewhat "prudish" nature.[19] "I went to Sunday school and church every Sunday," he once wrote. "I was desperately apprehensive of being thought of as a 'momma's boy' . . . I wanted my friends to think well of me."[20] As they spoke that day in Henry's restaurant, Ruth and Judd discovered they shared a certain unhappiness with their respective mates. He had been married for nearly ten years but was dissatisfied at home and yearned for something more. For several hours that day, Ruth and Judd conversed over drinks, revealing intimate secrets to each other and eager to share more. When their lunch had ended, they both realized that something special had happened in their lives.

Over the next few weeks, Ruth and Judd frequently met for lunch in Manhattan. Their first sexual union took place during August inside Gray's office at Thirty-Fourth Street and Fifth Avenue. His pet name for Ruth, repeated over and over again in later court testimony and the target of much ridicule, was "Momsie." In the months that followed, the new lovers romped in Manhattan hotel rooms where they overcame their repressed sexual desires and formed the emotional bonds that would lead them to disaster. "We went to the Imperial a few times; we did not like that so then we went to the Waldorf-Astoria," Ruth later said in her confession.[21] On several occasions, Ruth was forced to take her daughter along. The little girl would wait in the lobby of the Waldorf hotel for hours while Ruth romped in bed a few floors above with Judd, oblivious to time and the needs of her nine-year-old daughter. "I had sexual intercourse with him on a number of occasions," Ruth later told the court. "We got a room as Mr. and Mrs. Henry Judd Gray."[22] This fact, later revealed at her trial, denigrated Ruth as a mother and made her seem worthy of the most severe punishment. Women especially, saw this conduct as an abandonment of her maternal responsibilities and, in some ways, worse than the murder itself.

The afternoon rendezvous continued uninterrupted for nearly two years. Ruth and Judd seemed to have an insatiable desire for each other. Their trysts included visits to her home while Albert was at work. For perhaps the first time in his life, Gray experienced sexual fulfillment with a desirable woman and the feeling was intoxicating. Later, Gray's attorney described how helpless his client felt in the relationship. Ruth was a "poisonous snake . . . a serpent . . . who was abnormal, possessed of an all-consuming, all-absorbing sexual passion, animal lust, which seemingly was never satisfied." Judd Gray was "enslaved . . . like a human manikin, like a human dummy. Whatever she wanted, he did."[23] This image of Gray, as a defenseless victim in the grip of an oversexed and dangerous female, was one that was often repeated, and soon became the recurrent theme in media coverage of the case.[24]

Though neither Ruth nor Judd could remember who brought up the subject first, their conversations eventually drifted toward getting rid of Albert to pave the way for their own marriage. Talk of Gray's wife never approached that threshold, though Judd told Ruth many times that he was unhappy with her as well. From the very beginning of their relationship, Ruth was the dominant personality in their relationship. This view was emphasized through later court testimony and her own confession in which she highlighted plans to kill Albert. "We discussed various ways to get rid of my husband," she said. "We had talked about chloroform but Mr. Gray said he didn't know if that would be sufficient enough alone."[25] Ruth complained that Albert never took her out and frequently mistreated her. "Ruth regaled Judd with stories of her husband's brutal treatment of herself and the child. These stories may have been complete fabrications, at best they were exaggerations, but Judd believed in them implicitly. Once he exploded, 'I'd like to kill the beast!'"[26] After weeks—then months—of Ruth's stories of maltreatment at the hands of a man who did not love her, Judd grew to hate Albert although the two men had never met. In truth, Judd's entire impression of Albert was based on information that was supplied by Ruth.

Ruth's dissatisfaction with Albert was too much for her to bear, even if she could carry on with Judd without her husband's knowledge. Ruth tried on several occasions to get rid of Albert on her own. She put poison in his food but it only made him sick. She unhooked a gas line in the kitchen and filled the house with gas while Albert was sleeping. When Ruth later returned, expecting to find him dead, Albert was pacing up and down on the front lawn complaining of a severe headache. She tried carbon monoxide poison as well. Nothing seemed to work. As for Albert, he never suspected that his wife was trying to kill him. He remarked to friends and neighbors that he had a series of unfortunate "accidents." After several attempts to kill Albert failed, Ruth complained bitterly to Judd that her husband just wouldn't die.

For over a year, Ruth tried to kill Albert and failed each time. She then tried to convince Judd to help her. At first, he refused. But slowly, over time, he became accustomed to the idea that Albert had to go. When Ruth told Judd that Albert, in a middle of one of their arguments, threatened to kill her, it was the final straw. "Things became unbearable," she said in her confession. "I was looking for a way out and in talking with Mr. Gray . . . we discussed various ways of getting rid of my husband."[27] Judd decided to help her. His enthusiasm seemed to have increased when Ruth told him that she had taken additional insurance on Albert's life. If he died, she said, she would receive at least $90,000, an enormous sum in 1927 and certainly enough for the two lovers to begin a new life together.

In their discussions on how to kill Albert, Ruth and Judd studied several methods. They originally thought they should use chloroform to render him unconscious and then bludgeon him to death. The plan was to make it look like a burglary. But Judd was afraid he would not be able to control Albert while he smothered him with the drug. Albert was in fine physical shape, stronger and bigger than Judd. Ruth agreed it would be very difficult to overcome him. It became obvious that the only sure way was to render him unconscious by striking him over the head suddenly with a hammer, a bat, or an iron pipe. On March 7, after a day of heavy drinking, they agreed to try to kill Albert that evening inside his home. Judd drank nearly two bottles of whiskey before he was able to get up enough courage to perform the act. "I was quite intoxicated," he later told police. "I walked and walked and I walked fully two hours . . . there was no light in the cellar, no light upstairs, then I heard a knock on the kitchen window and I saw Mrs. Snyder motion for me to come in."[28] Judd met Ruth in the downstairs parlor where he drank some more whiskey. But he was unable to complete the plan. He and Ruth cried, holding each other, until they finally decided not to go through with the plan that night. Judd, feeling a sense of humiliation and failure, took a bus back to Manhattan.

Soon, they settled on another date for the murder: Saturday, March 19. On that day, Ruth and Albert, along with their daughter, Lorraine, were scheduled to attend a party at a friend's house on Hollis Court Boulevard, a few minutes drive from their home. They would be playing cards and drinking as well. Since they would be out of the house all evening, there was plenty of time for Judd to sneak into their home and hide in a closet until they returned from the party. During that same week, Judd visited a hardware store and bought a large window sash weight, a heavy, metallic object shaped like a pine cone that was used as a counterweight to open windows. He also bought a bottle of chloroform and later gave both these items to Ruth who hid them inside her bedroom where she and Albert slept each night.

On Saturday, Ruth, Albert, and Lorraine went to the friend's house as planned. But before she left home, Ruth secretly unlocked the cellar and kitchen doors. While they were at the party, Judd came into Ruth's home and hid in the upstairs spare bedroom where Ruth had left a bottle of whiskey for him. During the party, Ruth herself was careful not to drink too much. They left the party at 1:45 a.m. and headed back to their home on 222nd Street. When they arrived, Albert walked into the house and went directly to bed. Ruth put Lorraine to sleep and then walked through the hallway to her bedroom. As she passed the closet, she called out softly.

"Are you there, dear?" she said.

"Yes!" Gray replied.

"Wait! I'll be back shortly!"

Ruth then entered the bedroom, changed into a negligee and slipped into bed with Albert, who was already dozing. She lay quietly until she was sure he was sound asleep. Then she arose from the bed and joined Judd in the spare bedroom down the hall. Together, they drank the remaining whiskey and tried to encourage each other to follow through on their plans. Ruth handed Judd the sash weight and the bottle of chloroform which she had hidden earlier. She led the intoxicated Judd down the hallway into the bedroom where Albert lay under the blankets.

Judd was terrified. He had never even struck a man before that day and the idea of murder was abhorrent to him. "I have always been a gentleman and I have always been absolutely on the level with everybody," he later told the police.[29] As he stood over Albert, who was sound asleep, Judd hesitated for a moment. Then, while Ruth stood next to him, Judd brought down the sash weight with all his strength directly on Albert's head.

"He started to fight me," Judd later said in his statement to the police. "She got very much excited. He got me by the necktie and I think—I am positive—that she started to belabor him with this sash weight after that. She had the bottle of chloroform and handkerchief, which she poured on the bed." But they had underestimated Albert's ability to resist. He put up a strong fight. So much so that Judd couldn't handle him.

"Help, Momsie!" he pleaded to Ruth. "For God's sake help me!" Later testimony from both Judd and Ruth were in dispute as to what exactly took place during the assault. Ruth later told the court that she "could see Mr. Gray raise his arm, holding what I believed to be the weight in his hand, and in the darkness . . . I saw this weight in Mr. Gray's hand start to travel and immediately heard a thud, and my husband groaned twice." Gray contended that Ruth helped him kill Albert, a point which she later denied. But both agreed that while Albert lay mortally wounded in bed, Ruth and Judd tied his hands behind his back. Ruth took a handkerchief, laden with the chloroform, and pressed it against Albert's nose and mouth. They also wrapped picture frame wire around his neck as a garrote and tried to strangle him. "I am pretty sure," Gray later said, "that it must have been tied by her. I don't know whether it was around his neck or not, this I don't recall. I went right back to the bathroom."[30] Judd later said that he was so drunk, he wasn't sure what he did or when. "My movements that particular night are rather indefinite in my own mind," he testified. "She asked me if he was dead and I said I didn't think so. I started to mess up the room and she asked me to put some wire around his neck . . . I did try to help her but I was so shaky and intoxicated that I couldn't."[31] Albert soon lost consciousness and sometime over the next few hours, he died in bed.

Judd, feeling the effect of the whiskey he had consumed throughout the night, was befuddled, according to his confession. He found himself covered in blood and unsure what to do next, though he had the presence of mind to know that evidence of the crime had to be destroyed. Ruth's negligee was dripping with her husband's blood. Ruth took Judd into the basement where they removed their clothes and threw the articles into the furnace. Then Ruth went back into the bedroom where she put on a nightgown. She retrieved one of Albert's blue shirts from the dresser drawer and gave it to Judd who quickly put it on. The shirt later "proved to be the most damning piece of evidence against him."[32] According to their plan, the killing had to look like a burglary. Judd checked the rope on Albert's wrists and made sure it was secure. He then emptied the contents of the dresser onto the floor to appear as if a burglar had searched for valuables. They scattered other items across the room. Ruth took her jewelry, which was stored in a box on top of her dresser, placed it in a bag and then shoved it in between the mattress and the box spring.

Judd then tied up Ruth. "I bound up her ankles with some rope she brought up from the cellar," he said later, "and tied her hands behind her back loosely. I put some cheesecloth over her mouth . . . covered her up with her fur coat . . . I took two drinks from a bottle."[33] Ruth lay down on the floor in her bedroom. "It may be two months," he told her, "it may be a year, and it may be never before you'll see me again!"[34] They kissed each other with promises to reunite soon. Judd then put on his coat, left the house through a side door and walked over to a nearby bus stop. Still in a daze, he noticed a policeman walking a beat. Judd asked the cop when the next bus was due to stop, but the officer replied that he didn't know. He later boarded a subway for Grand Central station where he waited for the 8:45 a.m. train to Syracuse.

In the meantime, back at the Snyder residence, little Lorraine woke up after hearing a persistent tapping on the wall in her bedroom. It was 7:30 a.m. Since she had been out the night before at the party with her mother and father and didn't get to sleep until past 2:00 a.m., Lorraine was still groggy from getting to bed late. But she was able to hear a weak voice repeating, "Lorraine! Lorraine!" She soon recognized it as her mother's voice. The girl arose from the bed, opened the door and walked toward her parent's bedroom. The door was ajar. When she pushed it open, she saw her mother laying on the floor, her hands and legs tied with rope.

"Mommie!" she cried. "What happened?" Ruth had Lorraine untie her and go to a neighbor's house where they called the police. Soon the Snyder home was filled with uniformed officers, crime scene investigators, and detectives. By one count, over sixty police personnel were crammed into the Queens Village home. Even New York City Police Commissioner George V. McLaughlin responded. Inspector Arthur Carey, Chief of the Queens Homicide Squad, arrived on the heels of the commissioner. He was put in charge and, within minutes, Carey suspected something was amiss. The disarray in the bedroom was unlike any burglary the police had ever seen. Albert's loaded revolver was found under his pillow and when Ruth was asked why she didn't try to use it against the burglars, she had no answer. When police looked under the mattress, they found all of Ruth's jewelry which she placed there the night before. A handwritten phone book, which contained the name H. Judd Gray, was found hidden in a dresser drawer in the parlor. Ruth admitted the book was hers. When confronted with numerous questions about the name of Gray and the suspicious crime scene, she began to unravel.

"Do you know this Judd Gray?" asked Inspector Carey.

"No," she replied. "I never heard of him." It was an odd response from someone who had written the name in her phonebook. Ruth told police that when she returned from the party the night before, Albert went directly to bed. A few minutes later, she said, she joined him. She was awakened a short time later by footsteps. Thinking it was her daughter Lorraine, Ruth rose from her bed to investigate. When she entered the hallway, a stranger appeared who threw her down onto the mattress and that was the last thing she remembered. Ruth also said that the intruder "sounded foreign."

But Carey and his staff observed other details at the scene that immediately aroused their suspicion. There was no sign of a forced entry and detectives had never seen a burglary in which the entire house had been searched, including the couch. When Medical Examiner Dr. Howard Neail examined Ruth in her living room, no contusions or bruises of any kind were found on her head, despite the fact that she claimed to have been unconscious for several hours. While Albert's wallet had been emptied by the "burglars," Ruth's jewelry was left undisturbed. But most telling was the absence of a pillowcase on one of the bed pillows. When the missing pillowcase was found in the hamper, covered with blood, Ruth had no explanation as to how it got there. "After being questioned most of the day," the *Times* later reported, "Mrs. Snyder was taken to the old Jamaica Town Hall for further questioning. Mrs. Snyder fainted several times while the police questioned her."[35]

During the interrogation, detectives decided to take a chance. They used one of the oldest tricks in police work. They lied and told Ruth that Judd Gray was already in custody and had confessed to the murder. Ruth quickly gave in and admitted she helped to murder her husband. At first, she denied taking part in the killing and said she only assisted in the planning of the crime. Detectives sent out for a court stenographer from the Queens County district attorney's office. They transcribed a detailed statement from Ruth and, when it was finished, they had her sign it. She also supplied investigators with a crucial piece of information. Ruth said that, after the murder,

Judd had gone to Grand Central Station where he was to board a train for Syracuse. Up until the moment she told police, no one knew for sure that Judd Gray was involved in the killing or where he was. Without telling Ruth, Commissioner McLaughlin immediately dispatched Lieutenants Martin Brown and Michael McDermott to Syracuse.

In the meantime, the press began to hear about the Queens Village housewife who killed her husband for her lover. The *Daily News*, the *Daily Mirror*, and the *Times* sent over reporters to cover the story. Soon, the 222nd Street home was surrounded by reporters who combed the quiet neighborhood for background information on the Snyders. The *Daily News*, founded in 1919, had in a few short years grown into the nation's largest selling newspaper. Average daily sales of the *Illustrated Daily News*, which was its original title, easily exceeded 600,000 copies. Its most direct competition, the *Daily Mirror*, was not far behind and the two papers frequently engaged in circulation wars which demanded more sensational headlines. Both papers utilized the tabloid format which was defined by a paper that opened from right to left, one bold headline on the front page and, thanks to improving technology, an abundance of on-the-scene photographs. The New York City tabloids were a special kind of paper whose style attracted working-class readers who rejected the more sedate, conservative publications such as the *Times* and the *Herald*. Stories in the *Daily News*, whose approach to reporting was based on a British format, "were devoted almost entirely to love, violent death, and crime . . . [the stories] were short and ended on the page where they began. It had very little serious world or national news but many pictures, with an announced preference for pretty girls among the subjects"[36] Tabloids were easy to read, simple to understand, and folded neatly when carried onto the subway, all required characteristics of a paper that was favored by the average working man and woman in New York City.

Tabloids courted sensationalism by using lurid, exaggerated headlines that emphasized emotional content more than accuracy. It was a formula that worked well and made the New York City tabloids some of the most successful newspapers in the world. When customers bought the *Daily News* or the *Mirror*, readers knew what to expect: fast-moving stories, uncomplicated text, and above all, attention-grabbing headlines—even if they weren't exactly true. The public relied on the printed press as their primary source of information and it was not unusual for a newspaper to sell out three or four editions in a single day. The *Times*, though not a member of the tabloid community, reported heavily on crime, much more than today. During the Chester Gillette murder case in 1906, and the Lt. Charles Becker case in 1912, both extensively covered by the media, the *Times* devoted massive coverage to those events and placed the stories on its front pages nearly every day.

Stockholders of the *Times*, as well as its editorial board, were not blind to the financial benefits of using copious quantities of ink to report a murder story as sensational and sexy as Ruth Snyder and Judd Gray. When reporters learned that detectives were in Syracuse to arrest Ruth's lover, they hurried over to Grand Central Station to await their return.

By early evening, less than eighteen hours after the discovery of Albert's body, Lieutenants Brown and McDermott were already at the Syracuse police headquarters. After meeting with detectives, they took a car over to the Onondaga Hotel in the downtown section of the city where, according to Ruth, Judd had reserved a room. It was 12:30 a.m. and he had just returned from a dinner with his friend, Haddon Gray, who was no relation to Judd. There was a knock at the door,

"Mr. Gray? It's the police. We'd like to ask you a few questions about Albert Snyder."

"I don't know anything about it," he said through the closed door.

"We'd like to talk to you anyway," replied Lt. Brown. Judd opened the door and admitted the two men. They told him that Snyder had been murdered and they wanted Judd to go back to New York with them for further questioning. At first, he refused, insisting that he had never even met Albert Snyder, though he knew Ruth through a mutual friend. Judd treated the situation as some sort of a misunderstanding or even a joke. He reluctantly agreed to return to New York and soon, Brown, McDermott, and Gray were on an early morning train back to New York City.

During the train ride, Gray was affable and talkative. He was rarely without opinion on any subject that Lt. McDermott chose to discuss. As the talk eventually returned to the night before at the Snyder residence, Gray became quiet. When the men arrived at the City of Poughkeepsie station, dozens of reporters gathered on the platform while Brown and McDermott escorted Gray to the train bound for Grand Central. "Gray, smiling, composed, and debonair, he faced the trip always courteous and kind even to the cameramen . . . who in numbers plagued him for pictures," reported the *Times*. "He showed little interest in his fellow passengers. His air generally was that of an experienced traveler making an accustomed journey . . . he had only smiles for the detectives, few wants and obeyed their slightest orders."[37]

But within a short time after leaving the train station, Gray underwent a transformation. He became resigned to his guilt and suddenly confessed. The entire sordid story of his sexual obsession for Ruth, his compulsive need for her approval, and his rapid descent into murder came pouring out. "From that moment on he talked and talked and talked . . . he spared himself nothing, confessing freely to butchering Snyder with his own hands, but neither did he spare Ruth, exposing her complicity and attributing his moral disintegration to her influence."[38] Judd would eventually see Ruth as the cause of his deterioration, the reason he committed murder. He blamed her for the utter destruction of his life. "I would never have killed Snyder but for her," he later cried. "She had this power over me. She told me what to do and I just did it!"[39]

When Brown, McDermott, and Gray arrived at the Long Island City courthouse later that day, Gray was brought to the office of District Attorney Richard Newcombe. There, he repeated his confession and signed a formal statement. In the meantime, Ruth was brought to the same courthouse where she also gave a full confession to the District Attorney. The headline in the next day's *Times* was "Wife Betrays Paramour As Murderer of Snyder, And He Then Confesses."[40]

Within four days of their arrest, the Snyder and Gray case went before a Queens Grand Jury. "As the hand of the law rested with increasing weight on his narrow shoulders, Gray, half-crazed with remorse for his deed confessed again," said the *News*. "Helplessly floundering in the mire of his own confusion, Gray yesterday admitted his guilt again."[41] Lead prosecutor for the jury presentation was District Attorney Newcombe. Both defendants chose not to testify at the hearing, though eight witnesses were subpoenaed to the Queens County Courthouse for the Grand Jury inquest. They included Albert's brother, Warren Snyder, two police officers who responded to the murder scene and Emily Kulis, the stenographer who recorded the statements of Ruth Snyder and Judd Gray. The assistant medical examiner of Queens County, Dr. Howard W. Neail, testified to Albert's injuries and cause of death.

Haddon Gray, Judd's closest friend, told the Grand Jury of his movements the day after the murder and Judd's request for him to support a fictitious alibi. He admitted that he went to the Onondaga Hotel in downtown Syracuse on the morning of March 21 and mussed up the bedding in Judd's room to make it appear that someone had slept there the night before. He also said that he purposely make several phone calls from the room and also placed a "do not disturb" sign on the doorknob. But Haddon told the Grand Jury that he did not know he was doing these things to cover up a murder. Judd had told him that he was meeting a woman somewhere else and he needed help to deceive his employer and friends. Only later, Haddon said, did he find out that Judd was mixed up in a murder.

It was also made public that, prior to the murder, Ruth had surreptitiously taken out a number of life insurance policies on Albert's life. According to a *Times* report, in November of 1925, more than a year before the killing, the total amount exceeded $52,000. But Ruth had made certain that she included a double indemnity clause in a policy with the Prudential Life Insurance Company. This amendment stipulated that if Albert should die by accident, which included a homicide, the value of the policy would double. Since the original policy was for $45,000, this meant Ruth could inherit $90,000 upon Albert's "accidental" death. She was able to keep this information from Albert by instructing the insurance company to deliver any mail regarding the policies directly to her personally. When the policies arrived, Ruth placed them in a bank safety deposit box to which only she had access.

It was a compelling story and, once their confessions were presented to the court, Ruth and Judd were quickly indicted for Murder in the First Degree. If they were convicted of the charge, it carried a mandatory death sentence. But, on the same day the Grand Jury heard testimony, Ruth claimed her confession was all a lie. "They treated me brutally and worked me to death," she said of police detectives. "They gave me nothing to eat until yesterday. They worked me into a state where I would say anything, anything to make them let me alone!"[42] It was the start of a defense campaign to discredit her original statements to police. But she would have little success. Her statement was already published in several of the city's newspapers, including the *Times* which put the story on its front page for March 22.

The *Daily News* published a photo of Ruth, taken shortly after her arrest, which showed her in the typical "flapper" fashion of the day. To readers, it was a somewhat negative image because, according to contemporary standards, a married woman did not dare dress in that manner. A woman's role was to stay at home, take care of her husband, and do all things that a traditional wife was expected to do. "If there were more papas at the head of their homes and fewer mamas running around voting and playing cards, the United States would be in a better way," said one woman to the press. "I have no sympathy for the woman who cannot find enough to do at home."[43] It was beyond what was considered respectable for a married woman to cut her hair short, wear men's hats, fur coats, and form-fitting dresses. This sentiment was the hidden suggestion in the caption of a page three photo in the *Daily News*. It read: "Cold, clear eyes and an emotionless face. Can you see behind those eyes the beginning of a great fear?"[44] In case readers didn't get the idea, another photo on the same page had these descriptive words under an additional photo of Ruth: "Note here the cruel mouth of the woman who calmly plotted the murder of her husband with her secret paramour."

On March 24, 1927, Ruth had her first interview with the press at the Queens County Jail. In a story which appeared on page one, the *Times* made references to Ruth's physical appearance and expressed disappointment that she wasn't as alluring as expected. "Four sleepless nights had left little of the attractiveness which she is said to have possessed. Her eyes were red-rimmed. She carried a soiled blue handbag . . . her half-smiles were a little creepy under the circumstance, but nevertheless they improved her appearance. Her smile is said to have been her greatest asset in the days when her dash and gaiety won her the nickname, *Tommy*."[45] On the same day the *Daily News* described her as "a very tired woman who sat like a tigress at bay in the detective's room in the Long Island City courthouse submitting to an interview with the press."[46] This was one of the first of many references to Ruth as a "tigress" by the *News* which seemed preoccupied with her manner of dress and took care to describe carefully what the defendant wore each day. "She wore a vivid blue dress, a muskrat overcoat, a scarf and flesh colored stockings . . . she spoke with vehemence."[47] In a direct contradiction to the *News* report on the same conversation, the *Times* quoted Ruth, "she said in a half-hysterical voice that her husband, Albert Snyder, had been her "first and only love."[48] *Daily News* reporter, Jack O'Brian, had already told its readers that Ruth said, "I saw Gray on and off for ten months before our first intimacy . . . I grew to love him. I love him still. He is the only man I ever loved." The title of the *Daily News* article was, in fact, "I Still Love Judd," Cries Mrs. Snyder, Flouting Hint Gold Soiled Their Romance."[49] In a later press conference, Ruth appealed to public sympathy. "I am a mother!" she yelled at reporters gathered to hear her speak. "I love my child and I loved my child's father. God! Can you mothers and wives read this and appreciate the terrible, stifling ordeal I am going through at this time? Easter Sunday, Holy Week!"[50]

The interviews marked the beginning of an obsessive fascination with Ruth Snyder by the New York press. *The Daily Mirror* seemed to lead the way in malicious reporting on the case. Its pages were filled with negative, frequently bizarre interpretations of developments as they unfolded during the spring months of 1927. "Swedes are emotional and passionate," wrote one reporter. "Norwegians are cold-blooded and deliberate. Her [Ruth Snyder's] passion was for Gray; her cold-bloodedness for her husband."[51] Another *Mirror* reporter gave his bleak assessment of Ruth by declaring, "She is ice. But she is the ice of a filthy garbage-choked stream. If she could be melted down she would be a crawling mass of poisonous things."[52]

This characterization of Ruth as a "heartless bitch" continued throughout the trial, fueled by the media's dominant theme: she was a manipulative, sex-crazed woman who had an almost supernatural power over men. The press became convinced that she possessed a sexual prowess that was so irresistible, even a good man would kill for it. What chance could ordinary men have against such power? It may have been this deep, subconscious fear of female sexuality, emerging from under the shroud of Victorian protectiveness that generated the tabloid onslaught against Ruth Snyder. "The tabloids . . . emphasized Ruth's sexuality . . . they also cited evidence of her insatiable lust . . . the couple's wild lovemaking . . . delighted in the rumor that Ruth and Judd had engaged in steamy passion for over an hour with a corpse in the next room."[53] Despite the fact that neither the defendant, nor any of the investigating officers ever claimed that Ruth and Judd engaged in sex at that time, this scenario was repeated so often, it became a part of the story and required no additional proof.[54]

Though Ruth was branded with names such as "ice maiden," "granite woman," "fiend," "hard-faced woman," and worse, reporters couldn't help but dwell on the sexual aspects of the case. As more lurid details were revealed about Ruth's sexy afternoon trysts at the Waldorf while Albert slaved away at his magazine job, men everywhere wondered if their own wives weren't doing the same thing. Sex and murder made good copy and the tabloid editors knew it. "The tabloids increased their circulation by reporting every little kink . . . in the love affair, so that every reader could indulge vicariously in the forbidden; it was a heyday for voyeurs"[55] In almost every major story that appeared after Ruth's interview at the Queens County Jail, Ruth's clothing also became part of the story. "Mrs. Snyder wore a muskrat coat over a serge dress. Her hat was a green turban. About her throat was a gray silk scarf, which she fingered nervously during the interview. Otherwise, she was self possessed."[56]

Gray, on the other hand, was treated in very different manner by the press. He was most often portrayed as a victim; a good man who was ruined by the influence of a much smarter, diabolical woman whose charms and sexual talents led him into disaster. This theme, "a good man's life shattered by a female shrew," began in earnest on the day of the Grand Jury proceeding and was typified by a comment in a *Times* article on March 24. "The East Orange neighbors of Gray were still bewildered yesterday that a man of his good standing in the community and his outward evidence of good character and disposition could be guilty of the crime he has confessed to." Reporters even went to Gray's high school where they interviewed the principal, Wayland Stearns. "Judd Gray was a normal, healthy boy," he said. "He was not what I would call a world-beater in his studies, but not once, to my recollection, was Judd Gray ever disciplined by me during his stay at the school."[57] Support for Gray was evident even at the corset company where he worked. "We cannot believe this of our man Gray," said Vice President of the Benjamin-Johnes Company, L. G. Bell.[58] During an interview outside the courthouse, while the jurors heard testimony inside, Gray's attorney, William J. Millard, told reporters that his client "was irresponsible and that the disintegration of his mentality was due to his association with Snyder."[59] It seemed plain to anyone who read newspaper reports that Gray was apparently coerced, or at least manipulated, into committing a horrendous crime that he otherwise never would have done had he not fallen under the spell of "the Swedish-Norwegian vampire" as the *Mirror* described Ruth.[60]

While the press seemed to excuse Gray for his murderous behavior, they were repeatedly harsh against his wife who did nothing more than try to support her husband despite his public betrayal of their marriage vows. "Mrs. Gray was a shabby little wife," said one *Daily News* article. "She wore a beaver coat of inferior quality and there was a long wrinkle on the right shoulder. Her blue felt hat was not smart. Her black oxfords were a far cry from the nifty cream-colored slippers that Mrs. Snyder wore in court . . . but the swollen eyes and the red face told of the anguish to which she had succumbed. Her face was bleak with misery."[61]

Over the next few weeks, while the district attorney gathered evidence and prepared for trial, Snyder and Gray brooded in the New York jail known as "the Tombs," read newspapers, and sent handwritten notes to each other despite warnings from their respective attorneys. No one knew what would happen at the trial, though the press offered several scenarios to the public, all of which included the lovers turning on each other. Ruth's attorney, Edgar F. Hazelton, immediately asked the court for a separate trial, recognizing the legal danger of trying both defendants at the same time. That request was denied by Judge Townsend Scudder and after a litigious week of jury selection, testimony was ready to begin on the Monday morning of April 25, 1927.

District Attorney Richard S. Newcombe delivered his opening statement to the packed courtroom where seats were at a premium and only the most influential and wealthy people could attend. Newcombe said that Snyder and Gray deserve no mercy because their murder of Albert was cruel and premeditated. "And they concoct and conceive the scheme about having it appear as a robbery . . . though the crime was committed about three o'clock, they sat there planning and conceiving and scheming and God knows what else—I don't want to know—until six o'clock in the morning." It was a veiled reference to the frequently repeated, yet unsubstantiated, rumor that Ruth and Judd had sex while the body of Albert lay in the next room. "I am going to introduce before you the statement made by Ruth Snyder and the statement made by Henry Judd Gray and on the evidence before that the state will present to you we ask you to find the defendants guilty of a premeditated, deliberate murder."

During the next few days, Newcombe called a number of witnesses who testified to their sometimes limited knowledge of the killing. Warren Snyder, for example, was called to the stand to say, basically, that he was the victim's brother and little else, except that his brother was an upstanding citizen. Dr. Howard Neail, New York City's coroner, testified to the condition of Albert's body and cause of death. Gasps were audible in the courtroom when Newcombe called to the stand several employees of the Waldorf Astoria

Hotel. They testified to the defendants' frequent appearance at the hotel under the name of "Mr. and Mrs. Gray."

Damage was done to the defense when Leroy Ashfield, an agent with the Prudential Life Insurance Company, took the stand on the first day of testimony. He told the court that Ruth had called him to her home and wanted to buy lots of insurance on her husband's life. She insisted on large policies and also told Ashfield that she would pay for the premiums herself. After one initial conversation with Albert Snyder, Ashfield said, he never saw him again. All of his contacts since then were only with Mrs. Snyder and always in private. Ashfield said that Albert only asked for a $1,000 life policy. He eventually received $51,000 in insurance and one policy had the double indemnity clause which stated that if Albert died by accident, which included murder, the benefit would increase to $90,000. "Without dropping her classic masque of cold unconcern once, Mrs. Ruth Brown Snyder heard the first state star witness tell yesterday how she betrayed trusting Albert Snyder into signing blank insurance policies and then hurriedly dug up money to pay premiums on them just a week before he was murdered," said the *Daily News*.[62] Defense Attorney Hazelton tried to minimize Ashfield's testimony during cross, but was unsuccessful. The witness stuck to his story. "While the frozen-faced blonde with the edelweiss eyes looked on in approval, Edgar Hazelton attempted to shake the insurance agent . . . but didn't get far."[63]

The following day, while thousands of spectators milled outside the Queens County Courthouse, former New York City Police Commissioner George McLaughlin took the stand. He told the court that he interviewed both defendants shortly after the murder and they eventually confessed to the crime. "She had a handkerchief to her eyes," he said of Ruth. "But she was perfectly normal and composed."[64] Of Gray, McLaughlin told the court he had a remarkable memory and was able to recall the slightest detail of the crime. "McLaughlin, dignified and sure of himself, by far the outstanding figure in the crowded courtroom, described in a voice that sounded raucous through the amplifiers, how Mrs. Snyder on the day after the murder, told without coercion the full tale of tragedy."[65] After McLaughlin's testimony, Ruth's written statement was read into the record. As the first sentence of the confession was read, Ruth buried her face in her hands. But it was nothing compared to the anticipation and excitement when she finally took the stand on the afternoon of April 29, 1927.

Though she appeared stylish with her black coat, black hat, and matching beads, Ruth did not present the "flapper" appearance which certainly would have hurt her testimony to the all-male jury. "Her voice was musical and delightful," reported the *Daily News*, "smoothly rising and falling and audible all over the packed courtroom." As Ruth began her version of Albert's murder, spectators held their breath. "Mrs. Ruth Brown Snyder testified that she not only took no part in the murder of her husband," said the *Times*, "she fought to save his life."[66] Ruth said that she was terrified of Judd and she had no choice but to participate in the killing. "I was mortally afraid of him," she said. "I saw what a terrible man he was. I couldn't see any other way out than to what he had asked me to do." Her betrayal was the final blow to Gray who sat at the defense table, his head buried in his hands while Ruth's words moved him closer to the electric chair. "Watching her former lover narrowly out of her green-blue eyes and speaking with the self possession of an accomplished actress, Mrs. Ruth Snyder yesterday said: 'Mr. Gray did it!'"[67] Through her frequent sobs, Ruth accused Judd again and again, blaming him for the plan to kill her husband and claiming she had nothing to do with it. When it came time for Newcombe's cross-examination, Ruth was ready.

As Newcombe pounded away at Ruth, she held her own, standing up to the onslaught that had even the most seasoned trial watchers admiring her courage. "Even the openly antagonistic trial fans, who came to sneer, not to weep, left the trial chamber commenting on the woman's extraordinary courage and coolness under fire!"[68] The *Times* was impressed with Ruth's demeanor on the stand as well: "Mrs. Snyder defended herself on the stand with great spirit and mental agility, springing again and again out of traps in which she appeared to be securely caught." Eventually, when the subject got around to insurance policies on Albert's life, Ruth became more guarded and was unable to escape the obvious.

"Do you know of any reason on earth why Judd Gray would want to kill Albert Snyder?" asked Newcombe.

"Yes, for the insurance that he was after."

"Was there any insurance policy made with Judd Gray as the beneficiary?"

"No."

"Who was the beneficiary?"

"I was."[69]

When Assistant District Attorney Charles Froessel took over questioning, he hammered away at Ruth's story and soon had her in tears. "He was sarcastic, contemptuous and belligerent. There was no mock courtesy about him. He handled the witness without gloves. When he had her in retreat, his pursuit was vigorous and relentless."[70] When Ruth tried to answer his questions, Froessel would interrupt her with another question. She came across as deceptive and untruthful. "Once she broke down completely, wept and sobbed bitterly while her graceful frame shook with what was purported to be emotion," said the *Daily News*. When she left the witness stand after two days of testimony, she was a beaten woman and the plot to murder her husband rested squarely on her shoulders.

Judd's testimony was no better. His extended answers to all question proved that he did indeed have a remarkable memory. "The swarthy, black-haired lover of Mrs. Ruth Snyder came to the witness stand . . . and tried to damn her body and soul," said the *News.* "He consumed little time in verbally taking Mrs. Snyder by the shoulders and giving her several firm pushes toward the electric chair." Time after time, Judd blamed Ruth for every detail of the plot and said that he was helpless to resist. "His detailed, astounding description Wednesday of the manner in which he and Mrs. Snyder committed the crime seemed to have given him a superiority over which no question, no sharp interrogation could triumph."[71] From conversations that he had with Ruth almost two years prior to the night of the murder, Judd remembered almost everything, including their sexual romps in hotels, the backseat of his car, and even in Ruth's house while Albert was at work. "When he started unfolding the details of their first passionate adventure, the blonde on whom he once lavished endearments lifted her head and opened her eyes wide in horror . . . apparently she had thought he would lie for her."[72] When it came time for Judd to describe the killing, it was Ruth who led the way. "She took me by the hand and led me down the hall," he told the court. "I struck him on the head, as near as I could see, one blow. Then I hit him another blow. He raised up and started to holler . . . I was over on top of him. He grabbed me by the tie. I hollered, 'Momsie! Momsie! For God's sake help me!' She took the weight and hit him over the head." His testimony was summed up in a headline in the *Herald Tribune* the next day, "Woman Made Me Kill, Gray Insists, Steady Under Fire."[73]

When closing statements by counsel were presented, one of Ruth's attorneys, Dana Wallace, said Gray deserved no mercy. "This miserable filth of the earth is allowed to sit here, and before he makes his squealing appeal for mercy to you . . . he has defamed that woman!" Wallace called Gray "a diabolical fiend" and a "human anaconda." He pointed to Gray who was hunched over the defense table, his head resting on his hands. "There is the most despicable man that has ever walked God's footstool as far as I have known men."[74] Gray's attorney, William J. Millard, was no better when he attacked Ruth. "A sinister, fascinating woman came across his path," he shouted at the jury. "What a catastrophe! That woman, that peculiar creature, like a poisonous snake, like a poisonous serpent, drew Judd Gray into her glistening coils, and there was no escape. That woman! It was a peculiar, alluring seduction." Ruth sobbed quietly at her defense table while Millard berated her for the better part of an hour. "This woman, this peculiar venomous species of humanity was abnormal; possessed of an all-consuming, all-absorbing sexual passion, animal lust, which seemingly was never satisfied!"[75]

The jury received the case for deliberations during the late afternoon of May 9. At 7:04 p.m., after only two hours of deliberations, they had reached a verdict. "Mrs. Snyder was clenching her fists and her face was twitching nervously as she was led into the courtroom," said the *Times*.[76] "Gray came in, flushed, but looking about him with the bold and confident air which had carried since he took the witness stand." Ruth and Judd were found guilty of Murder in the First Degree. The *Herald Tribune* said, "Widow Sobs at Verdict, But Regains Usual Calm." The *Daily News* said that Ruth "slumped in her seat." But the *Times* reported that "Mrs. Snyder put her face in her hands and wept at the counsel table at the verdict."[77] Over two thousand spectators jammed into the courtroom which was designed for a few hundred. When the verdict was announced, the huge crowd overpowered the guards and swarmed around the two defendants for a better look at the nation's most famous killers. "It was one of the most dramatic and disgraceful scenes any court ever has witnessed," said the *Daily News*. "Determined to catch a glimpse of the frosty-blonde murderess and the cringing little corset salesman . . . spectators churned through the six resisting bailiffs and swarmed around the counsel table."[78] People in the aisles fainted as complete pandemonium erupted. After nearly thirty minutes of shouting, pushing, and more than a few punches thrown by panic-stricken guards, Ruth and Judd were removed from the riotous courtroom.

When Ruth arrived at Sing Sing, she was the first female to face execution in New York since Mary Farmer in 1909.[79] On the day Ruth was admitted into the facility, fourteen men were housed on Death Row and, already that year, nine men had been executed in the prison's death chamber. She had the misfortune to be in the midst of the "Golden Era" of executions in America and especially in New York State, where during the previous two years, twenty-eight men went to their deaths in the nation's busiest electric chair.

Though in operation for more than thirty years, the electric chair remained a subject of intense interest and speculation. Death by electricity had been a controversial subject during the late nineteenth century when many people wanted a change in the execution procedure. As a result, state authorities were under pressure to move away from hanging because many people saw it as a remnant from the Middle Ages. The idea of killing a man with electricity was first proposed by a Buffalo dentist named Dr. Alfred Southwick. After he read a newspaper story about a utility worker who was accidentally killed by electricity at his job the thought occurred to him that this would be an efficient method of execution.[80] Under Southwick's prodding, a Death Commission was formed by Governor David Hill to study the idea. In 1888, after months of debate, the panel recommended a change to the electric chair. But there were still many details to be worked out.

The development of electricity as a municipal power source was in its infancy then. Despite the tremendous success of the Chicago World's Fair in 1893, which featured a breath-taking display of never-seen-before lighting arrangements, municipalities struggled to introduce electricity into their cities.[81] Inventor Thomas A. Edison, who had developed DC current and harbored great ambitions for future municipal contracts worth millions, did not wish his current to be associated with executions. He concluded that it would scare people away from DC and lessen its marketability. He was also afraid that his competitor, George Westinghouse, would profit because he promoted AC current. In order to convince state officials that AC current should be the one used in the electric chair, Edison directed his staff to go on a bizarre campaign to kill pets and animals with electricity during public exhibitions.[82] Edison thought these efforts would increase the value of his current and lock Westinghouse out of the municipal contract market. For a time, he even used the term *Westinghoused* to describe death by electricity. Eventually, the use of the odd-sounding word disappeared and instead, two other words were combined to describe a death in the electric chair. Electricity and execution melded together to produce the new word of *electrocution*. As for the "battle of the currents," as it was called, Edison won the competition when Westinghouse's AC was later chosen to power the death chair.

New York's first official executioner was Edwin Davis, a man with a dark, mysterious appearance who sported a long drooping mustache. He always wore a tall top hat and a three-quarter length coat. Davis had never killed anyone before but had worked on the electric power plants in state prisons, especially at Auburn. He seemed to be the logical choice. Using a process of trial and error, Davis worked out the practical problems of conductivity, amperage, and the correct contact points that were needed to successfully kill a human being by electricity. Once he determined the best method, he kept the information to himself. "Davis carried the electrodes in a black bag, like a doctor on a house call. He guarded the devices jealously, allowing no one too close a view, and refusing to train a successor until very near the end of his career."[83] By 1913, when he resigned as the state's executioner, he had executed at least ninety-six men and women at Auburn and Sing Sing prisons.

He was replaced by John Hulbert, an introverted man who harbored a growing intolerance toward killing. Unlike Davis, who believed in the work he performed, Hulbert did it for the money. "He said that he needed the $150 he got for each execution," later said the prison physician. "He had responsibilities that would not permit him to give up that source of income . . . I never questioned that, but I felt that perhaps the very horror of the occupation of execution had a dreadful fascination from which he could not escape."[84] Although he performed at least one hundred forty executions in several states, the press was never able to obtain a photograph of Hulbert. That was because Hulbert took care to hide himself from public view and often took a circuitous route to and from Sing Sing whenever he was scheduled for an execution. He was sometimes referred to as "the man who walks alone."[85] His duties ended in January 1926 when he apparently suffered a nervous breakdown and refused to participate in any future executions.[86] His replacement, a distinguished-looking gentleman from Queens, was a one-time protégé of Davis and personally selected by Warden Louis Lawes. During the next thirteen years, this mild-mannered grandfather, who had a full head of long, gray hair and a deeply-lined face which contributed to his ominous appearance, would pull the switch on three-hundred eighty-seven men and women in four states. His name was Robert Greene Elliott.

Though he had no qualms about performing his job to the best of his ability, Elliott always claimed to be against the death penalty. "I hate like hell to do this job," he once told reporters. "I hope this thing (the Snyder-Gray executions) ends capital punishment in New York State."[87] His parents wanted him to become a Methodist minister but instead, he was drawn into a bizarre world of death by his curiosity about electricity. As a boy he expressed interest in the workings of the new science and read everything he could on the subject. "I distinctly remember hearing discussed the change in the method of executing murderers," Elliott wrote. In 1888, the State of New York did away with hanging and instead, opted for the electric chair. Edwin Davis was hired to operate the new machinery but Elliott dreamed of the opportunity of doing it himself. "Think of the executioner's great responsibility," he said to a friend. "That's a job I'd like to have!"[88]

By that time, Elliott had already decided to seek a career in electricity and attended a school to learn all he could about the new technological wonder that promised to change the world. He got a job at a local power plant where he excelled in the position and impressed his bosses. Elliott also maintained a growing, but clandestine interest in crime stories. He reveled in newspaper articles that reported on murders and became fascinated with the most famous crimes of the era. "The first murder case in which I became intensely interested was that of Lizzie Borden," Elliott once wrote. "Columns were devoted to her sensational trial at New Bedford and not a single detail escaped my eye."[89] His next job brought him to Clinton State prison where he was responsible for the facility's power plant. Soon, he was tending to the prison's electric chair and assisting the executioner, Edwin Davis. But when Davis retired in 1913, Hulbert took his place. It wasn't until Hulbert resigned suddenly in 1926 that Elliott finally landed the job he was destined to have.

Within a few days, on January 28, 1926, he threw the switch on his first execution. "Except for fear of a mishap, I do not recall experiencing any particular emotion while the deadly current streaked through the body in the chair," he later said.[90] On that very same day, Elliott also began to write a personal journal in which he recorded the name of every man or woman he executed over the following thirteen years. Sometimes, he included his observations as well as his personal feelings of the moment. Of his first execution, on January 29, 1926, Elliott wrote, "Luigi Rapito entered the chamber somewhat nervous and slipped into the chair. Convicted of killing Asa Kline in Cayuga County two years ago. Father Cashin attended him."[91] Elliott had to learn to write fast. By the time Ruth Snyder and Judd Gray were scheduled to die, he had already executed fifty-seven men in Massachusetts, New York, New Jersey, and Pennsylvania, an average of more than two inmates a month. And unlike his predecessors, Hulbert and Davis, who shunned publicity, Elliott did not shy away from the press, a practice that brought him much criticism during his long career. Ruth Snyder would be his first female, and as a result, Elliott would receive more publicity than he had ever received before.

Ruth and Judd sat on Death Row for the remainder of 1927 while defense attorneys filed several motions, all of which were decided by the New York State Court of Appeals in Albany. But at the prison, the presence of such a famous couple caused numerous problems for guards. "During her stay in the death house, many offers of marriage came for Mrs. Snyder," Warden Lawes later wrote. "For a week prior to the execution hundreds of newspaper reporters, feature article writers, and general nuisances, made the prison and its environs practically their domicile."[92] One newspaper reported that a plan was put into motion where Ruth would be revived after death with massive doses of adrenaline. She would then appear on a New York stage for a fee of $1 million. Hearst's *Daily Mirror*, the *American*, and *Cosmopolitan* magazine had even begun competing to sign her to an exclusive postmortem contract.[93] One of New York's most outrageous tabloids, *The Evening Graphic*, promised exclusive insights into Ruth's final moments. "Think of it!" announced an editorial on the day before the execution. "A woman's final thoughts just before she is clutched in the deadly snare that scars and burns and fries and kills! Her very last words! Exclusively in tomorrow's *Graphic*!"[94] The *Daily News* published a daily poll of its readers on the question of clemency for Ruth. The final results as of January 12, 1928 were surprising. Despite overwhelming negative press reporting, the majority wanted Ruth to live. The vote was 12,659 for death and 14, 948 for clemency.

By then, many newspapers articles had already appeared which described the execution process and the man who pulled the switch. Thanks to some ambitious reporters, the public knew the name and address of the state's executioner. As the date of Ruth scheduled execution grew near, the debate over the execution of a female intensified. Elliott received dozens of threatening letters at his home in Queens; more were sent to the warden at Sing Sing prison. "Dog Elliott," said one letter. "You should drop dead long ago for you are a cold-blooded butcher and murderer." Another writer said, "you are a disgrace to your family and to all mankind. It is bad enough that you kill, but you murder for money, and that makes your crime more terrible." A man from New York offered his personal observation with these words: "you ought to bury your face in the dirt. If there is any manly principle left in your inhuman carcass, you should blow out your brains . . . how can you look a man in the face? How can you look your wife or relatives in the face and call yourself a man?" Elliott later said that he never let these letters affect him. As the years went by, he expected them, though he said he never grew accustomed to the hatred expressed by some people. "When you die," one letter began, "nobody will shed a tear. It is wonder to me that somebody hasn't sent a bullet into you!"[95]

On the morning of Ruth Snyder's scheduled execution, hundreds of people began to gather outside the steel gates of Sing Sing. By late afternoon, at least three thousand people had assembled near the main entrance alone. Warden Lawes called in extra police to assist in crowd control and to take action if someone decided to interfere with the process. "It was pointed out at the time that the crowd at the prison . . . derived as much sensual pleasure out of the incident as in watching a spectacular fire, regardless of the tragic loss of life," he later wrote.[96]

The brightly lit execution chamber was hushed and extremely tense while the twenty-four witnesses, reporters, and prison officials awaited the arrival of the condemned. "Back and forth their gaze veered," said one report, "from the thing of metal and straps to the door opening from the corridor of the death house. The men against the walls looked neither at the chair nor the door. They stood like show-window dummies, wooden men with wooden eyes. Not a sound, not a movement in the whole room. You could hear your neighbor's watch ticking, his heart beating."[97] No one really knew what to expect when Ruth was brought into the room. "Once the gay, witty life of suburban bridge parties, "Momsie" Snyder moaned and twitched in her cell before the steady tramp of the guards came to signal her doom," reported the *Daily News*. "Constantly she assured the matrons of her innocence."[98]

Sitting in the front row of the death chamber was a photographer from the Midwest named Thomas Howard. He was hired by the *Daily News* for this one assignment. Howard had a camera taped to his ankle which he had smuggled into the prison because photographic equipment was forbidden by the warden, and had been for many years. A wire, which controlled the shutter switch, ran up his leg from the camera. The day before, he and his editor, Harvey Duell of the *News*, were in a Manhattan hotel room, practicing how to take a photo with such a setup. The angle and distance had to be carefully worked out to ensure a successful picture. After much trial and error, Howard felt confident that he could take a photo with the ankle camera.

As Howard shifted uneasily in the front row of the room, the green door to the right suddenly swung open and Ruth was brought in by two matrons. She wore a drab, brown smock over a dark green skirt and slippers. "Mrs. Snyder, her face tearful and eyes aghast entered between two prison matrons clad in black," said the *Times*.[99] The reporters who knew her from the trial were shocked at her appearance. She had gained at least forty pounds during her stay on Death Row. Her shapely body had become a shapeless form, accentuated by thick and pudgy legs; her blonde hair was lifeless, straight, and unkempt. "She came over the threshold and into the room like one deadened by hypnotism," said one witness. "She moved slowly and one could see there was no strength in her legs. Her steps were short and stiff, . . . her dull eyes stared straight ahead, seeing nothing—no thought in them whatever."[100] Father John McCaffrey, the Catholic chaplain, held a crucifix in front of him while Ruth prayed loudly. "This room seemed to be all there was in the world," said one reporter. "Our eyes fell upon the chair and the door and there was nothing else in the world, nothing. The place was a tomb, barely less dreadful to the living than to the living dead beyond the door."[101] She made her way to the chair, only a few feet away from the entrance door. "Her light blue eyes gleamed brightly. Her determined chin was held high and it trembled ever so slightly. Her lips quivered as she responded to the intonations of the priest who was reciting the Litany. Her shoulders sagged and there were deep, grief-stricken creases to her face."[102]

"Father! Forgive them!" Ruth cried over and over. "Father!" The matrons, their own eyes filled with tears, helped her to the chair and quietly strapped her into the seat. "Father, forgive them for they know not what they do!" Ruth said in a low, trembling voice. "And then a passion of weeping and broken words and eyes wide with terror darting this way and that over the room, seeing nothing in all human likelihood."[103] While Elliott made final adjustments to his machinery of death, Ruth sobbed loudly for all to hear. "I made the usual preparations," he later said. "I had brought my own electrodes for use on Mrs. Snyder . . . a feeling of repulsion swept over me. I was to send a woman, a mother, into eternity. The more I permitted my mind to dwell upon it, the more it cut deep into my heart . . . when her eyes fell upon the instrument of death, she almost collapsed."[104] A black leather mask was placed over Ruth's face. It gave her an eerie, medieval image which caused several of the witnesses to shudder. The matrons left the chamber, holding back their own sobs as Warden Lawes stood off to the side near the exit door.

Though he eventually witnessed one-hundred fourteen executions during his tenure as warden, Lawes never actually watched the procedure.[105]

The twenty-four official witnesses, crammed into the rows of wooden benches, waited breathless for the inevitable moment. One reporter later wrote, "they sat transfixed-fascinated by the ghastly scene!"[106] Elliott disappeared behind his partition and a second later, he turned the dial on the control panel in front of him. A loud crackling filled the room. Two thousand volts of electricity shot into Ruth's body at the speed of light. She pressed violently against the restraining straps as if to break free from the deadly chair. At that very moment, a nervous Thomas Howard snapped a photo using the camera strapped to his leg. A sizzling noise, much like a steak on a grill, emanated from behind the electric chair while the reporters were suddenly aware of a sickening smell. Ruth's neck and arms turned a deep crimson red. "Many in the room shuddered, others turned away."[107] After two minutes, Elliott turned the power off. He waited a few seconds and then switched it on again. "As the current surged through Ruth Snyder's body," Elliott wrote later, "I thought of her mother and her little daughter, Lorraine. My sympathies were more with them than the woman in the chair."[108] The cycle was repeated a third time until Ruth was motionless in the chair. Dr. Charles Sweet, Sing Sing's physician, briefly examined her and declared loudly, "I pronounce this woman dead." The matrons returned to the room and unfastened the straps. They removed the hideous mask and lifted Ruth from the chair. "The shocked spectators observed on the calf of her leg a red burn a little larger than a silver dollar."[109] She was lifted onto a gurney and wheeled into an adjoining room where an autopsy was immediately begun.

Several moments later, at 11:17 p.m., two large prison guards escorted Judd Gray into the death chamber. The five-foot-one-inch Gray appeared even smaller than he was and had to be supported by the two men. Wearing a gray suit and felt slippers, he was quickly taken to the chair and strapped in. Once a condemned prisoner was brought into the room, no time was wasted. Guards practiced the procedure continuously to ensure an efficient execution and minimize waiting time for the inmate. Judd's hair was combed back on his head and oddly, a handkerchief was tucked into his breast pocket. While Reverend Anthony Peterson prayed aloud, witnesses could hear Judd mumbling along in a meek, trembling voice. As the leather mask was lowered over his face, he tried to respond to the reverend's prayers but no sound came from his lips. "Lord have mercy on your soul!" proclaimed the minister.

After Elliott attached the electrodes to Judd's head and leg, he retreated into his hidden alcove off to the right. Following the direction of Lawes, he then turned the switch quickly and a loud hum filled the room. Judd's body stiffened in the chair as a spiral of blue smoke seemed to emanate from the back of his head. "There was pity in my heart for Judd Gray when I threw the switch to end his life," Elliott said of the execution. "I felt extremely sorry for this man who had forsaken his wife and daughter for the woman who lay dead a short distance away."[110] In two minutes, it was over. Dr. Sweet pronounced Judd dead and guards quickly removed his corpse from the chair. It was 11:19 p.m. "This was a very exciting night," Elliott wrote in his diary, "second only to the Sacco Vanzetti night in Massachusetts."

The witnesses and reporters slowly rose from their benches and paraded out of the dreary chamber, still acrid from the effects of searing human flesh. "How good the night air felt!" wrote reporter James Kilgallen. "Overhead the stars were twinkling in the sky and a full moon beamed benignly down upon the swirling waters of the Hudson River which backs up against the drab walls of Sing Sing."[111] Elliott packed up his electrodes and left the prison. But he was deeply affected by the executions and the pressures of placing a female in the electric chair, something he did only five times in his long career. "The executioner, who also suffered under the strain, denied at his Queens home that he had collapsed," reported the *Sun*, "but was treated by a physician."[112] Elliott claimed publicly there was no difference between executing men and women, but he took special care when the condemned was female. "The procedure is exactly the same," he once wrote. "However, I am probably more deliberate in the case of a woman. By that, I do not mean I am slower, but simply more painstaking in my efforts to avoid a mishap of any kind."[113]

Although Elliott took no pleasure in executing females, he had few reservations about granting interviews to the press. Though his immediate predecessor, John Hulbert, was the state's executioner for thirteen years, his photograph never appeared in the press. Elliott's image, however, appeared in the tabloids on several occasions and his name was well known to the general public. Immediately after the Snyder execution, the New York State Department of Corrections formally admonished him for posing for photographs and giving interviews to the New York City tabloids. The *Times* reported, "numerous complaints by private citizens over interviews attributed to Elliott were sent to authorities . . . the frequency with which his picture appeared in newspapers was also a cause of unfavorable comment."[114]

After the executions were completed, photographer Thomas Howard hurried back to the *Daily News* darkroom where the film was quickly developed. The resulting image was blurry and slightly out of focus, but there was no mistaking the subject. In a very real way, the lesser quality of the photograph added to its horror. It showed Ruth, strapped to the electric chair, a dark mask over her face and her body apparently rigid from the force of the deadly electric current. *Daily News* editors devoted the entire front page of the next morning's editions to the amazing photograph under the one-word headline: DEAD!

The reaction from the public was immediate and vociferous. Outrage was widespread while the *Daily News* was condemned from a variety of sources. Politicians, community leaders, and editorials denounced the publication of the photograph as an assault against morality. One minister called it, "the vilest piece of yellow journalism the world has ever known."[115] Department of Corrections Commissioner Raymond F. C. Kieb claimed the photo was a fake. "No permission was given to anyone to photograph Ruth Snyder in the chair," he said to reporters. "It did not take place, I'm sure. But I will start an investigation. Photographing such an occurrence is directly contrary to the intention of the law and is naturally a breach of good faith."[116] At Sing Sing, Warden Lawes was infuriated that one of the witnesses who he approved could betray him in such a public manner. "I trusted reporters," he said, "and one of them was unworthy of the trust. Naturally I did not search them for cameras. No reporter from that paper will be allowed to witness an execution again."[117] Lawes lobbied the state legislature to prohibit reporters to act as witnesses ever again and supported a bill that would make it a state law. He also took steps to make executions private and closed to everyone but prison officials. "Prison attaches announced today that changes are to be made in the lighting of the chamber that will prevent any person photographing surreptitiously a slayer in the electric chair . . . The white-frosted lamps now in use, which shade light so as to make photography possible in the chamber, will be removed."[118] But the *News* turned a deaf ear to most of the criticism. On the day the photo of Ruth Snyder appeared on the front page, the paper sold an additional 100,000 copies.[119] The publication of the photograph sealed its reputation as New York's most cutting-edge tabloid. By the end of the decade, circulation of the *Daily News* had, "hit an unheard of 1.3 million at a time when sales of all other New York papers were standing still."[120]

The Snyder-Gray case was over. But the reverberations of this tawdry murder, immortalized in endless columns of press coverage and hundreds of hours of radio broadcasting, would be felt far into the future. For decades, every woman who went to trial for murder faced inevitable comparison with Ruth Snyder. The notion of killing a spouse for insurance money was a novel occurrence in the 1920s and the social-sexual issues exposed by the Snyder love triangle, along with the symbolic representation of the out-of-control "modern woman," would not disappear easily. Gray's descent into murder and self-destruction while under the "spell" of a seductive, irresistible woman became a central theme in the case and one that resonated with the average man. "It was the detectives—all men—who first found Gray such a likeable fellow and passed on to the public as fact his story that he had been bewitched and dominated."[121] This theme was easily absorbed by the male-dominated press and accepted as fact without question. No further clarification was needed because all men ostensibly understood this concept. For her sins, which included the abandonment of her marriage bed, betrayal of her husband, and her unabashed enjoyment of sex, Ruth Snyder had to die. The morality play reached its final act. "It was a grand show," wrote a *Daily Mirror* columnist the next day. "It never failed once . . . it was the good old stuff done well and fiercely. It was grim and grand. It moved slowly and inevitably . . . and it came at last, last night, to the magnificent, the tremendous, the incomparable curtain that the audience was counting on. Everybody walked out with a satisfied feeling."[122]

The cultural significance of Snyder-Gray also attracted the attention of the artistic community. Novelist James Cain, among others, would later explore similar issues in two short novels, *The Postman Always Rings Twice* (1934) and *Double Indemnity* (1936). Both stories were inspired by the Snyder murder case; they would later become successful Hollywood movies in the *film noir* genre. So powerful is the connection between these two productions and *film noir*, they almost completely define this unique style of filmmaking. Like Gray's characterization in the print media, one of the essential ingredients in *film noir* is the innocent, helpless man caught up in catastrophic events not of his making.[123] "The principals of this new breed of crime films were not . . . professional criminals, defying the repressive institutions of their world, but hapless, sensitive, often passive amateurs with the sultry, treacherous heroines, femme fatales who had no counterpart in the man's world of Hollywood gangster films."[124]

Together, *Double Indemnity* and *The Postman Always Rings Twice* contain all the plot components of the Snyder-Gray case, especially the betrayal of the defendants as they tried to blame each other for the murder. "Out of the lurid gossip around the Snyder trial, Cain pulled the plots, probably the titles, as well as the circumstantial particulars."[125] But not all the scenes in his novels were taken directly from real life. Cain must have heard the rumors of Ruth and Judd's alleged lovemaking in her bedroom while Albert's body lay in her bed. In *The Postman Always Rings Twice*, Cain included just such a passage after Nora and her lover murder her husband:

> And the breath was roaring in the back of my throat like I was some kind of animal, and my tongue was all swelled up in my mouth, and blood pounding in it . . . Next thing I knew, I was down there with her, and we were staring in each other's eyes, and locked in each other's arms, and straining to get closer. Hell could have opened for me then, and it wouldn't have made any difference. I had to have her, if I hung for it.[126]

It could have been written by Judd Gray himself, so captured was he in the iron grip of a woman from whom he could not escape. Ruth Snyder became the iconic reference for the terrifying bond of sexual seduction and the helplessness that some men feel when confronted by its awesome power. It is this which is at the core of the Snyder story and why she inspired such revulsion and subconscious fear on multiple levels of Jazz Age society. Very few criminal cases ever reach the sort of notoriety that Snyder-Gray achieved. Its plot has become a fragment of our cultural mosaic, a permanent fixture in the literary world, and a disturbing glimpse into the hidden possibilities that exist in all our lives.

Dead a Thousand Times:
Anna Antonio

I am almost dead now. I feel at times, I am not breathing.
　　　—Anna Antonio at Sing Sing prison, August 8, 1934.

Anna Antonio, twenty-eight, was a battered wife and the mother of three small children. She was convicted of orchestrating the murder of her drug-dealing husband, Salvatore Antonio, on March 27, 1932. Though she was not present at the killing, Anna received the death penalty, as did the two men she allegedly hired to do away with her husband. But her conviction was just the beginning of an incredible ordeal for Anna. Following her trial, she would embark on a harrowing, twisting journey through the court system that was surely unlike any other before her. It included three reprieves from the governor's office and a dramatic rescue from execution just ten minutes before she was scheduled to die. In the eyes of many, her guilt was never firmly established and, because of those doubts, her death sentence seemed excessive and cruel. Public sympathy for her dilemma was intense, but the wheels of justice, once begun, are difficult to stop. Her story was never about the crime of which she was convicted, nor was it about her trial which took place in relative obscurity at the Albany County Court. Anna's story was about what happened afterwards, about how she became a pawn in society's seesaw battle with itself over the traumatic spectacle of a young mother who faced execution for a crime she may never have committed.

Physically, Anna was a small woman. She was five feet tall and weighed just one hundred pounds. She grew up in Albany, New York, the daughter of hard-working Italian immigrants who had little formal education. While Anna was a teenager, she met Salvatore Antonio, who was then thirty years old. A short, stocky man who weighed nearly two-hundred pounds, Salvatore was employed as a brakeman for the local railroad company. But, according to Anna, he also sold drugs as a side business and was well known to the Albany police. He had been arrested for crimes such as theft and assault and was considered part of Albany's criminal underworld in its notorious "Gut" district.

Once known as "The Tenderloin," the Gut was located on the eastern side of the city where the Dunn Memorial Bridge crosses the Hudson River. It was an area anchored by Dongan and Green Streets, long the center stage for some of Albany's most notorious criminals. During the Prohibition Era, the Gut was home to dozens of gambling dens and illegal saloons where customers from all walks of life gathered every night of the week. The run-down neighborhood also had an indigent population of hookers who roamed along Green Street at all hours of the day and night. The drug trade (mostly heroin) thrived along Bleecker Street, on various corners of Madison Avenue, and especially on Grand Street.

Anna was sixteen when she married Salvatore. Almost immediately, her life changed for the worse. He became lord and master over everything she did. Anna was forbidden to leave the apartment without his permission. When she disobeyed his instructions, Salvatore beat her. He placed restrictions over every facet of her life and treated her like his personal slave. Powerless to resist and with no other place to go, Anna resigned herself to an abusive, bleak, and unhappy existence. Anna had three children by Salvatore. Though he kept his regular job at the railroad, Sal continued to deal in drugs. "The house was always full of dope and guns," Anna later told police.[1]

During the early morning hours of Easter Sunday, March 27, 1932, two Albany Law School students were driving along River Road into the city of Albany. They were returning from a party in nearby Castleton. As they sped down the highway, the driver swerved to avoid an object in the center of the lane. "Antonio was waving one arm in the air as their automobile headlights disclosed him lying in the road."[2] When they stopped the car to investigate, they found a semiconscious Salvatore Antonio lying on the pavement. He was covered in blood but still alive. The students picked him up off the ground, tossed him into their car, and sped off toward Albany. He begged for a doctor but never said what had happened. By the time they arrived at Albany Memorial Hospital on Northern Boulevard, Salvatore was in a coma. Doctors rushed him into the emergency room where they vainly attempted to keep him alive while treating five gunshot wounds and at least fifteen stab wounds. Within a few minutes, Antonio died without regaining consciousness. The police soon arrived and began an investigation into his death. While detectives were interviewing the students, Anna suddenly appeared at the hospital. According to investigators, no one on the medical staff had notified her and it could not be determined how she found out her husband had died. Her appearance at the emergency room would later be used against her at her trial because Anna was never able to explain who told her that her husband had been shot.

At first, police assumed that Salvatore had received just rewards for his life of crime. One of his associates in the drug business was a man named Sam Faraci, thirty-two, an Italian immigrant who could not read or write English. He had been involved with Salvatore for many years and police immediately suspected him of involvement in the murder. But when police officers looked for Faraci at his rooming house in the *Gut* district, he had apparently vacated in haste. He was nowhere to be found. Police also knew that Faraci was rarely seen in public without his partner in crime, a Green Street thug named Vincenzo Saetta. Investigators were not surprised when they discovered that Saetta had apparently fled Albany as well.

Early on the morning of March 30, Police Officer John Campion of the Poughkeepsie Police Department was on patrol in his sector on the west side of the city. As he drove along Washington Street, a residential area of older homes, he noticed a vehicle occupied by two men pass alongside. The driver seemed to intentionally avoid eye contact with the young patrolman. Campion switched on his red grille lights, activated the siren, and moved behind the suspicious car. He pulled the vehicle over near Academy Street and requested ownership papers for the car. The driver said they were passing through Poughkeepsie on their way to New York City. But Campion noticed that they were on the wrong road for New York and were headed in the wrong direction. The men identified themselves as Vincenzo Saetta and Sam Faraci. Campion decided to bring the men into police headquarters for further questioning. After a phone call to Albany Police, Campion realized he may have made the most important arrest of his career. "The alertness of a Poughkeepsie Policeman John Campion started three persons along the trail to Sing Sing's electric chair," reported a local paper. "Doing patrol duty on Washington Street early on the day after the discovery of the body of the slain husband of Mrs. Anna Antonio, Campion stopped a car and brought the occupants to police headquarters."[3]

When Albany detectives arrived at the Poughkeepsie Police Department a short time later, they found Saetta and Faraci in separate rooms, smoking cigarettes and waiting to talk to them. But both men appeared to be sick, possibly due to drugs. "Within a short time both prisoners began complaining of stomach cramps, sweating profusely, and drinking large quantities of water—the typical withdrawal symptoms of confirmed drug addicts."[4] As questioning began, each man denied any involvement in the murder of Salvatore Antonio. But detectives were not convinced. After nearly three days of non-stop interrogation, which was a common and accepted police practice at that time, Faraci relented. "All right," he said. "I was with Vince when he done it, but I didn't do it. We stopped on the road outside Castleton. I went down the road a ways . . . when I came back, Vince says, 'I just shot and stabbed Antonio.'"[5] He insisted that although he was present when Sal was killed, Saetta was the one who actually shot him. Faraci said he had nothing to do with the actual murder. Investigators, unsure of which suspect had shot Sal, then placed both men in adjacent cells. While the two men conversed, police listened in. Saetta became enraged when he learned that Faraci had implicated him and demanded to talk to detectives. The story he told sealed both his fate and Anna's fate forever.

Saetta said that it was he and Faraci who had murdered Sal. They had killed him, he said, at the request of Anna, who told him that she had suffered enough at the hands of an abusive and violent husband. Saetta said that he met with Anna at the Leland Theater in downtown Albany a few weeks before the killing. There, they discussed a plan to kill Sal. "I have got to get rid of my husband and I want you to do it," she told him, "and if you won't do it, then I'll get somebody who will."[6] She said her husband had two insurance policies on his life. One was with his union, the Brotherhood of Railway Trainman, in the amount of $2,800 and another through Met Life for $2,500. According to Saetta, Anna said she would pay $800 if he would kill Sal as soon as possible. Saetta agreed and the deal was made.

Both suspects were taken back to Albany. Anna was quickly arrested and all three defendants were arraigned in Albany County Court on murder charges. Local attorney Daniel Prior was appointed by the court to represent Anna while Henry Lowenberg was assigned to Saetta and Charles J. Duncan to Sam Faraci. Daniel Prior was a well-known attorney in the capital district and highly sought after by many clients. His reputation soared after he obtained two acquittals for the notorious Jack "Legs" Diamond in 1931.

Diamond, a repetitive killer who survived four shooting attempts on his life and displayed an amazing talent for avoiding capture, was accused of the kidnapping and torture of a gangland rival in the illegal beer business. Prior represented Diamond during his sensational trial in Troy, New York during the summer of 1931, when people mobbed the courthouse just to get a momentary glimpse of the legendary gangster whose exploits rivaled that of Chicago's Al Capone. After less than two hours of deliberations, a local jury acquitted Diamond of all charges.

In December of that same year, "Legs" Diamond was arrested on kidnapping charges and, once again, represented by Prior. During the trial, Prior found witnesses who testified that Diamond could not have committed the murder because he was with them on the night of the kidnapping. A jury found him innocent of the charges and he walked out of the Renssalaer County Court a free man once again. But his freedom was temporary. "He is haggard, looks undernourished and . . . the pistol bullets and shotgun slugs that enemies fired into his body also have taken a toll."[7] As it turned out, his health was the least of his worries. Within hours of the verdict, he was found dead in his Albany rooming house with five bullets in his head. One newspaper report called it "the most appropriate end to a story more extravagant than anything that has been seen here or on the screen."[8] His killers were never found. When asked for a comment on his client's death, Prior declined. But his ability to get a defendant a favorable verdict was unquestioned and Prior became somewhat of a celebrity in upstate New York.

When the trial of Antonio, Faraci, and Saetta opened on the morning of March 27, 1933 in County Court, there was very little press coverage outside Albany. The New York City media took no notice of the trial and no reporters from any of the tabloids attended the proceedings. The *Daily News* and the *Mirror* had plenty of crime to write about in Manhattan, Brooklyn, and the Bronx. So, when defense attorney Prior told the jury that he was not interested in the guilt or innocence of Faraci and Saetta, only the Albany press was listening. "We have nothing to hide from you," said Prior in his opening statement. "What the district attorney leaves out, I will put in. Judge her as you find her here . . . it is not my concern what you may find concerning Saetta and Faraci."[9]

While opening statements were read, Faraci's family sat in the courtroom. "Five of Faraci's nine children and their mother arrived yesterday from Geneva, New York to witness the events which threaten to send Faraci to the electric chair. Three of the children are adults and one is an infant of one year," said the *Albany Evening News*. Anna's children, along with her brother, were also present and attended each day's testimony.

One of the first witnesses called to the stand was Police Officer John Campion of the Poughkeepsie Police Department. He testified to stopping the car operated by Vincenzo Saetta in downtown Poughkeepsie on the morning of March 30.

"You're a liar!" shouted Saetta from the defense table when he heard Campion's testimony. "He was driving!" yelled Saetta as he pointed to Faraci before the judge banged his gavel on the bench.

Marsh then called State Police Sgt. William Flubacher to the stand. He interviewed Saetta on the morning of April 13, nearly two weeks after Sal

Antonio's body was found alongside the Albany highway. Flubacher said that Saetta confessed that he was hired by Anna to kill her husband for $500 and later recruited his friend Sam Faraci to help him. "On the day before Easter, Saetta said, 'Mrs. Antonio called me at my room at 53 Columbia Street and said tonight was a good night. He is going downtown.'"[10] Flubacher told the court that Saetta, Faraci, and Sal Antonio drove to the city of Hudson that night for some drinks and food. On the way back, Saetta said, he saw the opportunity to act. "About a half a mile north of Castleton, we stopped. Faraci went to the side of the road . . . from there I shot Antonio and he fell into the ditch. I told Faraci go get your knife and finish him!"[11] Flubacher went on to say that Saetta and Faraci left Antonio for dead on the side of the highway and returned to Albany. While Faraci went to pick up his girlfriend, Saetta met with Anna at Columbia Street and Broadway. She gave him $40 as a partial payment for killing her husband. "When I get the rest," she told him, "I'll get it to you." According to Saetta, Anna was due to receive $5,300 in insurance money for the death of her husband.

On the following morning, it was Anna's turn to tell her side of the story. When her name was called, the frail defendant arose from the table and walked slowly to the witness stand. After taking the oath, she sat in the witness chair and crossed her arms on her chest. When Prior began to ask questions, she answered in a quiet voice and frequently turned to look at the jury. She said that her husband abused her for years and physically beat her almost since the first week of marriage.

"Did you live with him even after that?"

"I loved and feared him both," she said.

"You didn't say to yourself, 'Here's a good opportunity to get rid of him,' did you?"

"No, I did not."

"You didn't conceive of the idea to have two men murder your husband, did you?"

"No! I did not!!"

Anna said that she begged her husband to get out of the "rackets" and stop selling drugs at his job at the railroad, but he would not listen to her. She said she would not turn him in to the police because he did it to make for money for the children and to pay rent for their apartment.

"Did you, who loved Sal Antonio, call the police?"

"I'd be giving my own husband away if I did that," Anna said.

"How long was your husband in the dope racket?" asked Prior.

"Since August 1931."

"You took some of the filthy money and used it, did you not?"

"We had to live."

"You didn't care where it came from?"

"I didn't have anything to say about it."

"You never asked him about the money?"

"No, I didn't." Anna explained that everyone knew that Sal was selling dope, including the police. It was up to the police to arrest him, she said, not for her to turn him in. She said she did meet with Saetta and gave him $40 because she knew that he was her husband's friend and he asked for the money.

"Although there stood before you the man who killed your husband, you didn't call the police?"

"I didn't believe him," she answered.[12] Anna said that about two weeks before Sal was murdered, she heard that Saetta threatened to kill him. She said that she warned her husband but he said not to worry about it since he always received threats like that because he was in the dope business. When she was questioned about her statements to the police, Anna said she didn't remember saying some of the things attributed to her. She claimed that she was without food and water during that time and the questioning by police went on for days.

After Anna finished her testimony, it was Faraci's turn to explain his role in the killing. Once questioning began, he blamed Saetta for the killing and implicated Anna as well. Though he had no direct knowledge that Anna was involved in the plot, Faraci was convinced that she had hired Saetta to do the job. "Biting his nails continuously and speaking in broken English, Faraci told the details of Antonio's death in almost the same words as used in his alleged confession to police," reported the *Times-Union*.[13] But, he claimed, that confession was given to the police only after days of beatings and mistreatment. He said that he was thrown down a flight of steps at police headquarters, and deprived of food and water in order to get him to talk. When asked if he was telling the truth about the night of the murder, Faraci said that he was and that Saetta was the one who shot Antonio.

"You're trying to save yourself from the chair, aren't you?" said District Attorney Delaney.

"Yes, I am," he replied.

Faraci described how Saetta shot Antonio several times on the side of the road outside Albany that night and how they drove away from the scene thinking that Sal was dead. When asked why he packed his bags in his room and fled the city later that night, Faraci said that he thought it best that he return to Geneva to see his family. His testimony was unconvincing and Faraci left the stand under a cloud of disbelief. "Repeatedly wetting his lips and drinking great quantities of water, Sam Faraci battled doggedly the grueling cross-examination of D. A. Delaney today," said the *Albany Evening News*.[14]

After Saetta declined to take the stand, it was time for closing arguments. Prior told the court that Anna had nothing to do with the murder. He said that it was Saetta who wanted Sal Antonio killed because of his insults to him and the fact that he owed money which he refused to pay. Prior said that Saetta recruited Faraci and together they killed Antonio without Anna's knowledge. But when it was Delaney's turn to address the court, he vilified Anna as the mastermind of the plot.

"The woman is as much a killer in the crime as the man who fired the shots and the one who caused the eleven wounds in Antonio's body!" he said.[15] Delaney said Anna wanted him dead for the insurance money and to get rid of an abusive husband. "While the district attorney was addressing her, Mrs. Antonio, for the first time since the trial started, abandoned her calm demeanor and burst into tears," reported the *Albany Evening News*. "We expect a woman to be an ideal wife," Delaney said. "We do not expect a woman who will not a shed a tear for her husband, who will plot to kill. She is not a credit to motherhood . . . is not entitled to sympathy, she is entitled to condemnation!"[16]

After a brief charge by Judge Gallup, the case was handed to the jury for deliberations on the afternoon of April 15. Six hours later, the jury foreman announced they had reached a verdict. "The three defendants gazed fixedly at the floor as the jurors took their seats. The atmosphere was tense and electric," said one report.[17] While the full courtroom of spectators, friends, and family waited breathlessly, the jury foreman read the verdict. "Guilty!" he said loudly. It was guilty for Anna, Saetta, and Faraci of Murder in the First Degree, an automatic death penalty. "Relatives of the defendants pressed forward to where they sat with their lawyers," reported the *Times-Union*. "Mrs. Antonio's brother threw his arms around her and said in Italian, 'My poor sister!' At this the tears that had been welling in her eyes streamed down her cheeks and she burst into sobs."[18]

At Sing Sing, word quickly spread that a woman was coming to Death Row. It had been more than six years since Ruth Snyder went to her death in the electric chair in 1928. Matrons, who were traditionally hired from the nearby Village of Ossining, were summoned to attend to the new arrival. "Whenever a woman is confined at Sing Sing, facing death, there is a strange psychological reaction throughout the entire prison," wrote Dr. Amos Squire, a former prison physician. "Wretched men, outcasts from society, they experienced, in their animosity towards capital punishment and toward other suffering imposed by law, a grim sort of gratification over the fact that the world which had rejected them could also be capable of so barbarous a practice as executing a female."[19]

With Anna's execution set for June 28, Prior was under pressure. He knew that time was short. To complicate matters, the governor was also asked to decide the fate of four young men who were scheduled to die in the electric chair on the night of June 7. Frank Pasqua, Anthony Marino, Daniel Kreisberg, and Joseph Murphy, all under the age of thirty, were convicted for the killing of a skid-row derelict in the depths of the Bronx. It was their fourth murder for insurance money. Though Governor Lehman had a kind nature and a reputation for fairness, he also believed in the criminal justice system. After much consideration, he refused to order a stay. On the night of June 7, the executions began. "Three members of a murder syndicate who killed a derelict for $2,000 insurance died in the electric chair last night," reported the *Times-Union*.[20] "The fourth member . . . Joseph Murphy, was granted a last minute reprieve that his sanity might be investigated." After a review by psychiatrists, who found him to be sane enough to die, Murphy was executed on the night of July 5. Of the event, Elliott wrote in his death diary, "Joseph Murphy, convicted of slaying Michael 'Durable Mike' Malloy. He clung to the last to the thought that Governor Lehman would grant him another stay."

On June 20, Pasquale "Patsy" Capello, Anna's older brother, went to the governor's mansion in Albany. He was accompanied by Daniel Prior and Anna's three little children. That afternoon, they met with Governor Lehman in the executive chamber. District Attorney John T. Delaney appeared for the people and argued that the execution should go forward despite the fact that Anna had three children. That she was a mother should have no bearing on her sentence, he said, since it didn't prevent her from committing murder. While Capello sat behind the attorneys tending to the children, the men debated the case for more than two hours. Delaney called Anna a "cold and cruel plotter. She intended to throw suspicion on some other person. Our suspicions were first aroused when state police noticed she showed no emotion when informed of Antonio's death."[21]

Prior appealed to the governor for sympathy by pointing out that Anna was a long-suffering abused wife. "Her husband beat and abused her," he said. "Why, Governor, the wonder is she didn't kill him herself. I'm not excusing her, but women do those things."[22] Governor Lehman gave no indication of his feelings and stated his decision would be issued after he reviewed all the facts. While Anna waited for the governor's response, she sewed clothes for her children inside her cell, courtesy of Warden Lawes who allowed her to have a modern Singer sewing machine. On June 26, an unflattering photograph of Anna appeared in Albany's *Times-Union*. Though the image was not her best, it was offset by an accompanying photograph of her three children sitting together in her brother's home. In an article titled "Faith Helps Mrs. Antonio to Bear Ordeal," the *Times-Union* said that "she is not required to wear prison garb. Sewing dresses for her own wear is one of the diversions that distract her mind from the horror of the chair."[23] With less than forty-eight hours to her scheduled execution, her attorney kept pressure on Governor Lehman by calling his office several times a day. But Prior was concerned about Anna's mental and physical condition. "When I saw her last week she had lost a lot of weight," he said to reporters, "but was keeping up her courage."[24]

"If it is God's will that I die," Anna said. "It's God's will."[25] However, living conditions for females on Death Row were not as repressive as the male side of the cell block. Since she was the only occupant of the female section, Anna was not locked in her cell during the day. She had the freedom to walk in and out at will, played cards with the matrons, and ate her meals with them. Only at night was her cell door locked, and sometimes the matrons forgot to do even that. Warden Lawes was aware of the lenient procedures but did not allow similar privileges to the male side where crowded conditions prevented such lax security.

Invitations to the execution of Anna and her two accomplices were sent out during the middle of June. "There are surprisingly a large number of people who ask to be invited to witness an execution," Warden Lawes once pointed out. "The number in one particular case exceeded 1,000 and included three members of the jury which had brought in the verdict . . . those who seek an invitation are seldom invited, as it does not seem fitting to me that such a solemn and gruesome matter should be regarded in the light of a side-show for the entertainment of morbid-minded and abnormal people."[26] Lawes insisted that District Attorney John Delaney be invited to Anna's execution. It was common practice to invite the prosecuting attorney to the execution of a defendant he helped convict. It was also the law of the State of New York. Lawes believed that a D.A. should be required to attend such executions so that he could experience the reality of the death penalty. However, prosecuting attorneys were not required to attend; they were only required to receive an invitation. "Strange to say," Lawes once wrote, "I have never received a request from a district attorney to witness the execution of the man he prosecuted, or from a judge to attend the execution of the man whom he sentenced."[27]

While Saetta and Faraci pined away in their cells day after day on the male side of the death house, Anna was allowed outside occasionally where she played ball with the matrons and walked around the yard. Though the area was surrounded by a high wall and nothing could be seen of the outside world, Anna could see the sky and clouds drifting overhead. It was much more than what was available to the fourteen men on the male side. Though they had the opportunity to speak to other prisoners who shared the same fate, male prisoners were not permitted outside. In the meantime, Anna continued to proclaim her innocence. "I am innocent," she complained to the matrons, "but my children must suffer!"[28]

With the execution less than twenty-four hours away, Prior appealed to the newspapers and the public to help Anna. Because Governor Lehman had refused to intervene in previous death penalty cases, Prior didn't expect much. But for Anna there was always hope. "In the death house, she weeps for her children," said one news report. "She weeps also for her eighty-year-old father and through the grated door she screams, 'Somebody help me! Oh God! Somebody help me!'"[29] Her brother, Patsy, accompanied with their sister, Concetta, came to visit her during the late afternoon. They brought along Anna's three-year-old son, Frank. Lawes allowed mother and son to embrace for several minutes. Unaware that his mother was scheduled to die within hours, Frank played with Anna and kissed her as he would have if they were at home. "Wearing the pink cotton dress, trimmed with a white collar, that she had made in prison, Mrs. Antonio saw her brother and his wife today through a double row of screens in the visiting cage in the women's wing of the prison."[30] The guards and matrons, though long-accustomed to the execution process, were touched by the meeting between Anna and her son.

Though she was a mother of small children like Ruth Snyder, Anna generated much more sympathy from the public. Unlike Snyder, who was seen as a traitorous wife who abandoned her marriage bed for the "flapper" life-style, Anna was seen as the dutiful wife who remained with her husband despite his mistreatment. Public perception of the two women could not have been more different. Snyder attended her trial usually dressed in contemporary fashions and embraced the Jazz Age image attributed to her by the tabloid press. Anna arrived in court dressed in street clothes, wore no makeup, and symbolized the stereotypical Italian immigrant. Snyder was glamorous and she knew it. Anna was ordinary and never sought to be anything else. She was like a lot of women who felt powerless, dominated by men, and at the mercy of a society who seemed not to care too much about her welfare.

On the male side of death row, Faraci, a painter by trade, was visited by his wife, Mary, and his four-year-old son. She had traveled from upstate Geneva using money that was given to her by the Mutual Welfare League, a prisoner's advocacy group that assisted families of the condemned. During her visit at Sing Sing, Mrs. Faraci visited the office of Warden Lawes where she requested to have her husband's body shipped home after the execution. Lawes agreed, as long as the League provided the funds. Once the final arrangements were made, Mrs. Faraci said good-bye to her husband and left Ossining to return home.

As nighttime approached and the hour of Anna's execution grew near, tensions rose inside the prison. More guards were called in and the prison chaplains were notified to be on the ready. Inside her cell, Anna, a devout

Catholic, set up a crucifix and lit candles supplied by a matron. She prayed on her knees for redemption, convinced that only God could save her. "All day long in her cell, Mrs. Antonio, although weakened physically and mentally from lack of sufficient food, loss of sleep, and anxiety, had clung tenaciously to the hope her life would be spared."[31] She dictated a will to matrons who wrote the document for her in English. She left whatever possessions she had in this world to her children. Anna asked that her brother, Patsy, get full custody of her three children to raise them as he saw fit. "He has been very good to them, and me," she said. "If I could only live to comfort my children. It's them, more than myself, that I'm thinking of!"

Saetta, though only yards away, had no physical contact with Anna. The construction of the death house was such that both the male rows of cells were at a ninety degree angle with each other while the three female cells were in another corridor separated by a door. If that door were left open, the inmates could talk to one another but not see their cells. On occasion, if a female were allowed outside into the yard area, the men could catch a glimpse of her as she passed through a mutual hallway. Saetta lay on his cot throughout the night, resigned to his fate. "I don't expect anything," he said. "I'm willing to pay the price." Faraci told the guards he told the truth and he had nothing more to say.

At 10:00 p.m., a guard appeared in Anna's cell. Accompanying him was the local barber who was to shave a spot on her head to ensure proper contact with Elliot's electrodes. After matrons calmed the hysterical Anna, she sat on the bed while a barber cut her hair off in a four by four inch area. Anna had long, thick, brown hair that draped past her shoulders. Once the barber finished his work, her clear scalp was very noticeable on the back of her head. When she was able to see it in a mirror, Anna became panic-stricken all over again. Prison chaplain Father McCaffrey was summoned to the cell where he tried to soothe her with prayer. It was 10:51 p.m., nine minutes before the scheduled executions were to begin. Warden Lawes went to the death chamber where he greeted witnesses who were gathered for the ordeal ahead. Dr. Charles Sweet, the prison physician, conversed with Robert Elliott behind the wooden panel where the controls for the electric chair were located. The lights in the death chamber were dimmed which made the room darker than it had ever been before. Lawes wanted less light to make it more difficult for anyone to take a photograph as a reporter did in 1928 during the Ruth Snyder execution. Lawes never forgot that public betrayal and made a vow it would never happen again. All reporters were carefully screened and searched; if they didn't submit, they were barred from the execution chamber.

In the meantime, Saetta was grim while he prepared for death. But he was not totally finished with all he wanted to do. At the very moment Anna was praying with Father McCaffrey, Saetta demanded to see the warden. At first, guards refused. But Saetta carried on so violently, that the guards thought it best to summon Warden Lawes. When he arrived, Saetta blurted out that Anna was innocent. "Mrs. Antonio is absolutely innocent of this crime," he said. Lawes was skeptical but Saetta went on to say that he had a dispute with Sal over money that was owed to him. The two men argued for several weeks during March 1932. During this time, Sal went around to saloons and pool halls in the *Gut* telling everyone who would listen that he had cheated Saetta out of his money. Saetta said that he felt he had to do something about that kind of disrespect. He told Lawes that he, Faraci, and Antonio took a ride over to the city of Hudson where the three men drank all night. On the way home, Saetta said he shot and killed Sal on the road back to Albany. He said that Mrs. Antonio had nothing to do with the murder and never paid to have Sal killed.

Lawes immediately called for a stenographer to put Saetta's words into writing. "His statement was long and rambling," Lawes later said. "I could have helped him out, but I thought it was fairer to let him tell his story in his own way."[32] As the stenographer prepared the statement, Anna waited in her cell, unaware of the developments a few yards away. The execution deadline of 11:00 p.m. passed while the statement was typed. As soon as he had the signed paper in his hand, Lawes returned to his office and called Governor Lehman personally. He read Saetta's confession over the phone to Governor Lehman. He then conferred with his legal staff who suggested a temporary postponement of the executions. A short time later, Lehman sent a telegram to the prison in which he "directed the warden of Sing Sing prison to postpone the electrocutions of Vincent Saetta, Sam Faraci and Anna Antonio until Friday night, June 29, in order that I may have time to study and consider the long statement made by Saetta just before 11 o'clock tonight."

When word reached Anna that she had been given a second chance, she collapsed to the floor in a dead faint. "It was hellish hot in her cell," Lawes said later. "She had been under terrific strain. Everything was ready for the execution."[33] But Anna was not as well as thought. She had lost much weight and appeared very sickly. Throughout the day, she had paced in her cell and constantly asked the guards the time. She had not slept the night before and was hysterical over the thought of her children having their mother executed in the electric chair. "By the time word came from the governor that he would grant a stay, she had fainted," said Lawes to reporters. "When she came to, she looked about her in great surprise. In a weak voice she asked the matron to say something. I am sure she thought she was dead and needed the reassurance of a human voice to convince her that she was still on this earth."[34]

But Lehman granted only a twenty-four-hour reprieve. Anna still faced death on the following day. "A crudely phrased, ungrammatical statement, babbled out by a man who thought he had only a quarter of an hour to live, today occupied the rapt attention of Governor Herbert H. Lehman."[35] The governor, who spent most of his time at his Park Avenue home in Manhattan, refused to talk to reporters and declined comment. Daniel Prior and the other defense attorneys waited in their respective offices for further developments. They remained in contact with the governor's office by telephone and provided each other with frequent updates on the situation. For Anna though, the countdown to death began anew.

"Today her hope is growing stronger that she may be permitted to live to see her children even though she may look at them only from behind prison bars," said Albany's *Times-Union*. "Even life imprisonment would seem a glorious release to her who is now in the Valley of the Shadow of Death."[36] Warden Lawes came to visit Anna the following morning. He saw that she was in a sickly way and ordered the physician to examine her immediately. Anna ate hot soup that the matrons had brought her, but little else. Once again, she insisted that she was innocent of the crime and wished to speak to the governor. Lawes told her that was impossible but assured her that her attorney was in contact with Lehman's office. "Her shaved head covered with a silk bandana handkerchief, Mrs. Antonio bore the marks of her ordeal of being within a few minutes of the electric chair," said one reporter. "I can never go through that terrible experience again," she said. "If have to go again; they'll have to carry me!"[37]

While she waited in her cell, attended by the matrons, Anna prayed in front of the burning candles and a small crucifix that hung on the wall. Reporters gathered outside Sing Sing's gates, anxious to record the final moments of prison life before the execution. "Mrs. Antonio had borne up well during the day," said one report. "She had been so brave that her brother, who brought her three-year-old son for a visit, said that she made him feel ashamed of himself."[38] In the meantime, District Attorney John Delaney blasted Saetta's confession as a "fabrication of lies which did not agree with anything that was brought out by our investigation of the murder or that was testified to at the trial."[39] Saetta responded by telling the warden that "District Attorney Delaney had double-crossed him by promising a commutation of the death sentence."[40]

But unknown to Delaney, Sam Faraci had also made an oral statement to prison authorities which corroborated Saetta's confession. This fact was brought to Lehman's attention and throughout the day, his office struggled with the problem of a triple execution. Lehman did not want an innocent person to be executed, especially when she was the mother of three young children. But Lehman tended to accept the decision of the jury and knew the case had gone through the appeals court where the conviction was affirmed. Day passed into night and still, no decision was announced.

At Sing Sing, Robert Elliott arrived through the back entrance for the second time in two days. He hurried to the execution room where he unpacked his bags and placed his precious electrodes on a table. As he cleaned the items, he made sure their points were shiny and smooth for maximum contact with human skin. Then, as was his custom, Elliott checked all the equipment in the death chamber. "In examining the chair, I make certain that it is hooked up and that no wires are broken," he once explained. "I inspect the adjusting screws, test the strength of the straps and determine if the buckles work freely. A strap did break during an execution, and I try to prevent a repetition of this."[41] He also checked the conductive quality of the electrodes by placing them in a bucket of salt solution and turning the current on. If the water heated up, he knew that the electric current worked properly.

Across the yard, Warden Lawes worked in his office coordinating the procedures for the execution, which was again scheduled for 11 p.m. In the meantime, Anna lay on her cot almost too sick to stand up. She embraced her brother Patsy at 8 p.m. and said her farewell. "Good-bye, Patsy. Perhaps I will see you in the morning. And if I don't, we'll both try to be brave."[42] At 9:30 p.m., Father McCaffrey arrived and began the prayer vigil. Anna steeled herself for her death which she was sure would come within the next hour. She held the crucifix in her hand while she pleaded to God for another chance.

At 10:15 p.m., less than forty minutes before Anna's scheduled execution, a matron hurried over to the death house. When she entered the female cell block, she shouted out the news. The governor had granted another reprieve. Anna could not believe her ears. She fell to the floor unconscious. Warden Lawes rushed to her cell a minute later. Anna came to quickly. "Oh, thank God!" she cried. "Thank almighty God!" On the other side of the wall, Saetta and Faraci took the news impassively and showed no reaction. Lawes told Elliott that he could return home at his leisure.

After a review of the Saetta confession, Governor Lehman, District Attorney James Delaney, and Defense Attorney Daniel Prior agreed that a reprieve should be granted to all defendants in the interests of justice and to afford enough time for the defense to put together a formal motion for a new trial. "The District Attorney, while expressing the opinion that the statement of Saetta had no merit, concurred that a reprieve should be granted," said Governor Lehman. "Therefore, in accordance with the request . . . I am granting a reprieve until the week beginning July 9, 1934, in the case of all three defendants, Vincent Saetta, Sam Faraci, and Anna Antonio."[43] The Albany *Times-Union* reported that "hope for a new trial and possibly for a new lease on life, today exalted the spirits of Mrs. Anna Antonio, for whom the stroke of death at Sing Sing prison has twice been stayed by the stroke of Governor Lehman's pen."[44]

While her family and friends rejoiced, Anna lay in her cell nearly paralyzed with fear. She had lost ten pounds due to the mental strain and lack of nourishment. Anna did not eat solid food for three days and looked emaciated. Everyone who saw her during that week remarked on her sickly appearance. She was barely skin and bones and was unable to get up from her cot. "For the first time in three days, she had toast and coffee . . . she said today that she was too weak to sweep and wash out the woman's section of the death house which she had previously done."[45]

Prior, Duncan, and Lowenberg had to act immediately. The three defense attorneys filed motions asking for a new trial based on the revelations of Anna's alleged innocence. Duncan also secured a second statement from Saetta which added to his claims on June 29.

> I know the facts to be that Mrs. Antonio in no way asked me to kill her husband. In no way did she encourage me to kill her husband and never at any time promised me money to kill her husband. I want to add that whatever statements were made by me to authorities before my trial were made after I was beaten continuously by the police. The statements were suggested to me by the police. I was told by the police what to say and then promised immunity.[46]

Duncan was also able to secure an affidavit from Michael D'Ambrosio, a records clerk at Sing Sing, who processed the three defendants into the facility. He said that on the day they entered the prison, he heard Saetta say that he expected a commutation of his sentence and if he didn't get one, he would make a last minute statement in an attempt to get a delay.

From the day Anna arrived at Sing Sing until the time her case made it to the appeals court, twenty-four men died in the electric chair. Tensions at the prison were high because executions affected everyone at Sing Sing, not only the condemned. "So long as the men in prison are in proximity to the death house, thoughts of what goes on there are bound to exert a morbid influence upon them," a prison physician once wrote. "The sight of the building itself—which they can view from various points—has a depressing and degrading effect on them and naturally news from the death house seeps back to them through numerous channels."[47]

Arguments for a new trial were heard by County Judge Earl H. Gallup, the judge who presided over the original trial. District Attorney Delaney told the court that the defendants were convicted by a jury after a trial in which all the available evidence was presented. Prior argued that Saetta's posttrial statements changed everything and absolved his client of any wrongdoing. He stated that if the jury had heard these statements, a different verdict could have resulted. But Gallup disagreed.

> The court, in determining whether or not a new trial should be granted on this proposed newly discovered evidence cannot adopt the humane rule of giving the prisoner the benefit of any reasonable doubt . . . the proposed new evidence must raise a reasonable presumption that its reception would have changed the verdict of the jury or that on a new trial it would produce a different verdict . . . the court is satisfied that if the case were retried the same verdict would probably be rendered.[48]

It was a tremendous blow to the defense. Saetta's confessions, upon which Anna had relied to save her life, meant nothing. According to the court, it did not change anything. "Twice saved from death, in Sing Sing prison's electric chair by last minute reprieves, Anna Antonio, mother of three small children, must die next week," reported the *Post*. "Last hope for the doomed mother apparently faded today when County Judge Gallup denied Mrs. Antonio's appeal for a new trial."[49] But Prior moved forward. He prepared another motion to the State Court of Appeals even though the court was already in recess and was not due back until after the summer. Delaney responded by indicating that it didn't matter if the court were out, the decision made by Judge Gallup was final and there was no right to appeal. Legal experts in the state disagreed, but tended to give the defense the benefit of the doubt and encouraged Prior to file the papers with the court clerk.

In the meantime, Anna waited. "Hopeful that Governor Lehman would grant her a third reprieve, Mrs. Antonio . . . today washed clothes in her cell," reported the *Post*. "I'd rather be doing this washing than lie in bed and think," she said to matrons.[50] Her execution was set for the night of July 9 and again, she prepared herself for the worst. She refused to see her daughters that day though, afraid of the effect it may have on their lives to see their mother in prison. "No matter how much time I spend here," she said, "I would rather they did not see me in here."[51] Encouraged by the news that the governor's office seemed receptive to the appeal, Anna had genuine hope for the first time in weeks. "I believe Governor Lehman will give my lawyer time enough to appeal to a higher court."[52] She was right. Later that same night, Governor Lehman decided to grant a third reprieve. When Anna heard the news, she was on her knees in her cell. "Thank God!" she cried to matrons. "My prayers have been answered. My children will be happy!"[53]

Disturbed by the idea that Anna might go to her death because the appeals court was in recess, Lehman asked Chief Judge Cuthbert W. Pound to recall the court specifically to hear the Antonio case. "It is evident that there is only one body that can determine the right of Mrs. Antonio to an appeal . . . that is, your court," he wrote to the Chief Justice. "I am of the strong opinion that unnecessary delay in this case and in other cases where similar questions may arise should be prevented. I feel it to be of great importance that the administration of justice be definite, certain and expeditious."[54] District Attorney Delaney was not impressed and ridiculed the idea that Saetta's later statements were more important that the first confession he made to police. "It is not to be believed," Delaney told reporters. "Look at the record of the trial. In his original statement, Saetta gave a full, detailed confession which cannot be contradicted. This last minute statement doesn't change the guilt of the three defendants in one iota [sic]."[55] Lehman thought otherwise and decided the prudent thing to do was to give the defense more time and an opportunity for additional review. He put the execution off until the week beginning August 6.

After he received the letter from Governor Lehman, Chief Justice Pound concurred that expediency was paramount in this case and he decided to recall the appeals court to hear all the issues raised by Saetta's last minute statement. "My Dear Governor," he wrote in a telegram sent on July 11, "your letter of July 10 is at hand. Special session of Court of Appeals is hereby called at urgent request of Governor for July 16 at two o'clock to consider Antonio case. Please notify judges and attorneys. Signed, Cuthbert W. Pound, Chief Justice."[56] By then, Saetta and Faraci, battered by the on-again, off-again execution dates, were about to go mad. To make matters worse, other executions went forward as planned. As Saetta and Faraci cowered in their cells, never sure if they would be alive the next day, the other condemned prisoners had to pass them on their own way to death.

On the night of July 12, Frank Camora, a fifty-one-year-old Italian gas station owner from Lodi, New Jersey said his last prayers. He had been sentenced to death for the murder of his estranged wife, Lena, on January 26, 1933. On that day, he picked up his wife and feigned reconciliation. They had lunch and headed back toward the small town of Ramapo, New York. When they stopped to admire the scenery, Camora stabbed Lena without warning. He dragged her behind a large boulder where he dumped a five gallon can of gasoline on top of her. He then tossed a lighted match onto the unconscious woman. Lena exploded into flames and was burned alive. Faraci was friendly with Camora and the two men frequently confided in one another. When he was removed from his cell to walk the last mile, Camora said good-bye to Faraci and encouraged him to be brave. Faraci burst into tears as he watched his friend enter the chamber through the dreaded green door. Elliott, who had executed two hundred-fifty-two men and women by then, was unmoved by the experience. "Camora did not speak after entering the chamber," he wrote in his diary. "Like many others, he just seemed to give up and let the normal proceedings take their course."[57]

On July 16, the State Court of Appeals met in Albany to consider the perplexing problem of what to do with Anna Antonio. Daniel Prior argued to the panel that his client had a right to another trial based on newly discovered evidence, which consisted of Saetta's last minute confession. He contended that the State Court of Appeals had the power to order a stay of the execution and a new trial. But Chief Justice Pound rejected that argument, pointing out that only the governor of the state can order a stay after a lower court affirmed the conviction as Judge Gallup did on July 11. "The motion for reargument must be denied. It presents no points overlooked or misapprehended by the court on the original verdict," he said. Judge Pound also went one step further. "For the guidance of future cases," he wrote in his decision, "the court states the following rules. After affirmation of judgment of death, no stay of execution can be granted except by the Governor . . . the appeals must, therefore, be dismissed."[58] In other words, the new execution date of August 6 would stand.

Prior asked his investigators to return to Albany to search for additional evidence while he prepared still another motion. Though he did not expect to find anything new, he was surprised a few days later when his staff reported they found the man who telephoned Anna to come to the hospital on the night Sal was killed. At her trial, Anna said she did not recognize the voice. But prosecutor Delaney told the court that the phone call was made up because Anna planned the killing and therefore already knew Sal was at the hospital. Investigators told Prior the man was Father William Brown, the pastor of St. Joseph's Church in Albany. He was at Memorial Hospital the night Sal was brought in to administer the last rites. Following the ceremony, he telephoned Anna at her home and told her that her husband was in the emergency room.

Prior asked for another trial because a new witness had been found. He said this witness helped to show that Anna was telling the truth all along and that Delaney was incorrect when he said Anna had prior knowledge of the killing. Prior submitted his papers to Supreme Court Justice O. Byron Brewster of Elizabethtown who reviewed the defense issues. On August 2, he ordered District Attorney Delaney to appear in court to show cause why a new trial should not be ordered. On the following Monday, three days before the scheduled execution, defense and prosecution argued their case before Judge Brewster. While her fate was debated in court, Anna sewed a birthday gift for her daughter, Marie, who would be seven years old on the day her mother was to die in the electric chair. "Mrs. Antonio quit her tireless sewing yesterday," said the *News*. "She has completed enough clothing to last her three children a year."[59] The hours passed slowly while Anna realized that this might be her last chance for life. Two days went by with no word from Judge Brewster. "Mrs. Mary Manning, a matron at the prison, escorted Mrs. Antonio on a morning walk along the corridor of the death house. 'I'm anxious to learn what will come of me,' Mrs. Antonio said to her keeper."[60]

On the night of August 8, less than twenty-four hours before her date with death, Judge Brewster announced his decision. He said he was perfectly aware of the gravity of the situation before the court and accordingly, addressed the issues with careful review. "I find however," he wrote in his decision, "that the difficulty of its rendition is due to considerations that have no proper place in the stern administration of justice, eloquent and potent as they may be."[61] There would be no new trial. Anna received the news while she was taking an exercise walk. She was reading a handwritten letter from her daughter Marie. "I will have a birthday tomorrow, if you get good news mother," said the note. "Mrs. Antonio was unable to speak when Justice Brewster's decision was told to her," reported the *Post*. "She looked open-mouthed at Mrs. Lucy Many, the matron. The child's note fluttered from her hand. Gently, Mrs. Many led the distracted woman back to her cell."[62]

The prison staff knew from experience that hope was running out for Anna. They knew that the governor rarely granted a commutation after so many courts and judges had decided the case before it reached his desk. In order for Lehman to interfere, he would have to act in direct opposition to three courts who had decided that Anna received a fair trial and no additional evidence thus far uncovered would have resulted in a different verdict. Furthermore, it would be extremely difficult for him to grant such a privilege to Anna without doing the same for Saetta and Faraci who were convicted at the same trial and received the same penalty. Privately, Lehman wanted the Appeals Court to order a new trial and thereby relieve him of the responsibility. As the hours went by, Anna realized her situation was bleak. "It looks as if they've all turned me down. God alone can help me! I'm not thinking of myself, but of my children. You don't know how terrible it is to be here."[63]

Saetta and Faraci brooded in their cells, convinced they were about to die. For his last meal, Saetta feasted on roast chicken, Italian sausage, ice cream, pineapple pie, salad, and orangeade. Faraci ordered steak, French fries, strawberry shortcake, apple pie, and ice cream. Cigars were requested by both men. When matrons tried to get Anna to order her meal, she declined. "Nothing, thanks," she replied when asked what she wanted for supper. A cup of coffee was her only meal today. She has refused solid food since

Tuesday night.[64] Matrons had given up trying to give her regular meals. Each day, trays of food would sit outside her cell door on the concrete floor until someone would take it away.

"Most of the night she sat on her cot, staring in front of her," wrote the prison physician of her last evening. "Occasionally, her eyes would droop and she would be on the point of drowsing, when she would awaken with a start, and begin staring straight in front of her again."[65] The matrons would periodically relay her condition to the principal keeper who, in turn would feed the information to reporters gathered at the front prison gate. Periodically, the press telephoned the warden's office for an update. "All afternoon Mrs. Antonio appeared to be in a trance," reported the *Daily News*. "It seemed probable that if she is executed tonight she will be too weak to walk the few feet from her cell to the chair."[66] With the execution set for 11:00 p.m., Anna declined to see her children. "No, just thank them," she said. "I just want to be quiet."[67] That day, August 9, was Marie's seventh birthday and surely one she would never forget. But mother and daughter would not see each other for the occasion. Instead, Anna sent Marie a box of candy and a home-made dress that she put together in her cell. "Just because I must die, is no reason that little Marie should suffer on her birthday," she told the guards. "Maybe it would have been better if I had died the night she was born. The children would have been spared the disgrace."[68] Later that night, Patsy came to see his sister for the last time and with him, he brought Anna's son, Frank. "I am almost dead now," she whispered. "I feel at times, I am not breathing."[69] After her brother and son left, Anna was finally alone with her thoughts and resigned to the worst.

"In a state bordering on catalepsy, Mrs. Anna Antonio, Albany mother of three, today sat moaning on the edge of her cot in the women's wing of Sing Sing's death house," reported the *Post*. "This bright breezy summer day is the last on this earth for the woman convicted of slaying her husband Salvatore, for insurance money."[70] Though Prior spoke to Governor Lehman that very night, he had no hope that the governor would intervene. Nevertheless, Prior tried, even though he knew that it would be highly unlikely a reprieve would come. Father McCaffrey arrived at Anna's cell and began his vigil. While he prayed in the background, the matrons laid out Anna's clothes for the night. At 9:30 p.m., the prison barber arrived and cropped her hair in order to make better contact with Elliott's electrodes." I've been through enough to kill a million people," she said to the barber.

In the meantime, excitement was building outside at the gates of the prison. Like many other executions that received a great deal of media publicity, Anna's was attended by a large crowd of curiosity seekers, local residents, reporters, and an odd mixture of death penalty supporters and detractors. A dozen guards stood at the entrance to the prison in full gear to discourage any ideas that pedestrians might have of walking onto the grounds. One newspaper described the crowd as "A curiously excited mob of men, women, and even children, who would have fought their way into the execution chamber if they had been able to, made merry to a ghastly modern version of a Roman holiday. They chattered, laughed, screamed at ribald jokes, around hot dog and beer stands."[71]

At 11:00 p.m., when the principal keeper came to her cell, Mrs. Antonio was on her knees praying with Father McCaffrey. "I have stood the suspense as long as I could," she cried. "Surely the governor won't let them do this to me!"[72] She looked up in terror at the guards and knew that this time; there would be no last-minute rescue. "She was attired in a dress which she had made during her imprisonment," said Elliot later. "It was a pretty garment— blue with bits of white trimming on the sleeves and across the front. As she stepped from the cell, guards started to carry her; but she indicated that she would not need any assistance."[73] She rose to her feet and grasped the trembling hand of the priest.

With tiny, faltering steps, Anna began the walk to the death chamber. As she prayed, her chin rested upon her chest. "The young woman's demeanor was one of brave resignation to the inevitable. Her countenance was grave, but there were no tears in her eyes and she appeared to be in complete control of herself."[74] She was painfully weak and weighed less than ninety pounds. Her voice quivered as she spoke the words of prayer. "The priest and the principal keeper led her down from the women's wing to the circular arena of cells that the condemned, with sardonic humor, had dubbed 'the dance hall' and along the fabled last mile through the green door."[75] When she entered the death room, guards quickly placed her into the chair. "Anna is clad in a blue dress with a large white collar," later said one witness. "She has one light colored stocking on, on the right leg. The left is bare for the electrode. Several guards close in a circle so you can't see them place the black hood down over the praying woman's head."[76] Elliot then stepped from behind the control panel. "Approaching from the back to affix the head electrode, I could see that she was extremely nervous," said Elliott. "A wave of pity for this frail little mother swept over me," he wrote.[77] But Elliott, ever the professional and not about to let personal feelings interfere with his dedication to duty, was not deterred. Pity was not one of his stronger points.

After the guards attached the electrodes and the straps were securely tied across her chest, arms, and legs, the men stepped back. "I always affix the head electrode," Elliott later said, "which is attached to the base of the skull and is held secure by a strap under the chin . . . about a minute passes from the instant the condemned enters the death chamber until he is fully strapped in the chair and the electrodes and the mask are adjusted."[78] Father McCaffrey gave a final blessing and retreated behind the rows of witnesses. "The two matrons, with a guard between them, stood in front of the chair," later wrote an eyewitness, "not over four feet away from her, blocking the view of the witnesses. Only these three, two women and one man—no one else in the room—actually saw her die. Any witness who might have secreted a camera upon his person . . . would not have succeeded in taking a picture of Anna Antonio."[79] As soon as the area around the chair was clear, Elliott turned the dial up to the maximum and a loud crackling filled the room. Within two minutes, it was over. Anna was dead. In his diary, Elliott wrote:

> #254 New York. Thursday Aug 9, 1934
> 9 amp.
> Anna Antonio # 87513-28 yrs old
> Convicted with #255-256 of hiring two men to slay her husband. She walked to the chair unassisted although nervous. She sat in the chair calmly and repeated the catholic prayers with Father McCaffrey.

The *Herald Tribune* reported that Anna "died with a sober, resigned expression on her thin face . . . and weighed no more than ninety pounds at the end . . . she was too preoccupied with prayer to make a farewell statement from the chair, but earlier she had protested innocence."[80] Another report said, "A slim 29 year old mother sat down to death in Sing Sing electric chair tonight with a final word to the warden of her love for her three children."[81] The *Post* told its readers that "the woman, who because of our extraordinary legal system, died four agonizing deaths through months of postponements, delays, appeals and last minute reprieves, and at times almost lost her reason as a result, was calm and resigned in the face of the inevitable."[82] The *Albany Evening News* said, "The state had avenged the death of Salvatore Antonio. Perhaps it was right. But if you sat in that room you had a frantic urge to cry out against it."[83] After the physician pronounced her dead, Anna's tiny body was quickly removed from the wooden chair. There was still more work to be done.

Sam Faraci was brought in next, flanked by two guards but standing on his own feet. When he first entered the chamber, he closed his eyes against the overhead lighting. "He entered easily, but sullenly as one who feel he is punished for another's fault," reported the *Troy Record*.[84] The witnesses, already unnerved by the spectacle of Anna's death, shifted uneasily in their seats. Faraci motioned to the guards that he wanted to say something. "I'm going to the chair," he said loudly, "but I am innocent. That is all I can say. I wish all of you good luck—all of you—all of your life."[85] Faraci had barely finished the sentence as the guards quickly strapped him into the chair.

Father McCaffrey gave his blessing and stepped back. Elliott made a final check around the apparatus and abruptly turned the dial to full power. At 11:23, prison physician Dr. Charles Sweet pronounced Faraci dead. In the background, witnesses could hear the faint sounds of the autopsy saw working on Anna's body in the adjacent room. Suddenly, there was a loud thud from the second row of seats. One of the spectators had fainted in the aisle and had to be carried out of the chamber.

In the meantime, Faraci was lifted from the chair and rolled into the autopsy room. No sooner had he disappeared when Vincenzo Saetta was brought in through the green door. "He was cheerful. 'Hello Guard!' he called out. He was smiling. He was the worst of the three, to hear him tell it, yet it was he who tried to shoulder all the blame."[86] Saetta had no final statement; he simply sat down in the chair and waited for the end to come. At 11:28 p.m. he was declared dead and removed from the chamber. Elliott, his work finished for the evening, began to pack up his gear. The witnesses filed out of the room. Reporters scribbled notes on their pads and rushed to make telephone calls to their editors.

"DOOMED MOTHER DIES" was the headline in the New York *Daily News* the following day. The page-two story described Anna's last torturous hours on Death Row while she hoped for a reprieve that never came. "Once, with a piercing shriek, she started from her coma and leaped to the bars of her cell, her body tense and shuddering in agony, silent and strange after the wail that startled the death house. Then she relaxed and fell back on her cot in a swoon."[87] The *Times* was less emotional and reported, "Her two men accomplices took matters much more calmly than Mrs. Antonio. Both were visited by relatives during the day and both asked repeatedly whether any word had come from the governor for the woman."[88] The *Post* follow-up story on the triple execution concentrated on Anna's children. "The children are three-year-old Frankie, whose mother played ball with him in the Sing Sing death house a few hours before she sat in the electric chair, Marie, who celebrated her seventh birthday the day her mother was electrocuted and Phyllis who is nine."[89] The *Poughkeepsie Eagle News* described Anna's physical condition as "pale and wan, her weight reduced 15 pounds since she entered the death house 15 months ago. Mrs. Antonio was supported by two matrons as she was brought to the chair."[90] The *Troy Record* said that "she walked the rest of the way, a bit defiantly, drawing on a reserve of nerve which doctors had said she did not have."[91]

In Albany, Governor Lehman was feeling the effects of weeks of contemplation on the fate of Anna. Though he was sympathetic to her predicament, Lehman decided not to issue the reprieve solely based on emotion and the fact that Anna was a female. "The case of Anna Antonio has received my most painstaking and careful consideration," he said in a released statement. "The responsibility of carrying out the death penalty on a woman is so distressing that, frankly, I sought to find any fact which would justify my interference with the course of justice."[92] But, he said, he could not find any redeeming factor in her attorney's motion or in the trial record that would condone an additional reprieve or a commutation of her sentence. The *News* later reported that Anna was "the costliest death felon." After an interview with Sing Sing prison officials, it was determined that "her incarceration of fifteen months cost the State $4,650 for the service of matrons."[93] They said that "more money was spent for the supervision and maintenance of Mrs. Antonio than was ever spent for any other Sing Sing prisoner."[94] However, some of the press noticed the long range effect of the multiple executions. "Three people had died for the murder of Salvatore Antonio," said the *Post*. "Today, twelve children are fatherless."[95]

"The three children of Mrs. Anna Antonio . . . today will get their mother back—dead," said the *Post*. "They lost their father the night before Easter 1932 when he was stabbed and shot to death . . . they lost their mother last night when the State of New York took her life in the electric chair at Sing Sing."[96] Anna's body was claimed by her brother, Patsy, and taken home to Albany where she was buried in a local cemetery. The exact location was kept a secret to avoid curious crowds who would be sure to congregate at her grave.

Many people believed, right up until the moment of her execution, that Anna would be spared once again. "Women's alleged sixth sense of curiosity came to the fore last night or the number of telephone calls concerning the electrocution of Mrs. Antonio coming to the *Eagle News* office would indicate."[97] The same article pointed out that four of every five callers were female, and the inquiries continued until two o'clock in the morning. The odds seemed to have been in Anna's favor. "Morbid bettors had a field day offering odds of 3–1 that the twenty-eight-year-old mother would be granted a reprieve."[98] After the execution, Anna's children were not told exactly how their mother died. "It won't be so hard now," her brother told reporters. "But later, when they get older . . . I guess now we'll just tell them Anna got sick and went to heaven."[99] The day after Anna's execution, an Albany newspaper published the following editorial. "The gain of lawlessness in this country can be checked only when there is a general understanding that the administration of justice is definite and certain," said the *Evening News*. "Unhappily, there is justification for such belief in too numerous instances of lax administration of justice. Make it definite and certain and the crime problem will be near solution."[100]

By the following Monday, just four days later, the name of Anna Antonio was gone from newspaper tabloid headlines. She quickly faded from public consciousness. Media attention was now focused upon the rather obscure city of Oneonta in upstate New York. There another female had been arrested for a killing involving insurance money. On the very day Anna was executed, a woman with the unlikely name of Eva Coo prepared for her trial in Otsego County Court for Murder in the First Degree and was about to discover for herself, the agonizing struggle for life amid the horrors of Death Row.

Eva Coo and Murder on Crumhorn Mountain

She got a rotten deal all around . . . rotten!
—Sing Sing Warden Lewis E. Lawes to reporters
after the execution of Eva Coo in 1935.

The tumultuous march to death by Anna Antonio ended the nearly seven-year hiatus of female execution in New York. In the years that followed, societal resistance to women in the electric chair would be severely challenged. By the mid-1930s, the print media, long the most reliable source of information for the masses, lost acres of ground to radio, though the sensationalism associated with the tabloids still existed. In the realm of crime reporting, the New York City press, led by the *Daily News* with the impertinent *Daily Mirror* not far behind, relished in fast-breaking developments across the nation.

The *Daily News* set the standard by which all the big city tabloids would be judged. Ruth Snyder's execution photograph, revered in some circles as an example of American ingenuity, was already a journalism legend and raised the level of sensationalism to new heights. The *Daily News* offered sparse coverage of national events, and limited international news. The editors cared little for society's problems, unless they could boost circulation. In business since 1920 as the *Illustrated Daily News*, "the *Daily News* was perfect morning reading for anyone who did not want to ponder the world's troubles . . . it had very little substance and evidenced slight concern for social justice."[1] But subway riders, who appreciated its easy-to-read vocabulary and stories that began and ended on the same page, made it the most popular newspaper in New York and, therefore, one of the biggest in the nation. By 1930, barely six years after it began publication, the *Daily News* was selling one million copies a day. Its editors attributed success to its no-holds-barred reporting—the work of a twenty-four hour a day staff of reporters who frequently hung around Manhattan's busiest police stations in the hopes of catching a crime story in progress.

Meanwhile, the so-called gangster era, epitomized by criminals like Chicago's Alphonse "Scarface" Capone and New York's Charles "Lucky" Luciano, saw the beginning of its decline in 1934 when bank robber John Dillinger, George "Baby Face" Nelson, the maniacal "Pretty Boy" Floyd, and the much-reviled "Bonnie and Clyde" were killed in shoot-outs with police. But the "gangster," a term invented during the frantic years of the Jazz Age, was still very much an object of fascination for the general public. "I respected the cops," said one death row inmate. "But I respected the gangsters too. They were a fact on the lower East Side. To lots of us, especially the kids, they looked like the only ones who'd managed the long, hard climb out of the pit of poverty."[2] Thanks to Hollywood, which released *Little Caesar* (1930), *Public Enemy* (1931), and *Scarface* (1932) in quick succession, the popularity of crime films and the emergence of the outlaw as a sort of mythic hero, became an indelible part of American culture.[3] "Central to the gangster film's appeal was its criticism of Prohibition . . . widely resented across the classes, and the gangster emerged as an object of . . . empathy, to the extent, that as a bootlegger, he resisted a very unpopular piece of legislation."[4] In the eyes of a beleaguered population, hungry for good news amid a dreary economic landscape, the gangster represented a glimmer of hope. "The gangster was uplifting, awe-inspiring and grand, even in death. Movies created dreams and fantasies that made a hard life bearable."[5]

During the 1930s, as the Great Depression ravaged a bewildered nation, millions of movie fans sat in darkened theaters where a few pennies bought a temporary escape from the harsh realties of everyday life. The biggest films of the time were *I Am a Fugitive* (1932), *King Kong* (1933), *It Happened One Night* (1934), and *The Thin Man* (1934) with William Powell and Myrna Loy. The top box office stars were Clark Gable, Paul Muni, Mae West, Joan Crawford, Marie Dressler, and the adorable Shirley Temple. The hit song in 1934 was *Blue Moon*, while Benny Goodman, at age twenty-four, brought big-band swing to his National Biscuit radio audience. But in New York, Wall Street was a dismal place. The Dow Jones high for the year was one hundred ten and national unemployment was a staggering twenty-two percent. But a room for a month at the uptown Barbizon Plaza Hotel was only sixty-eight dollars and a meal at Rosoff's famous restaurant, including dessert, cost an average of one dollar, though few people could afford it.

In upstate New York, the small city of Oneonta, located fifty miles west of Albany, was feeling the brunt of the depression as well. But it wasn't always so. Before those bleak years, Oneonta, like many other cities in America, was in the midst of a boom era. During the 1920s, it was recognized as the epicenter for several railroads and a major destination for truckers on the way to Albany, Utica, and Binghamton. Each weekend, hundreds of blue-collar workers converged on Oneonta's saloons and hotels where a night of relaxation or fun could be had for the asking. Back then, the Delaware-Hudson Railroad employed legions of workers in Otsego County, which maintained one of the largest rail houses in the world. Oneonta, known as the "City of the Hills," was a comfortable, scenic town that had minimal violent crime, few major problems, and a friendly reputation. The surrounding valley consisted of dairy and vegetable farms where people tilled their land, grew a diversified selection of crops, and patronized Oneonta's many supply stores.

During this exciting era, a decade before the gloomy years of the Great Depression, Oneonta was prosperous. Hollywood stars Zasu Pitts and Ken Maynard, along with his lovable horse, Tarzan, made personal appearances in area theaters like Smalley's where first run films ran every week and long lines were a frequent sight. Becker's Bakery on Oneonta's Main Street had rye bread for a dime a loaf and sold layer cakes for twenty cents. Downtown, Finnigan's market sold five pounds of sweet potatoes for twenty-five cents and a dozen Barlett pears for thirty-nine cents. Laskaris, already in business for over thirty-five years, sold ice cream by the gallon, while down the street at Kandyland, a one-pound box of assorted chocolates cost twenty-nine cents and a half-pound of taffy went for a quarter. All along River Street, hundreds of rail workers resided in small, two-story homes, hastily built during the previous decade when housing was scarce and badly needed. It was a short walk over to the rail depot at Broad Street where busy restaurants, saloons, and flophouses were plentiful and catered to workers who flaunted their generous paychecks every Friday night. The Windsor Hotel on Chestnut Street maintained a thriving business thanks to out-of-towners and other professionals who serviced clients in the area. The Wilson Hotel, where out-of-town truckers gathered because of low rates and its willingness to look the other way when a working girl made her way upstairs, was located nearby. It was also suspected that just down the street from the Wilson, in a three-story apartment building, a woman named Eva Coo was running a brothel.

Eva Currie-Coo was born in Ontario, Canada, sometime in 1888. She once told reporters that her birthday was June 17 but Eva often lied about her background. She was one of nine children who, at the age of eighteen, married a Canadian Pacific Railroad worker named Bill Coo. By 1920, they had divorced and gone their separate ways. Not much is known about Eva from that time until she turned up in the city of Oneonta in early 1924, the year she purchased an apartment building on Chestnut Street. Police later claimed that she ran a profitable speakeasy whose clientele included some of the most respected people in Otsego County. "Little Eva," as she came to be known, was an outgoing, gregarious woman with a boisterous sense of humor and a discreet mind that knew when to keep quiet about her customers. Because of this, she was successful and profited during a time when other people could not. "She was free and easy," said one reporter who knew her. "And generous to a fault . . . anyone hard up for a meal, a bottle or a little cash could come to Eva and be pretty sure to get what he needed."[6] By 1928, she had saved enough money to buy her own restaurant. She purchased a vacant roadhouse in a small town called Maryland, located a few miles northeast of Oneonta on a busy state road. The building had several bedrooms on the second floor and a large front room with a bar that faced the busy road outside. Eva called it the Woodbine Inn.

She moved into the dilapidated roadhouse and began renovations. Soon, the tavern was open for business and, using her contacts in downtown Oneonta, Eva built a steady clientele. The Woodbine Inn became notorious throughout Otsego County as "Little Eva's place." But the title was not meant as a compliment. "Eva Coo became "Little Eva" in open ridicule and contempt; for she was a big, stout, flamboyant woman . . . she had been proprietress of a speakeasy and the leading procuress of the vicinity."[7]

The inn became popular when it was rumored that the barmaids were serving more than just cold beer. For the right price, Eva could set up a customer in a private room with one of her girls. Soon, even high Otsego County officials frequented the inn for some bootleg gin, a little gambling, and if they were in the right mood, an hour with one of her girls. Local politicians drank there, and city businessmen frequently stopped by, as did police officers and many of the local railroad employees. The Woodbine Inn became the place to be on a Friday night when rail workers had lots of cash and cruised the city bars looking for some fun. Its ground floor was usually jammed with customers during those times and not an empty parking space could be found.

A frequent customer at the inn was a man named Harry Wright, a jobless alcoholic who walked with a limp. Everyone knew him by the nickname, "Gimpy," and knew that he could be found at Eva's place at anytime during the day or night. Eva had taken Harry in when his mother died in January, 1931. She let him stay in one of her rooms in exchange for keeping the inn clean and the bar stocked with booze. He swept the floor, removed empty beer bottles, and took out the garbage. After Harry moved in, Coo purchased an insurance policy on Harry's life from the Prudential Life Insurance

Company, naming herself as the beneficiary. During the spring of 1933, Eva convinced Harry to sign over the deed to his mother's house since he wouldn't be needing it anymore. After he agreed, Eva went to another insurance broker in Oneonta and bought two more policies. Within the year, Eva had purchased at least eighteen insurance policies on Harry. In every case, she named herself as the sole beneficiary.

In nearby Cooperstown, the *Freeman's Journal* later reported that "approximately $16,000 in life insurance was carried by Mrs. Coo on Mr. Wright's life . . . a will, leaving the entire estate to Mrs. Coo, was drawn two months later."[8] She once asked a broker what would happen if Harry died by accident, such as being the victim of a car accident. She was told that the benefit would double in the event of an accidental death. Apparently, Eva was a believer in insurance; she bought policies on the inn, her car, and on the lives of the people who worked for her, including her current boyfriend, Harry Nabinger.

Another employee at the inn was a young woman from Pennsylvania named Martha Clift. She was an attractive brunette who came to Eva in 1933 when she was twenty-three and recently divorced. Martha had two small children who she left with her mother while she worked at the inn. She and Eva became good friends and were frequently seen together in the streets of nearby Oneonta, running errands and buying supplies for the Woodbine. Though she lived with Eva for a short time, Martha moved into an apartment on Main Street in downtown Oneonta during the spring of 1934.

By then, the Great Depression, which had begun symbolically on October 29, 1929, when the New York stock market crashed, had taken its toll on Otsego County. Hundreds of rail workers lost their jobs, local businesses closed, and home foreclosures increased. The Woodbine Inn managed to remain open, but the high-spending days of the past were gone. Customers were few and far between because most people had no money to spend. Eva began to realize that her business and even her home were in jeopardy. She couldn't pay the mortgage and barely had enough money to survive. She had to do something.

On the afternoon of June 14, 1934, Eva told Harry Wright that she had recently visited nearby Crumhorn Mountain where she saw a number of cherry trees that she wanted for the Woodbine property. When Harry agreed to dig up the trees, he and Eva picked up Martha and began the ten-minute drive to the mountain. Crumhorn was a sparsely populated area that contained a few abandoned buildings along its narrow dirt roads. When they reached an old, deserted farmhouse on the south side of the mountain, Eva said that she had to go inside the building to retrieve a tool to dig up the trees. Harry got out of the car and waited by the passenger door. When Eva returned, she carried a large wooden mallet under her sweater. As Harry turned to get back into the car, which was driven by Martha, Eva brought the mallet down on his head. He fell to the ground in front of the two-ton Willys-Knight automobile. As he lay there, he managed to cry out, "Now I know why you brought me here!" According to Eva's later statement, Martha then drove over Wright's body, crushing his chest under the wheels. Then she backed up over him again.

As Martha was driving over Wright, a man named Ben Hunt, Hunt's wife, and five children came upon the scene. They were accompanied by the owner of the property, Mrs. Fink. Hunt had heard about the abandoned farmhouse and was interested in buying it for his family. When they saw Martha and Eva, Mrs. Fink immediately became suspicious. "Mrs. Fink, soon joined by Mrs. Hunt, rushed up to the death car, demanding to know why the women were there . . . there were sharp words between the two parties because the house owner thought that the trespassers were there to steal. Mrs. Fink knew Mrs. Coo."[9] While the owners and Eva argued over her intentions, Wright's body lay a few feet away from Mrs. Fink, hidden under the car in which Martha sat, behind the wheel. For nearly fifteen minutes, they parried back and forth, while the owner checked her property and Hunt questioned the two nervous women. Eva, sitting in the passenger seat, tried to explain that she stopped at the farm just to relieve herself. Although Mrs. Fink seemed satisfied, Eva dared not move the car because Wright's body would be clearly exposed. She stalled for time while Hunt and his family piled back into Mrs. Fink's car. Martha then told Hunt that Eva was a very stubborn woman and wouldn't leave until they did. Reluctantly, Mrs. Fink agreed and drove off with the Hunt family.

As soon as they were out of sight, Martha and Eva wrapped Wright's body in a blanket and loaded it into the back of the Willys. They carefully drove down Crumhorn Mountain and back to the Woodbine. About two hundred yards north of the inn, they dumped the body on the shoulder of the road. When Eva got back to the inn, she called the police. She told them that she hadn't seen Harry all day and was worried about him. A short time later, state police began to search the area. The following morning, Trooper W. B. Caldwell found Wright's battered body in the ditch where Eva had dumped it.

Police immediately surmised that Wright was drunk and stumbled out onto the busy state road where he was run down by a speeding car or truck. Everyone seemed satisfied by that explanation, and Wright was buried the following day. "The [coroner] issued a verdict of accidental death, stating that the man had evidently been struck by a hit-and-run truck driver. This theory was advanced on account of the injuries apparently sustained on the back, near the shoulder. Wright's left side was crushed and fractured ribs penetrated his lungs."[10]

Feeling a little more secure now that Wright was in the ground and the police had decided his death was a hit-and-run accident, Eva decided to collect on the insurance. She went to the office of Metropolitan Life Insurance in Oneonta where she promptly submitted a death claim. But she couldn't contain her nerves. The agent noticed that Eva was shaking and seemed very worried. On a hunch, he called the funeral director who prepared Wright's body for burial. During their conversation, the director mentioned to the agent that Wright's body did not look like a typical car accident victim. The agent then called the local coroner to voice his suspicions. Soon, police began a full investigation into the death.

Otsego County Sheriff George Mitchell, working with State Police, told reporters he questioned whether Wright died in a vehicle accident. "It looks fishy to me," he told reporters.[11] And he wasn't the only one who thought so. The Oneonta *Daily Star* reported "there was no broken glass to give the troopers the impression the victim had been struck by a truck or automobile and so far they have been unable to find any eye-witness of the fatality."[12] Because Oneonta was not a big city, word soon got out that Eva had bought multiple insurance policies on Wright's life. "There was some suspicion attached to Wright's death when his body was found Thursday," said Sheriff Mitchell. "Everyone knew he had considerable insurance."[13]

Things were rapidly getting worse for Eva. When police originally interviewed her, she told investigators she was at home during the previous night. She never left the Woodbine, she said. But unknown to her, Mrs. Fink had filed a trespassing report with the State Police after she left Crumhorn Mountain. Mrs. Fink described her encounter with Eva Coo at her farm that night and voiced her suspicions that she was there to steal something. As soon as police realized her alibi was a lie, Eva became a suspect in Harry's death.

On Monday, June 18, she was asked to come to the Oneonta police station to prepare for a coroner's inquest. Eva initially denied everything, including being at the Crumhorn Mountain farmhouse. But as the questioning went on, Eva decided to elaborate on her story. She told police that Harry was killed by accident in front of her inn while making repairs on the building. She said that while he was up on a ladder, Martha ran into the ladder with a car, knocking Harry to the ground and killing him.

> When Martha and I came back from town June 14, Harry was fixing the eves on my road stand at the west end near the rain barrel. Martha hit the ladder and Harry fell in front of the car. Martha went right over him. We put the quilt in the car and was going to take him to the hospital. When we got ready to put him in the car, he was dead . . . I didn't know who moved Harry and don't know even now . . . Martha told me never to ask . . . that's why the quilt was in the car . . . we were going to take Harry to the hospital . . . but I don't

think Martha could admit running over him. I wanted to get the troopers and she didn't want to for she had been drinking and asked me to wait till she asked advice from someone what to do.[14]

But while Eva sat in the detective's office, two state troopers went to the Woodbine to look for evidence. Although they had no search warrant, the troopers entered the building and searched Eva's bedroom. They found several insurance policies, all on Wright's life and all of which listed Eva Coo as the beneficiary. Ultimately, police learned that Eva had purchased no fewer than nineteen insurance policies on Harry Wright, and they included the double indemnity clause. When confronted with this information, she refused to budge. "All the policies were with the Prudential, Metropolitan and American Mutual, according to authorities," reported the *Albany Times Union.* "They had been taken out by Mrs. Coo . . . who said she had obtained the policies herself because Wright was always talking about taking out insurance, but never did anything about it."[15] But still, Eva Coo told police she had nothing to do with his death.

In the meantime, police had located Martha Clift in the nearby village of Franklin and brought her to police headquarters. At the beginning of the interrogation, Martha was nervous and scared, but she held on. Threatened with the death penalty, then a very real possibility, Martha relented. During the early morning hours of June 20, she confessed to her role in the killing. "Establishment of the fact that murder had been committed in connection with Wright's death came with startling suddenness at 1:15 yesterday morning when Mrs. Clift finally said she would make a statement," reported the *Oneonta Daily Star.*[16] In her confession, Martha told police that Eva promised to pay her if she would help kill "Gimpy." The *Freeman's Journal,* a small-circulation newspaper published in Cooperstown, reported that according to Martha, the murder was premeditated. Mrs. Clift said that she was to get $200 toward a secondhand car and that Mrs. Coo told her the insurance was only $1,000. Plans were discussed, in which Mrs. Clift was to attract Wright's attention by helping him light a cigarette after he left the car and then Mrs. Coo was to run the car into him."[17]

Once Eva learned of Martha's confession, she gave in. She told police they killed Harry on Crumhorn Mountain for the insurance money. But Eva believed that she couldn't be charged with murder because she didn't actually kill Wright. She just hit him on the head with a mallet, she said. It was Martha who drove the car over Wright and killed him. But District Attorney Don Grant knew that both women could be charged with murder since they had acted in concert and conspired to kill the victim. The *Oneonta Daily Star* reported that one of their plans was to "drive a car part way down an embankment, get out to look for a flat tire, release the brake and let the machine and its human cargo go to its death in the creek."[18] Martha and Eva were taken into custody and locked in jail for the night. But the Sheriff decided not to formally charge the suspects at that time. While Eva sat in her jail cell, local reporters were allowed in for interviews. "Reposing behind the cold iron bars of the Otsego County Jail here tonight, Mrs. Eva Coo, of near Maryland, who faces the supreme penalty if convicted of First Degree Murder, maintained a stoical calm . . . she did seem to be slightly overcome by the publicity."[19] Although Eva and Martha eventually signed statements that same night, Sheriff Mitchell was unhappy with some of their discrepancies.

Early the next morning, under a veil of secrecy, Wright's body was dug up from the grave and brought to the Oneonta Police station in the rear of a pickup truck. Police parked the vehicle behind headquarters and out of view from street traffic. Local reporters got wind of the exhumation and tried to get a photograph of the coffin, but they were unsuccessful. "The *Star* was told last night by a reliable source . . . that the body of the murder victim was exhumed yesterday at the Portlandville cemetery where it was buried Saturday."[20] By nightfall, after a contentious day of accusations and retractions by the defendants, the stage was set for one of the most bizarre interrogations in the history of American criminal justice.

Together with Sheriff Mitchell, a few deputies, and the corpse of Harry Wright in the bed of a pickup truck, Eva and Martha Clift were driven up to the abandoned farmhouse on Crumhorn Mountain. By the time they arrived, it was near dark and the grounds had to be illuminated by the vehicles' headlights. Police asked Coo and Clift to reenact the crime by placing Wright's body where it was on the night of the murder. Eva removed the corpse from the pickup truck and with the help of Martha, dropped the body a few yards away from the barn house. To add to this macabre scene, a thunderstorm swept over the mountain, peppering the area with an occasional bolt of lightning. Throughout the reenactment, police insisted the women move the decomposing corpse to the exact spot where it was during the killing. "Unbelievable as it sounds," reported the *Star*, "both also failed to show the least bit of emotion as the crime was enacted in the driveway of the farmhouse on Crumhorn Mountain Thursday night while lightning played about . . . revealing the body of the victim lying in the spot where the accused pair said he had fallen."[21] According to witnesses who later testified at trial, Eva and Martha were subjected to this medieval style of interrogation while Harry's corpse was carted around the scene to ensure accuracy.[22] The *Albany Times Union* reported that "surrounding their activities with the utmost secrecy, Otsego County authorities pushed their investigation into the death of Harry Wright with as strange and eerie practice as characterized the suspected murder itself."[23] When investigators were satisfied, the defendants were taken back to Oneonta police headquarters where additional statements were taken. Wright's coffin was taken back to the Portlandville cemetery where it was dropped back into the ground and quickly covered with fresh soil.

But upon review by District Attorney Grant in Cooperstown, it was decided that still more clarifications were needed in the defendant's admissions. Since not all the details in the statements were the same, it could mean trial problems for the D.A.'s office. "Mr. Grant, feeling that the truth had not been given in statements made by both women here Wednesday morning after an all night grilling, spent all of Friday night and Saturday morning in Cooperstown talking with them," the Star reported.[24] The Times Union reported that "Mrs. Clift . . . said the plan to kill Wright was worked out after two or three months of discussion between Mrs. Coo and herself."[25] Eva had said that she wanted to put Wright in a car and send him over a cliff. "Plan after plan was considered for making away with him so as to have no trace . . . one plan was to take the victim on an outing, lure him near a creek, hit him on the head and hold him under water until he was drowned . . . or to render him unconscious and set him in a tightly closed garage in a car with the motor running."[26] And in her confession, Eva told police that she wanted "to give him a bump and put him in the car in gear and let it go down the hill and then it would go in the river."[27]

Finally, on the morning of June 25, after being held for nearly thirty-six hours without being charged, Eva and Martha were arraigned on First Degree Murder charges in Otsego County Court at Cooperstown. "District Attorney Grant drove the questioning of these women relentlessly through the days and nights until the case was established. When the others would have abandoned the quest, he drove on . . . and was finally rewarded," reported the Freeman's Journal. "It is a horrible story of horrible greed and avarice."[28] At the same time, prosecutors hastily assembled a Grand Jury to indict both defendants. According to a story in the Daily Star, "Neither woman showed any signs of strain as each was led separately into the district attorney's office in the county courthouse to be arraigned before Justice of the Peace Harold D. Carpenter, who held them on information furnished by Sheriff George H. Mitchell."[29]

By that same afternoon, the Grand Jury began to hear testimony. Everett Holmes and James "Sunny Jim" Byard, two attorneys who were well-known in the Oneonta area, were appointed to represent Eva and Martha. For the next three days, the jury heard from thirty witnesses who described the events surrounding the death of Harry Wright. The confessions from Eva and Martha were also read to the jury. Upon advice from their attorneys, each defendant declined to testify. Mrs. Fink and Ben Hunt were asked to tell the story of their accidental meeting on Crumhorn Mountain with Eva and Martha.

On the evening of June 27, both defendants were indicted for First Degree Murder. "The women, accused of one of Central New York's most ruthless crimes, were arraigned immediately . . . and pleaded not guilty . . . the composure of the prisoners, which has been shaken but once . . . remained calm during their arraignment."[30] The *Freeman's Journal* reported that Eva's "personal appearance, which included a new haircut, revealed marked improvement over that which was apparent when she first entered confinement. She showed no concern as she entered the courtroom and maintained her unmoved demeanor throughout the proceedings."[31] The defendants were remanded to the county jail; the trial date was set for early August. In the meantime, the Sheriff's Office contacted Canadian authorities for additional information on Eva. "The blonde matron, whose past was being checked by American and Canadian police to learn if she had ever speculated in life insurance policies before opening her hotel at Maryland, was apparently unruffled at the prospect of facing a murder charge."[32]

Jury selection began on the morning of August 6, when one hundred citizens gathered at the county courthouse, which is located in the Village of Cooperstown at the southern tip of Lake Otsego. By then, the case had attracted a great deal of attention due to the possibility that another woman could receive the death penalty. At that time, the ongoing life-or-death drama surrounding the execution of Anna Antonio was reported in each day's newspapers. Eva read the stories while she waited in her cell at the county jail, but probably never believed that she herself would be convicted of murder and would one day be in exactly the same position as Anna Antonio.

Reporters from across the state began to arrive in droves to cover the upcoming trial. One was Dorothy Kilgallen from New York City's *Journal American,* who would make the name "Eva Coo" nationally known through her emotional coverage of the trial. "She was . . . an inveterate liar," Kilgallen wrote of Coo. "Maybe it was good for business . . . or maybe she really did have a heart as big as it seemed . . . there was some evidence that indeed, Eva knew too much about too many. But nonetheless it was true that she received no help whatsoever from anyone."[33]

On that very Thursday, August 9, the unthinkable happened; Anna Antonio was executed at Sing Sing prison. The following morning, while jury selection continued, Eva sat in the courtroom numb with apprehension and fear. She may have realized that if the state could execute Antonio, the mother of three children, the same could happen to her. For the first time, Eva knew she was in a fight for her life.

On August 11, at the insistence of Defense Attorney "Sunny Jim" Byard, Wright's body was dug up yet again. Since the exact cause of death remained in dispute, the defense team wanted the body reexamined. "The body of

Harry Wright was taken from its grave for examination today . . . defense counsel sought to determine from the body whether the 54-year-old handy man was hit with a mallet before he was slain."[34]

During the same week, jury selection moved slowly with many of the prospective jurors claiming that they had already formed an opinion on the case. The *Freeman's Journal* reported that "of the first 100 called, all but forty-six furnished satisfactory excuses and were relieved of duty by the court." Just about everyone in Otsego County had heard the name Eva Coo, knew her, or had visited the Woodbine Inn. The possibility that one of her customers would sit on the jury to decide her fate was on the mind of her defense attorneys as well as Judge Riley Heath. It could easily be used as an excuse for a mistrial later on. Adding to their concern was the unpredictable Eva Coo, who was cocky, boisterous, and always eager to display her earthy, sarcastic sense of humor. "Whenever Eva was paraded past a group of local onlookers, either within or outside the courthouse, she would slowly walk by, calling each man by his first name . . . few managed to avoid recognition and more than one husband had some explaining to do."[35] She posed for photographers, chatted with everyone, and was never at a loss for words. "She was dressed to the nines in a suit of brown with a figured-vest effect . . . a brown straw hat with a narrow rim and band of yellow organdy about its crown, brown hose, brown suede oxfords, and black kid gloves."[36]

After a few difficult days of jury selection, a twelve-man panel was chosen, along with two alternates. District Attorney Grant asked each juror if he believed in the death penalty for females. If they answered in the negative, Grant excused them without further inquiry. But it was Eva herself who selected most of the panel. "She stood over her gray-haired attorney and speeded selection of jurors so capably that the list was exhausted early in the afternoon."[37] Judge Heath knew most of the men selected and seemed confident they could render a fair verdict. Arrangements were already completed at a Cooperstown hotel, where the jury would retire after each day's testimony. "Do not feel we are locking you up," Judge Heath told the panel. "Laugh and chat; get plenty of exercise. You are good sports and good citizens and I appreciate what you are doing!"[38]

The New York tabloids had their own interpretation of the drama in Cooperstown. "The list (of jurors) includes two alternates in addition to the dozen who are expected to decide whether the buxom, blue-eyed "Diamond Lil" shall die in the electric chair, or return to her famous little roadhouse on the Albany-Oneonta Highway to continue filling gas tanks . . . with her assorted libations."[39] Local newspapers in Otsego County saw the case from a different perspective and frequently criticized the New York City press for their erroneous and sensationalized reporting. "The tabloids, to appeal to the sordid nature of their readers, resorted to devices to which no local newspaper would descend," said the *Freeman's Journal* in an editorial. "For example, they spoke of a haunted house on Crumhorn Mountain. There is no such thing as a haunted house and no one ever called the Scott house haunted until the sob sisters thought of it."[40]

By August 16, trial preparations were complete and testimony was ready to begin. Thanks to Dorothy Kilgallen and the other tabloid reporters from New York City, the Coo case had become well-known by the first day of trial. The *Daily News* sent one of its top crime reporters, Grace Robinson, to Cooperstown during the week of jury selection. Her lively but opinionated reports appeared daily in the city's most popular newspaper. Like many of her contemporaries, Robinson immediately seized upon comparisons with Ruth Snyder. "Mrs. Eva Coo, who has frosty blue eyes like those of Ruth Brown Snyder, and who like her is accused of murder for insurance, went on trial for her life today," read a story on August 14. In the same article, Robinson referred to Coo as the "blonde backwoods innkeeper," as the "robust-looking defendant," and as having a "ruddy face."[41] And like Snyder, Eva Coo's manner of dress became an essential part of the reporting on the trial. The *Daily News* described Coo as "a calm and capable looking woman as she sat in court all day in her brown knitted dress, brown hat . . . brown suede slippers, and gay yellow beads . . . her bobbed and naturally blonde hair was waved slightly and she appeared equal to any situation life might offer."[42]

Crowds began to gather outside the Cooperstown courthouse early each morning, and some people camped out on the lawn overnight so as not to miss any part of the show. "Monday noon Sheriff George H. Mitchell cleared the courtroom and locked it for an hour so that those who had brought lunch baskets with the idea of eating their mid-day meal in the court room, in order to be sure of a seat at the afternoon session, were foiled in their plan and compelled to seek pleasant places on the lawn and everyone had an equal chance to gain admission."[43] When Eva Coo finally arrived, it was an event. The *Daily News* called her the "blonde, blue-eyed "Little Eva."[44] Eva didn't help matters by dressing as if she were appearing at a movie premiere, smiling for the cameras, and making wisecracks to her friends and customers, of whom there were many in the crowd. "Although something of the air of nonchalance which she had borne last Monday . . . had disappeared, she appeared composed and fortified for the ordeal. She sat quietly in the chair and seemed to take an active account of what was going on."[45] The *Times* reported that "Mrs. Eva Coo, road-house proprietress, learned today that she alone faced execution for the murder."[46] This was because Prosecutor Grant announced that in exchange for her testimony, Martha Clift would be allowed to plead to Second Degree Murder and thereby escape the electric chair.

Defense Attorney Byard stated that he would ask the court to reject the confession of Mrs. Coo because it was obtained as the result of torture. He referred to the bizarre interrogation at the summit of Crumhorn Mountain orchestrated by the D.A. and Sheriff Mitchell. "In that reenactment, Wright's body, removed from the grave without a court order six days after his death, was taken from its coffin and suddenly thrust before the roadhouse keeper," reported the *Star*. "She was forced to take hold of that body and lift it up . . . other sources said she was also forced to shake hands with the corpse."[47]

On that first day of testimony, the courtroom was packed while the state presented seventeen witnesses including Cooperstown National Bank teller, Milton Shepard, who was called to the stand during the afternoon session. He told the court that, in 1933, Harry had a bank account containing $1,500. He said that during the spring and summer months, Harry came into the bank and cashed a series of checks. When he came into the bank, Shepard said, he was usually drunk and always accompanied by Eva Coo. Prosecutor Grant also called several local agents to the stand to describe how Eva purchased life insurance policies on Harry, naming herself the beneficiary.

When Harry Nabinger entered the court room, expectations were high. Everyone knew that Nabinger was Eva's lover and, if anyone knew exactly what she was planning in the months before the murder, he did. After a few minutes in the witness chair, it became obvious that he had turned on her. He described Eva as being cruel and abusive to Harry Wright during the months before the murder and also stated that he had driven Eva around to buy insurance on Harry's life. "Husky-looking Eva's lower lip trembled a little when Nabinger confessed the intimate details of his association with her," reported the *Daily News*.[48] Nabinger's testimony went on and on, each revelation about their life together at the Woodbine more damaging than the one before. Eva came across as a heartless, money-grubbing individual who would stop at nothing to get what she wanted. "Her fair head dropped a little further into her shapely hand . . . but in a moment the flutter of emotion was over . . . she resumed her gum-chewing."[49] But Nabinger had nothing good to say about the woman he had lived with during the preceding year and had planned to marry someday. He told the court that Eva frequently beat Harry Wright and locked him out of his room. During his testimony, Nabinger described Eva as a "tigress who whipped the ailing handyman once when she found him drunk and treated him cruelly on many other occasions."[50] Most of the press did not approve of Nabinger; their distaste of the man who turned on his lover so completely was demonstrated in newspaper stories that described his testimony. "Nabinger is the sleek, 39 year old father of five children who admitted that he was repaying

Eva's favors and hospitality during months of unemployment with his story of insurance manipulations by her that may send the buxom innkeeper to the electric chair."[51]

Outside, hundreds of spectators who could not get a seat waited on the front lawn. The crowds grew bigger each day. Vendors walked along Main Street hawking ice cream and souvenirs, including mallets that resembled the one Eva had allegedly used on Harry Wright. Parking became a problem as hordes of out-of-state vehicles descended on Cooperstown each morning to catch a glimpse of the famous defendant as she strolled into the courtroom for the day's proceedings. Sheriff Mitchell issued numbered tickets so that everyone would have an equal chance to gain entrance to the court. The Woodbine Inn became a local tourist attraction as curiosity seekers visited the bar, which remained open under a different owner who made the most of his opportunity to make some fast cash.

New York's *Daily News*, eager to top its rival, the *Daily Mirror*, maintained a team of reporters on-site for the duration of the trial. "Atop Crumhorn Mountain, even more exciting scenes were enacted," the *Daily News* told its readers. "Mrs. Fink . . . auctioned off family heirlooms . . . sold for sums far in excess of their value as antiques."[52] By the second week of testimony, the Eva Coo trial was a sensation, reported in all New York's major papers and by the European press as well. The *Daily Mirror* enlisted the aid of physiognomist and cartoonist Cleanthe Carr to study the face of Eva Coo for clues to her criminal behavior. In an article published on August 19, she reported her findings to New York readers. "While drawing Eva Coo's crude primitive face . . . I am struck by her wide, short neck, like a bull's," Carr wrote. "A brutal jaw reminds me of a steel trap. It is the mouth of a woman interested in the things around her only as they affect her material advantage." How Carr arrived at this conclusion was not explained in the article. "There is nothing remarkable about her forehead, although it was never made to balance the reckless determination of her heavy jaw. Her eyes are large and cold," she went on to say. "At one time they probably represented her one claim to beauty . . . her face as a whole expresses natural cunning rather than cleverness . . . and confidence in her colossal nerve."[53]

Every morning at the county jail, the guards delivered large amounts of mail to Eva, who took the time to read every letter and stacked them neatly in the corner of her cell. "Despite the general disgust aroused by the killing of which she is accused, Mrs. Eva Coo now on trial at Cooperstown for the murder of Harry Wright, has found there are persons interested in her spiritual welfare."[54] To some people, the trial was an event that provided entertainment and a welcome break from the bleak years of the Great Depression. The diversified show of vendors and opportunists who packed the front lawn of the courthouse each day added to the merriment. Inside, some witnesses cracked jokes on the stand, which frequently caused spectators to erupt in laughter. "The stark grim tragedy of a murder trial was interspersed with some bits of humor that drew restrained merriment from the audience and even brought a smile to the face of the judge."[55]

Prosecutor Grant called a surprise witness to the stand on August 20. Mrs. Gladys Shumway, who had been held at the Otsego County Jail as a material witness, was a former boarder at the Woodbine Inn and knew Eva well. "She had stayed at the Coo place last fall and while there had been engaged more or less in looking up names of insurance agents."[56] She told the court that Eva hated Harry and remarked more than once that it would be easy to kill him. Mrs. Shumway said that on one occasion, Eva held up a wooden mallet and said, "Wouldn't that be something to hit somebody on the head with?" The defense responded by trying to show that Mrs. Shumway was a friend who betrayed Eva's trust and generosity. "In retaliation for her damning witness stand narration," wrote the *Daily News*, "Diamond Lil's lawyer . . . visited on the Shumway woman as cruel an excoriation as veteran trial observers had ever heard."[57]

Bayard brought out the fact that Shumway had come to the Woodbine Inn when she found herself pregnant with nowhere to go. The baby was later born dead and in the following weeks, Eva cared for the young girl. "Gladys Shumway, whom Eva befriended in her most dire emergency, today turned on the innkeeper and gave testimony that may send the Diamond Lil of these Otsego Hills to the electric chair as a cold blooded murderess," the *Daily News* told its readers.

"Eva Coo took you in and took care of you when you didn't have a friend, didn't she?" Byard shouted at the witness.[58] Mrs. Shumway could not respond and burst into tears.

"You don't get any sympathy from me!" said Byard as he backed away from the witness stand.

"I didn't ask for any!" cried Mrs. Shumway.[59]

The real drama was reserved for the following day, when Eva's best friend and accused accomplice, Martha Clift, took the stand. Though she had confessed to the crime and admitted that she was the one who actually ran over Harry at Crumhorn Mountain, Martha escaped a death sentence because of her deal with District Attorney Grant. Allowing her to plead guilty to a lesser charge, Grant knew that her testimony would support a murder conviction for the person he felt was morally and legally responsible for the crime: Eva Coo.

"With the mallet in her right hand," Martha told the court, "she pushed Wright in front of the car with her right hand and hit him with the mallet. He fell down . . . the car was in low gear and in motion and I was nervous and kept right on going. I ran over the body, went out into the lot . . . and turned around."[60] Martha said that's when Ben Hunt and Mrs. Fink showed up at the farmhouse and asked the two women what they were doing on her property. After the confrontation was over and Mrs. Fink left, Eva loaded Harry's body into the rear of the Willys and drove down the mountain. "That's the hardest work I ever did!" said Eva, according to Martha's testimony. The two women then drove over to north of the Woodbine Inn where Eva threw the body onto the side of the road.

But Defense Attorney Byard was relentless in his cross-examination, and emphasized the plea deal being a form of payment. "Referring to the witness as 'the self-confessed murderess' attorney Byard put Mrs. Martha Clift . . . into the crucible of a burning cross-examination . . . in a determined endeavor to find any flaws in her version."[61]

"You knew if you didn't tell this they would roast you alive?" he asked as Martha sat demurely in the witness chair.

"Well, I am telling the truth!" she replied.[62]

"You're getting paid for this testimony aren't you? Paid for with your life?"

"It's the truth though."

For the next few hours, Byard pounded Martha with shouted questions designed to show that she had betrayed her friend and that she was the real killer of Harry. But Martha held on and refused to budge from her claim that it was Eva who carried out the murder. She said that when she ran over Harry it was unintentional.

"It was purely an accident?" Byard asked.

"On my part it was," Martha replied.

"You hadn't any intention like that?"

"I hadn't planned on running him over. I was gonna' stop and Eva motioned me on."

"You have lied about things in this matter haven't you?"[63] Again Martha broke into tears and sobs. But the damage to Eva had been done. Jurors took it all in while Martha came across as a pathetic patsy to Eva's diabolical plan to kill Harry. "While a jammed courtroom hung on her every syllable, Mrs. Clift described the casual manner in which Eva continued her preparations for snapping Wright's frail hold on life—how the women plotters ate, drank, and slept in their accustomed manner while Wright's life hung in the balance."[64] When court recessed, Eva complained to reporters. "If I take the hot seat, I won't be the only one to burn," she said. "Why, that girl would have been kicked from one end of this county to the other if I hadn't taken her in and fed her, treated her like a younger sister . . . now look at her! To save her own skin she makes a bargain with the state to put me on the spot. Talk about blood money!"[65]

A succession of prosecution witnesses followed Martha to the stand, including Deputy Sheriff Owen P. Brady, who described the nightmarish interrogation of the defendant on Crumhorn Mountain.

"Did you see a coffin there?" asked Byard.

"Yes"

"Who was in it?"

"It wasn't opened when I saw it."

"Did you see the body of Harry Wright after it was out of the coffin?"

"Yes, I did."

"Where did you see it?"

"It was lying in the road," said Brady.[66]

Byard again asked that Coo's statements be disallowed due to the circumstances of her interrogation. When Prosecutor Grant protested that the statements were not coerced, Byard appealed to Judge Heath to settle the matter by putting Eva herself on the stand. After much discussion, it was agreed by all parties that Eva could only be questioned about the conditions in which she gave her statements. When she took the stand, Eva told the court that she was permitted to sleep in her cell only a few minutes at a time and if she dozed off, guards immediately woke her up. This abuse continued, she said, until the night of June 21, when she was removed from her cell and told she was being taken back to Crumhorn Mountain.

"It was raining," Sheriff's Deputy Brady stated, as they arrived on the mountain. "She observed the dead body of Harry Wright there and she was told by the district attorney to pick him up and stand him up."

Eva said one of the deputies told her to wipe her hands on the grass after she touched the body, which she did. "After she had picked up the body on the mountain," the witness stated, "it was moved about from spot to spot in the driveway. There were no lights there at the time except the car lights."[67]

Eva also stated that Grant had promised her immunity if she implicated Martha in the murder. Judge Heath then decided to put Grant on the stand to respond to those charges.

"In so far as I can recall," Grant told the court, "I never was alone with the defendant and on no occasion did I ever mention immunity to her or make her any promises. I further state I never promised that she could go home."[68]

After nearly a week of reviewing the facts in the case, Judge Heath gave the defense a partial victory. Eva's second statement, given at Oneonta Police headquarters the night she was arrested, was ruled inadmissible. However, Eva's other two statements were allowed and read into the court record. "The hill-billy Diamond Lil' squirmed, toyed nervously with a pencil, and her face and neck flushed as the words she had poured out to District Attorney

Donald Grant last June came back to torment her in her battle to escape the electric chair," reported the *Daily News*.[69]

When State Trooper Ernest Maynard took the stand, he told the court how he retrieved the insurance policies from Eva's home the day she was arrested. "The officers gained entrance to the Coo place by removing a screen from a rear window and raising the sash . . . The witness narrated how he examined the contents of a bureau and also a vanity dresser in the room, in the top drawers of which were found three or four insurance policies."[70] Though the officer's entry into Eva's home had been illegal, the evidence was allowed into testimony. Objections were later raised by defense counsel, but again Judge Heath denied the motions.[71]

On September 4, after presenting seventy-four witnesses over a period of two weeks, the people rested their case while outside, a huge throng of spectators had taken up residence. "Each day the crowd grew larger and more unruly. They trampled down the lawn between the courthouse and the jail, brought picnic lunches to eat on the shores of Lake Otsego and vied with one another to secure tickets of admission to the courthouse."[72] While court was in recess, local excitement centered on Smalley's Theater in Cooperstown, where Shirley Temple's new movie, *Baby Take a Bow*, premiered in late August. "The story contains a great deal of human interest and comedy," said the *Star*. "It affords Shirley an excellent opportunity to display her singing and dancing talents."[73] Lines of movie-goers waiting to see the show ran down the street, and during their wait, the topic of conversation was always Eva Coo. The *Freeman's Journal* reported that "here and there a local face may be discerned in the crowd, but by far the larger proportion are strangers who have been attracted here by the widespread publicity which the trial has received."[74]

On September 5, the defense opened its case by calling for the immediate arrest and arraignment of Martha Clift for the murder of Harry Wright. "Sunny Jim" Byard told the court that Martha was a "self-confessed murderer" and should be the one on trial. Byard also asked for immediate dismissal of all charges against Eva based on several issues. First, the evidence against Eva had been obtained illegally by police and should therefore be rejected by the court. Second, "the District Attorney, by repeatedly making improper remarks during the trial for the purpose of misleading and prejudicing the jury," was guilty of prosecutorial misconduct. Third, holding Eva Coo for thirty-six hours without charging her with a crime was a violation of her civil rights. And finally, Byard declared there to be "no corroborated evidence holding up the accomplice Clift's testimony" and that "the death of Harry Wright was caused by an accident resulting from the unaided acts of Martha Clift."[75] Judge Heath saw things differently and quickly denied all defense motions. "The defense lost . . . today in opening the active part of its effort to save Mrs. Eva Coo, blonde and buxom, from the electric chair for the murder of her handyman," reported the *Daily Star* the following day.[76]

After calling a total of sixteen witnesses, most of who were ineffective and could offer little in substance for the defense of his client, "Sunny Jim" Byard was forced to close his case. Judge Heath told Byard and Grant, "If you boys finish up tomorrow, I believe I'll be able to complete my charge to the jury before dinner time."[77] In the meantime, Eva could hardly contain herself with reporters. "I ain't afraid of anything but God—and He won't punish me because I never harmed a soul," she said. "Don't think I'm mad at Martha for what she done to me . . . although I wouldn't have done it to her. But I ain't mad at nobody!"[78]

After summations by Grant and Byard, Judge Heath charged the jury. "Don't be influenced by feelings of gallantry because the defendant is a woman," he said. "The law against murder applies to a woman as well as a man."[79] The jury received the case for deliberation at 3:05 p.m. on the afternoon of September 6. "Eva Coo was the picture of nervous terror as she left the courtroom for the noon recess . . . several times her bright blue eyes filled with tears and she wept quietly to herself, seeming on the verge of collapse."[80] At 5:02, the foreman announced they had reached a verdict.

Eva Coo was found guilty of Murder in the First Degree. "If the law exacts its penalty from Eva Coo, she will be the fifth woman to die in the electric chair," reported the *Daily Star*. "The state has yet to exact the death penalty from an unmarried woman."[81] The *Times* reported that "for the first time during the sensational four-week trial, the 47-year-old roadhouse proprietress, Canadian-born, lost her composure. She shuddered violently. When she was led before Justice Riley H. Heath . . . she walked unsteadily. Her lawyer, gray-haired James J. Byard, gravely offered her his arm."[82] The *Daily News* described her as "a forlorn figure as she sat at the defense table with no friends." The same article was careful to say that she was "attired in a dark blue dress with small white beads and a dark blue straw hat . . . over her blonde hair."[83] Judge Heath immediately sentenced Eva to die in Sing Sing's electric chair on October 18 and then cleared the room. "Except for a fluttering of the eyelids, an involuntary shudder shook her body and a little unsteadiness of gait as she left the courtroom."[84] Once Eva left the room, Martha Clift was brought into the court, where she was allowed to plead to Second Degree Murder and receive a sentence of twenty years to life.

As reporters later gathered around her cell in the county jail, Eva fielded their questions with typical candor. "One look at the jury when they walked into the courtroom and I knew," she said. "Their faces were hard and I knew they were gonna' make me die. But I didn't cry when I heard the verdict. And

I didn't cry when the judge said it would be the chair. I didn't want Don Grant to see me cry!"[85] But she railed against what people said about her in the court and the way she was treated. "The state troopers, those bullies! They said I smuggled myself into this country from Canada . . . I had $13,000! With dough, baby, you can go anywhere you want!"[86]

At 10:00 a.m. the following morning, Eva and Martha were taken from the Otsego County Jail and placed into two separate vehicles. Martha was taken to the women's prison in Bedford in Westchester County while Eva was taken to Sing Sing. "Both in tears, they were taken in separate motor cars . . . while two other friends of the condemned innkeeper . . . also weeping, watched from the second floor of the jail."[87] When she arrived at Sing Sing, Eva's only remark was "Well, I'm here at last!" After processing, she was led to her death row cell—one which had an ominous history. "Mrs. Eva Coo arrived at the prison here late today and was assigned to the centre cage which was occupied by Mrs. Ruth Snyder, seven years ago, and more recently by Mrs. Anna Antonio."[88]

In the meantime, the *Freeman's Journal* assured its readers that Eva Coo got what she deserved. In an article titled "Steps to Save Eva Coo From Chair," which appeared on September 12, 1934 on page one, the final paragraph may have encapsulated the feelings of the editorial staff. "It was a very sad and sordid picture of a type of life that is not pleasant to realize exists in Otsego County . . . there can be but one verdict as to the result of such living. It is to be hoped the lesson has sunk home in several quarters."

Byard filed an appeal based on the fact that Eva's statements were obtained illegally and that the statement of Martha Clift was not corroborated by supporting evidence. The notice of appeal automatically postponed the original date of execution (October 15, 1934). In the meantime, a newspaper article, allegedly written by Eva Coo, appeared in a Sunday edition of the *New York Mirror*. It purported to be her life story. When Eva obtained a copy of the article, she denied writing the piece and felt that because it portrayed her in a negative way; it hurt her chances for a successful appeal. She complained to Warden Lewis Lawes, who investigated the matter. It was later determined that Eva's lawyer, "Sunny Jim" Byard was paid $3,000 by the *Mirror* to get the story during his interviews with Eva. He had smuggled in a man named John Kobler without disclosing to Eva and prison authorities that the man was actually a newspaper reporter. Though he had done nothing illegal, Byard's actions were perceived as unethical and a betrayal of his client. In the prisoner activity log at Sing Sing, Warden Lawes wrote, "It is disclosed that John Kobler is a reporter and he is not to be admitted under any circumstances."[89] Eva was "greatly disturbed and even hysterical when she read the article and felt they would do her more harm than good."[90] In January, the court decided to appoint a new defense attorney for Eva. He was David Slade, a well-known lawyer from New York City, who immediately went to work on her appeal motion.

Slade's efforts were in vain. On April 30, 1935, the New York State Court of Appeals denied all the issues raised by the defense and affirmed the conviction. The most serious allegation, that the confession was obtained by coercion, was rejected by the appeals court, thus clearing the way for Eva's execution. "Donald Grant, District Attorney of Otsego County, insisted that the trial of Mrs. Coo had been eminently fair and that she was given every opportunity to clear herself of the [murder] charge."[91] In her cell at Sing Sing, Eva was devastated. She remained firm in her belief that she was convicted by a vindictive district attorney who had promised her life if she would cooperate. "What do you think?" she said. "I've been turned down. Every one thought I would be granted a new trial but I think the Governor will do something."[92] In reality, that would be a slim hope because only a few months before, Governor Herbert Lehman had refused to save the life of Anna Antonio when he was under much greater political pressure than he would receive on Eva's behalf. The execution date was set for the week of June 27. "She sits dumbly on her cot, knees widespread, her body slouched in exhausted dejection, but in her eyes is a gleam of faith that a stay will save her from that dreaded last night," reported the *Sun*.[93]

Clemency hearings took place in Albany during early June. On the day Slade presented his case to the clemency board, Eva celebrated her forty-third birthday. In his presentation, Slade argued that she deserved mercy because it was unclear who actually killed Harry Wright. Statements from both defendants indicated that it was Martha who drove the car and struck the victim, causing his death, and yet Martha escaped the Murder First Degree conviction. "If she (Eva Coo) had been permitted to tell her whole story," said Slade at the hearing, "I feel sure she would not be in the death house now."[94]

Eva's sense of humor never failed her. "My friends say they can't get in to see me at Sing Sing," she told a reporter. "But I didn't have any trouble getting in." David Slade told reporters, "This is the greatest miscarriage of justice I have ever seen."[95]

As the day of execution grew near, Eva spent most of her time stitching fancy handkerchiefs for the matrons, who had become her constant companions and provided emotional support. Eva also found an unlikely friend on Death Row. He was an inmate scheduled to die the same day as Eva. He had been convicted of the murder of a police officer in Troy. His name was Leonard Scarnici, a twenty-nine-year-old compulsive killer who spent nearly his entire life in and out of jails. He claimed to have murdered a dozen men in the Albany area during his crime sprees. Robert Elliott, the state's executioner, called him "one of the toughest criminals I have ever seen."[96] Scarnici received several reprieves from the chair, and he gave Eva hope that she, too, could be saved with a little luck. "Gaunt and drawn, with lines of terror etched deeply around her frightened eyes, and trembling mouth, she waited for the word which would tell her that she is not to die tonight."[97] But it was not to be. Governor Lehman declined to grant a reprieve; her execution would go forward as scheduled.

On the morning of June 27, crowds began to assemble outside the gates of Sing Sing. Warden Lewis Lawes, accustomed to such demonstrations, had stationed more guards in and around the prison. It was well known that Lawes supported Eva's quest for clemency and was an outspoken opponent of the death penalty. But his personal opinions could not stop him from his official duties. "Not only does capital punishment fail in its justification, but no punishment could be invented with so many inherent defects," Lawes once wrote. "It has never been and never can be anything but an uncertainty. It is a punishment for revenge, for retaliation, not for protection."[98] In Oneonta, Sheriff Mitchell and D.A. Don Grant told the press that they were satisfied with the successful prosecution of Eva and saw no irregularities at her trial. But Eva was bitter over the deal between Martha and the district attorney's office and over Grant's promise of lenience if she were to cooperate. "I can't see why they should take my life while *that one* over there should be treated so much better," she said to the press.[99]

The *Daily News* reported that "the once buxom and blondined [sic] Diamond Lil' of Otsego County, sat sleepless and in growing terror in her Sing Sing death cell last night with Governor Lehman ominously silent on her plea for clemency."[100] Eva ordered a last meal that consisted of toast and tea, which she barely ate. "I don't want to eat," she told the matrons. "It's bad for my figure. I'm on a diet."[101] In the meantime, the shadowy figure of Robert G. Elliott appeared at a rear gate of Sing Sing under the cover of darkness. He proceeded directly to the execution chamber where he began his preparations. Coo and Scarnici would be his 279th and 280th executions. But Elliot was not happy about his pending work.

"Throughout her imprisonment, Eva remained good-natured and cheerful," he later said. "She had a pleasant word for everybody. Consequently, she was liked by those who came in contact with her . . . When I arrived . . . gloom was everywhere I went. Nearly everyone I met was hopeful that the governor would intervene."[102] Eva spent a fitful night in her cell. She talked incessantly with the matrons, who had become very close with her and considered her a friend. In the prison there was a great deal of sympathy for Eva and no one wanted to see her die. "Sleepless and in growing terror of the electrodes which will send a charge of death into her fear-aged body tonight, Eva is staking her all on the chance that the governor may send emissaries to Martha Clift, the chum who saved her own life at the expense of Eva's."[103] But after a last-minute phone plea to the governor's office by the warden failed, hopes were crushed. "Eva Coo and her gangster prototype in murder for profit, emotionless Leonard Scarnici, made their last bids for life late yesterday, and lost."[104]

At 10:30 p.m. Eva was taken from her cell and marched down the corridor to the dreaded green door. "Just beyond the green door at the end of the dance hall was hell, or as close to hell as most men would ever come," said one of the condemned prisoners. "Push the door, there's the chair looking almost as ugly empty as it will look later . . . to your left a row of witnesses: newspaper people, police, prison officials. Straight ahead, the chair!"[105] As she passed Scarnici's cell, she called out to him.

"Bye Lenny!"

"Keep your chin up, Eva!" he replied, aware that within a few minutes, he would be next to walk through the same door.

Eva entered the death chamber, looking frail and haggard, while thirty-four witnesses waited nervously in their seats. She had lost thirty pounds during her time on Death Row. "Eva Coo stepped through the little green door alone and unassisted . . . she stopped momentarily. She gave a quick glance about, the harried, defiant look of the hunted animal. The tigerish look was gone from her eyes but instead was the appearance of a wounded deer, defiant to the end."[106] The matrons, weeping uncontrollably, brought her quickly to the fearsome chair and strapped her in. "You've been good to me," she said to the matrons. "Goodbye darlings!" Eva said loudly. The mask was placed over her face, muffling her voice as she appeared to say something more. "I could feel Eva shudder as I affixed the headpiece. When the mask was placed over her face, she gasped, 'Oh!'"[107] Once the cap was attached to her head, the matrons left the room. When everyone was clear, Elliot, obscured from view behind a control panel, turned the dial firmly, sending 3,000 volts into Eva's trembling body. "Only her nose was visible as she sat strapped in the electric chair. She moaned slightly when the straps were pulled tightly. She gave spasmodic jerks . . . her chest heaved slightly after the first jolt."[108] He repeated the procedure twice while the witnesses cringed from the awful sounds and smells of electricity cooking a human body. In his execution diary, Elliott made this entry: "New York June 27, 1935 11 PM. Eva Coo #89508–42 years-9 amps." That year, Elliott executed thirty-six men and women, a personal record. After the prison physician pronounced Eva dead, guards unstrapped her from the chair. She was placed on a gurney and wheeled into the adjoining autopsy room where the postmortem examination began.

In the meantime, Scarnici was brought in through the same green door through which Eva had entered a few minutes before. One reporter later wrote, "Leonard Scarnici, the putty-faced hoodlum who likewise killed for money, swaggered in with a smile on his face, a wisecrack for his attendants, and a wad of chewing gum in his mouth."[109] The *New York Sun* reported, "Scarnici, his shoulders lifting insolently and a cigarette drooping between his lips, walked into the death chamber one minute after Mrs. Coo's body had been wheeled away."[110] He sat down in the chair, half-smiling, and made his final statement. "All I want to say to those double-crossers up in Albany is that I'm a better man than they are."[111]

Although Eva still had family, including her mother who was living in Canada, no one came to Ossining to claim her body. "Sing Sing prison authorities are awaiting word today from the family of Eva Coo as to the disposition to be made of the body of the woman who was executed last night for the murder of her handyman."[112] The family never arrived, and Eva was eventually buried in a potter's field in the nearby city of Peekskill. Many felt this was a fitting end to a person who was forgotten by her friends, betrayed by her own attorney, and ridiculed throughout her prosecution and trial.

Eva Coo was surely no saint. During an interview with a reporter, former boyfriend Harry Nabinger had this to say: "Eva was the hardest woman I ever met; she was so hard, you couldn't believe it," he said. "She stole and cheated and ruined men's lives. She ruined mine."[113] Others, including journalist Dorothy Kilgallen, while not defending Eva Coo, had doubts about the sort of treatment she received in court. Kilgallen asked, "Did she receive—no matter who or what she was—the kind of justice supposedly guaranteed every human being? I don't know."[114] Warden Lawes summed up her case during a post-execution interview in which he lambasted the prosecution. "I don't know if she was innocent or guilty," he said. "But I do know she got a rotten deal all around, rotten . . . and I'm not defending her, she may be guilty as well, but she got a raw deal. Her trial attorneys, do you know what? One of them wrote to me, saying he'd like four invitations to her execution. That's the kind of defense she had!"[115]

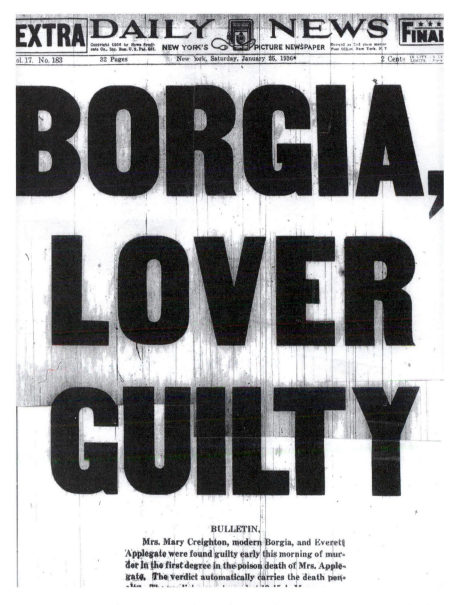

The front page of the New York *Daily News* for January 25, 1936. The lead story reported on the guilty verdict of Mary Frances Creighton and Everett Appelgate. Courtesy of Ossining Historical Society.

An accurate reproduction of Sing Sing's electric chair on display at Ossining Museum. The electric chair at Sing Sing was first used on July 7, 1891 for the execution of Harris Smiler, 32, who was was convicted of the murder of his girlfriend. Photo by author.

Typical cell door at the original Sing Sing prison. These
cells measured seven feet long, three feet wide, and six
feet-seven inches high. They had no running water and
no heat. Photo by author.

Robert Elliott. Courtesy of Ossining
Historical Society.

Death row cell at Sing Sing prison. There were 24 of these cells in the death house for male prisoners and 3 for female prisoners. Photo by author.

Harold King, Chief of Detectives, Nassau County Police Department, ca. 1936. Courtesy of the Nassau County Police Department.

Rough on Rats:
Mary Frances Creighton

I think of the disgusting sexual lives [that] their utter lack of any moral
sense whatsoever allowed them to enjoy . . . [H]ere was a pair "made for
each other" in a most peculiar and revolting way.
—Reporter Dorothy Kilgallen
on Mary Frances Creighton
and Everett Appelgate

After the executions of Anna Antonio and Eva Coo, as traumatic as those
events were for the public, there was no respite in death penalty cases. At least
eighteen male inmates waited outside Sing Sing's "dance hall" for an identical fate. After two female executions in the preceding eleven months, New
York had equaled the total number of women executed in the state during
the previous thirty-five years. Within a few months, another female would be
on trial for her life. But unlike the pathetic Antonio, this woman had a long
and complex history with the law in two different states. She had been
accused of homicide before. Twice she had been tried for murder. She had
been acquitted both times. Her name was Mary Frances Avery-Creighton.
But in New York City, millions knew her by her other name, a sobriquet
assigned by the tabloids in stories that crucified her each day with sordid
accounts of sexual perversion and medieval murder plots. That name was
"Black-Eyed Borgia."[1]
   Her story of child sexual abuse, poisoning, and murder was lascivious and
repellent by any standard. In many ways, Creighton was an enigma, a contrast

in style and substance to all who knew her. She was a compulsively neat housekeeper who frequently hosted card parties for her neighbors. She liked to cook and knit, and seemed devoted to her husband. But when provoked, she could be vicious and unforgiving. She probably murdered her in-laws and later, her own brother. And, there could easily have been more. Three of her neighbors escaped death by poisoning when they were rushed to the hospital after becoming ill after swallowing a drink prepared by Creighton. Medical treatment probably saved their lives. Police tried to stop her before she killed again, but Frances, as most people called her, had been through it all before and was difficult to trap. Only when she murdered her boyfriend's wife to allow him to marry her sexy fifteen-year-old daughter was she finally stopped. Her husband, who some people believed participated in her crimes, supported her to the day she was executed and never betrayed her, even though Frances was strongly suspected of killing his mother. Of all the women executed in New York during the twentieth century, Mary Frances Creighton received the least sympathy from the public—and this may be deservedly so.

Mary Frances Avery was born in the suburban city of Rahway, New Jersey, in 1899. When she was a teenager, both her parents died, a devastation that probably had a lasting effect on the young girl whom everyone called "Frances" or "Fanny." During her school years, she did not achieve much academically and made few friends. She never participated in any sport, club, or activity, and mostly kept to herself during her high school years. Frances moved to Newark when she was fifteen, and finished her education in public schools. In 1917, she met John Creighton, a handsome young sailor on his way to fight in Europe during World War I. They soon married and moved in with John's parents, Walter and Anna Creighton, on North Seventh Street.

A few years later, Frances's brother, Raymond Avery, decided to move in, and soon the house became somewhat crowded and uncomfortable. To make matters worse, John's mother and Frances constantly battled each other for supremacy in the Creighton home. Frances was a matronly woman who was always meticulous about her appearance. She never used foul language and was mindful of her manners. But she also had a bad temper and did not get along with her in-laws, who invariably took the side of their son against his new wife. Frances, who could be domineering and manipulative, spread baseless rumors about her in-laws to neighbors. She said that her mother-in-law was a disturbed woman who was determined to commit suicide.

Coincidentally, after Frances repeated this rumor for a few weeks, Anna Creighton became seriously ill. She suddenly developed a fever and rampant diarrhea and vomited continuously. Despite attempts by doctors to save her, Anna Creighton died on December 1, 1920. One investigator's report surmised the episode with a single sentence: "Mrs. Frances Creighton said that her mother-in-law, Anna Creighton, was going to destroy herself. Shortly thereafter, Anna Creighton became sick and within a week, died."[2] Walter Creighton blamed his daughter-in-law, though he could not articulate why. In the meantime, while Frances attended bridge parties with her neighbors, she told friends that her father-in-law Walter was becoming ill and seemed to have the same illness as his wife. He quickly developed severe abdominal pains and vomiting. Within days, he was dead. John Creighton was shocked at the sudden passing of his father and mother, though he never seemed to suspect Mary of any wrongdoing. "I know that Fanny is guiltless of killing my mother," he later told the press. "If my mother died from unnatural causes, I know in my innermost heart that my wife is innocent of responsibility for her death."[3]

During the summer of 1923, Raymond, Frances's nineteen-year-old brother, also became violently ill. He doubled over with stomach pain and suffered hallucinations. Over the next few weeks, his condition worsened greatly. He was treated by doctors and brought to a Newark hospital for further testing. As a patient, he seemed to improve and later returned home. But like Anna Creighton, he died a few days later in May, 1923. Frances later remarked that her brother was "a pervert and better off dead."[4] Over the family's objections but encouraged by Raymond's friends, an autopsy was performed. The postmortem examination revealed large amounts of arsenic in Raymond's internal organs.

Arsenic, even in the 1930s, was an antiquated drug whose use as an instrument of murder was something of a mystery, given its limitations and risks. Arsenic poisoning is a painful way to die and its presence in the human body after death is easily determined. The volatile substance attacks the internal organs, such as the liver, kidney, and lungs. It does not dissipate quickly after death and, if a coroner suspects arsenic as a cause of death, chemical tests can readily reveal its presence. As far back as 1809, scientists knew that a postmortem examination could find arsenic in the human body. Historically, there were many cases of poisoning murders in France, England, and especially in Germany. For example, Anna Maria Zwanziger, who may have killed simply to watch her victims die, catapulted into the headlines in 1910 when she was convicted of several murders by arsenic. She was beheaded in Nuremberg in 1911.[5]

Though it is an extremely toxic substance and a powerful tool to cause death, several problems are associated with the use of arsenic for murder. The killer can never be sure exactly how much of the poison to give the victim. If he or she administers one massive dose, instant and painful death will result—a sure sign the victim has been poisoned. The killer is most often forced to administer small amounts over a period of time. This usually results in a prolonged and severe illness that exposes the killer to additional risk. Murder by arsenic usually follows a well-known sequence of events that investigators are familiar with: sudden sickness, death, burial, suspicion, exhumation. This is exactly what occurred in the case of Anna Creighton. All these factors came into play during Mary Frances's two trials for murder, although the pivotal question of who actually administered the poison was left unanswered.

After the deaths of Mr. and Mrs. Walter Creighton and Raymond Avery, police investigated all three incidents. The bodies were exhumed and tested for the presence of arsenic. Traces were found in Anna Creighton's and Raymond Avery's bodies, but not in Walter Creighton's. Police decided to arrest Frances and her husband John, and to charge them both with the murder of Raymond Avery, which they considered to be their strongest case. The two were indicted in Newark, New Jersey, for the murder and their trial began—under an avalanche of publicity—in the Essex County Court.

"Creighton's North Seventh Street neighbors were among the most important witnesses for the State and its contention that Avery was poisoned so that his sister and brother-in-law might inherit his insurance of $1,000 and his estate of $1,800."[6] Prosecutors also called two doctors, who testified that Avery died from arsenic overdose. But Defense Attorney James W. McCarthy told the jury that these men were mistaken and even if they weren't, it was simply their own opinion and not fact. The tests were not conclusive, the defense asserted.

"And you can't send this young woman and this young man to death on an opinion," he declared. "Look at this young woman. Is she a murderess? Is she one who would administer poison to her own flesh and blood? Is she such a cruel and heartless woman to murder her brother for $1,800? Oh, good God! Judas sold Christ for thirty pieces of silver, if she sold her brother's life for $1,800, she is worse than a thousand Judas!"[7] The prosecutor told the jury that the Creightons were monsters who would do anything for money, including murder. While he spoke, Frances sobbed loudly in her chair, causing the judge to admonish her. The *Daily News* reported that "Mrs. Creighton closed her heavy lidded eyes and bowed her pretty head, while her husband hid his face in his hands."[8]

After the jury deliberated just fifty-two minutes, they found Frances and John not guilty of murder charges. "The words yesterday afternoon beat upon the stillness of the packed Newark courtroom—the room into which men and women had fought like stampeded cattle to gain entrance a short time before as the dramatic trial of the black-eyed woman and her weak-featured husband drew to a thrilling end after five wearing days."[9] But Frances was still not free. During the trial, she had also been indicted for the 1920 murder of her mother-in-law, Anna Creighton, and immediately after the verdict, she was remanded back to the county jail to await another trial on that charge. John Creighton, however, was not under indictment and was a free man.

Less than three weeks later, Frances was on trial again for murder in the same Essex County courtroom. "The courtroom was crowded when she entered, dressed in black, which is appropriate to her dark complexion and immovable expression," reported the *Daily News* on July 10. The Creighton's family physician, Dr. Thomas Boyle, testified that he was called to the home on December 1, 1920. He said that Anna Creighton had suddenly become ill after drinking a cup of cocoa prepared by Frances. He said that Anna's vocal chords were paralyzed and he found her unable to speak. She was in great pain, suffering from intense stomach pain, he told the court. Despite medical treatment in the home that morning by Dr. Boyle, Anna died later that same day. "Fear crept into the black eyes of Mrs. Mary Frances Creighton and her pretty swarthy face became pinched and drawn yesterday . . . it was the first sign of weakening of the inscrutable woman."[10]

But Defense Attorney McCarthy managed to secure the cooperation of Dr. Alexander O. Gettler, a Bellevue Hospital toxicologist and an occasional staff member for the Manhattan District Attorney's Office. On the second day of the trial, he took the stand to testify that although he found traces of arsenic in Anna's body, it was not, in his opinion, enough to cause death. When asked what did cause her death, Dr. Gettler could not say with certainty.

On the afternoon of July 13, the case went to the jury. After only four hours of deliberations, the jury announced their verdict. Frances was brought into the courtroom on the arms of two matrons. She was almost too weak to stand. "Her swarthy face was corpse-hued in the pallid light of the courtroom," reported the *Daily News*. "Her pretty head swung drunkenly on the slender throat."[11] When the judge asked the jury foreman for the verdict, he replied "Not guilty, your honor!" Frances fainted to the floor. She had to be carried out of the chaotic room where spectators had both cheered and booed the controversial verdict. As for Walter and Anna Creighton and Raymond Avery, their deaths would forever remain a mystery. No one would ever be prosecuted for their murders.

After Frances was acquitted at the second trial, the Creightons decided they had little to look forward to in New Jersey. In the spring of 1924, they moved to the small village of Baldwin on Long Island, where John maintained friendships from his years in the army. He later joined the American Legion and attended meetings each month, socializing with other members. He felt comfortable with men who had shared similar experiences during the war. John became friendly with another Legionnaire named Everett "Appy"

Appelgate, who was an investigator for the Veteran's Administration earning thirty eight dollars a week.

Everett lived with his wife, Ada, their teenage daughter, Agnes, and his wife's parents in a small cottage on the west side of the village. Ada was an obese, extraverted woman who battled weight problems most of her life and stayed in bed all day. By 1934, she weighed nearly two-hundred-fifty pounds and was a lasting source of embarrassment to her husband. Ada had a hostile disposition backed up by a sharp tongue which she often used on Everett. Her complaints were directed at the American Legion where she thought her "Appy" spent too much of his time. Ada's parents supported their daughter's side in any family argument which frequently infuriated Everett. But the Legion was very important to him since a major goal in Everett's life was to become a County Commander. After a loud argument in November 1934, Everett decided to move out of the house. He desperately needed a place to live and for that, he turned to his friend and fellow veteran, John Creighton.

At that time, John and Frances were living at 12 Bryant Place on the west side of Baldwin with their two children, Ruth, thirteen, and Jack, nine years old. The home had two bedrooms and one bathroom, all on the ground floor. Living space was cramped, even for just four people. Nevertheless, the Creightons permitted the Appelgates and their fourteen-year-old daughter, Agnes, to move in. Because money was tight, the two families agreed to share the expenses. According to a police report, "the Appelgate family pays 3/7 of the general expenses of the place and the Creighton family pays 4/7 according to the number in each family."[12]

From the very beginning, life was chaotic inside the cramped household. Because there was not enough space for everyone, sleeping arrangements were unpredictable. Ada, needing more space than anyone else, slept with Everett in the front bedroom on the first floor. John and Mary Frances slept in the back room of the house while the two teenage girls, Ruth and Agnes, frequently retired to the dark and dingy attic where there was no electricity or heat. Jackie Creighton, age twelve, slept on the floor wherever he could find space. When the family settled in, John was able to get a job as a surveyor while Everett turned to one of his favorite enjoyments in life, the pursuit of very young girls.

Though Ruth Creighton was only fourteen at the time, she was a very pretty girl who had the body of an adult woman. Dr. Richard Hoffman, a psychologist who once interviewed Ruth, wrote about their first meeting. "Her blonde hair caught the morning light," he said. "Her eyes were pale blue with just enough strabismus to make her cute. She had a small well-shaped mouth and a little nose above it. Her face was oval, her cheeks rounded . . . a poster of innocence."[13] Ruth was a rebellious teenager and frequently showed up at school wearing shorts and makeup. She was fresh to teachers and had a spoiled demeanor. For months before the Appelgates moved in with the Creightons, Everett drove Ruth around town to do errands and took her to school in his car. The impressionable teenager was flattered that a man his age would show so much attention to her. "One night when he came home for dinner and found Ruth alone in his bedroom, he put his arm around her and kissed her passionately on the mouth. The girl experienced an ecstasy that she had never known before."[14] Not long afterward, Everett and Ruth had their first sexual encounter inside a motion picture projection booth during an American Legion social affair. "I came into very much contact with her," Everett later explained to police. "It caused me to do things that were natural to my desires . . . showing her affection and the same being returned . . . I knew that she was only fifteen years of age but as she was a willing party to the acts . . . I presumed it was a matter of confidence between us two . . . in other words . . . I had sexual relations with her."[15]

Living conditions at the Bryant Place home grew progressively worse. Everett and John were busy at their jobs and often attended Legion functions which left the rest of the family to fend for themselves. In addition, Everett frequently brought guests home who would drink and play cards throughout the night. For the children, there were no scheduled meals, bedtimes, or household chores. It was complete chaos. The two girls disappeared for hours at a time; no one knew where they were or what they were doing. Ada screamed at Everett when he was home, degrading him in front of his friends, the Creightons and Ruth, his secret lover. In the meantime, Frances, who was by nature, a neat and organized person, tried to maintain some semblance of order in the household. She tried to keep the place clean and picked up after everyone. Everett, perhaps seeing an opportunity for another sexual conquest, never missed a chance to tell Frances how much he appreciated her efforts.

"He tried to become familiar," she later told police. But I tried to resist and did not quite succeed." Everett was a determined man. In January of 1935, he had sex with Frances for the first time. "Mr. Appelgate and I were intimate almost as soon as he and Ada came to live with us," she later claimed. "The first time was one day when I was in bed with a cold. Everybody was out and Mr. Appelgate came in about three in the afternoon and into my room . . . he lifted the covers and got into the bed."[16] Over the following months, Everett continued his sexual relationship with Frances, while at the same time, and unknown to each other, he was having sex with her daughter as well. But during that period—it is unclear exactly when and how—Frances found out about Ruth and Everett. But instead of being angry, she accepted it. Though Frances did not approve of the situation, she did nothing to stop it. "I asked him if he didn't think it was bad enough the way he was carrying on with me without doing a thing like that to a child," she told police. "I told him if the father found out he would kill him."[17]

On one particularly hot evening in June, 1935, Everett returned from a Legionnaire convention after dark. He had been drinking and when he arrived home, he found Ruth awake. He asked her to join him in his bedroom and the teenager agreed. They quietly got into the bed where Ada was awake. "She told Ev to take off my nightclothes," Ruth later recalled. "I was perspiring and she thought I was asleep but I heard it."[18] And there, while his wife lay next to them, Everett had sex with Ruth, according to her statement. Ada never objected and was fully aware of what was going on. The next morning, while Everett was in bed, Ruth began to fondle him. "Look," he said to Ada, "Ruth is trying to rape me." Ada then told Everett to show her what rape means. He then pulled Ruth on top of him and had sex with her while Ada watched. According to Ruth, this situation continued for months with Ada's full knowledge and approval. Ruth later told police that her mother was also aware of it because she had caught them in suggestive situations on many occasions.

Over time, the unusual relationships inside the Bryant Place cottage became volatile and unpredictable. At some point, Ruth found out that her mother was having sex with Everett. Though Frances never admitted it to her, Ruth said that she could tell by the way they acted. "Their actions spoke louder than words," she told police. "She couldn't keep away from him. Oh, she was mad about him, if you ask me."[19] John Creighton knew there was something wrong in their marriage but apparently never suspected that Everett was having sex with his wife. "Oh, he kept getting mad," Ruth later said. "Mother would say no and he wanted to know what was the matter with her, if she had gone nutty or something. That is what he said one night. He said he was going to have her head examined."[20]

But Ada, who desired sexual relations with Everett despite his obsession with a fifteen-year-old girl, could not contain her growing jealousy. She began to talk to neighbors about Ruth. Ada said she was a spoiled child, a brat, and worse. She said that Ruth's behavior was her mother's fault because she raised her that way. Soon, the rumors of the scandalous affair between Everett and Ruth began to circulate in the village of Baldwin. It wasn't long before these stories got back to Frances, who was humiliated that the entire neighborhood seemed to know about her promiscuous daughter. And worse, that Ruth's conduct reflected upon her as a failed mother. Later, when Frances found out that the rumors were spread by Ada herself, she became enraged. "I would have given anything to get rid of them [the Appelgates] only I was afraid if I put them out, my husband would find out the real reason,"

Frances later told police. "I didn't like Ada very much and Appy told me he couldn't stand the sight of her."[21]

But Frances knew how to deal with difficult people. Her mother-in-law and her brother were once a problem to her, that is, until they died from unexplained arsenic ingestion. Frances knew that arsenic had an objectionable, metallic like taste. She was aware that the deadly powder had to be mixed with food or drink to disguise that taste. For her, this dilemma was already solved. She knew there was a type of arsenic, sold legally over most drug store counters, that was already premixed with other substances, a special kind of poison that was used to kill rodents. It was called *Rough on Rats* and luckily, it was on sale in a nearby drug store in Baldwin for twenty-three cents.

On the morning of September 17, 1935, Ada became severely ill. She suffered stomach pains that made her scream and she constantly threw up in her bed. Everett called a doctor who decided to send her to the Nassau County Hospital. Over the next few days, with treatment, her health improved dramatically. She was then discharged and sent home. That same night, Frances cooked dinner for the family. Afterward, she and Everett prepared a glass of eggnog for Ada. Frances took the glass to the bedroom and left it on a night table. Everett then came in and while he propped Ada up in bed, he held the glass to her lips and she drank it. Then he and Ada went to sleep.

Hours later, Everett was awakened in the middle of the night by Ada's screaming. She was pacing the floor like a madwoman, moaning in pain, and experiencing hallucinations. She had vomited in the bed and awakened everyone in the house. Everett, with help from Frances, cleaned up the mess and put Ada back to bed. But a short time later, she awoke again with intense abdominal pain. She complained of seeing odd things in her room and then suddenly fell to the floor. According to Everett, he tried to revive her but his efforts failed. At 6:25 a.m., the police were called. The officers summoned an ambulance. When the medical crew arrived, Ada was already unconscious and near death. The family physician, Dr. Spencer Caldwell, was then summoned to the scene and by the time he arrived, Ada was dead. He made the pronouncement of death while Dr. Alexander Zabin, who had been treating Ada for obesity, was contacted and agreed to sign the death certificate. It was surmised that Ada suffered a heart attack and the matter seemed closed.

That afternoon, at Nassau County Police Department, Patrolman Joseph O'Connor went to see Inspector Harold King, commanding officer of the detective division. He carried with him copies of old newspaper articles from the *New York Daily News*. The articles, published in 1923, detailed the consecutive trials of Mary Frances Creighton for the poisoning of her mother in-law and her brother in Newark, New Jersey. O'Connor explained that a neighbor on Bryant Place became suspicious of the Creightons when she heard rumors of the New Jersey case. She obtained copies of the newspaper articles and turned them over to Officer O'Connor.

"Get hold of Applegate," King told his detectives. "Have a talk with him but be sure the Creightons don't know about it. And go back and talk to the woman who provided these newspaper articles."[22] Later that day, when investigators returned, they were told an interesting story. A neighbor said that she suspected Mrs. Creighton had stolen some cash from her home during a visit. When the neighbor confronted her, she denied it. But later, Mrs. Creighton brought a cake over as a peace offering. After the neighbor ate the cake, she became violently sick and suffered vomiting spells. She accused Mrs. Creighton of poisoning her. Frances responded by telling the neighbor she was "accused of that once before and they couldn't prove it."

When Dr. Zabin was contacted in reference to Ada's death, his response raised further suspicions. "I wouldn't be surprised if there was something odd about that death," he said. "I signed a death certificate only a few hours ago but I signed it against my better judgment. I was treating the woman for one thing and apparently she died of something else."[23] When Dr. Zabin detailed his treatment of Ada and described the time that she spent at Nassau County Hospital, detectives noticed a very strange fact. "Almost as soon as the woman reached the institution, she responded to treatment—the same treatment that had been ineffectually administered to her in her home," King later said. "She had been back in her home only a few hours when the violent sickness began again."[24] Dr. Zabin also told police that every time he visited Ada's home, Mrs. Creighton hovered over her bedridden friend and would not leave even for a moment, as if she was afraid that Ada might say something out of line. That was enough for Inspector King, who immediately suspected a murder had been committed.[25]

Nassau County District Attorney Martin Littleton was advised of the situation and, sensing the case might generate headlines, entered into the case with all the enthusiasm of an aspiring detective. Young, handsome and extremely ambitious, Littleton took charge of the investigation immediately. He ordered police to bring in the Creightons and Everett Applegate for questioning. Littleton had a habit of conducting such interviews in the middle of the night. He thought the procedure would put people at a disadvantage. The three suspects were brought to his office at midnight by county investigators led by Inspector King. "At first glance," said King, "Mrs. Creighton appeared to be a typical, middle-class housewife—except for her eyes. They were dark and forbidding, and had a hypnotic quality. Closer scrutiny of the woman's face marked her as a person of strong will, an individual accustomed to dominating others."[26]

Over the next several hours, while Frances and Everett dodged Littleton's questions and tried to explain the sudden death of his wife, Ada's body was being transported to the coroner's office for an immediate autopsy. Everett was adamant; he knew nothing about the death and could offer no new information. "God alone knows," he told investigators. "I certainly don't!"[27] Frances stood her ground as well. She was under the impression that Ada died from heart trouble. But during the questioning, preliminary results from the postmortem exam arrived. Ada's body showed positive signs of arsenic poisoning. Littleton was convinced that it was murder but agreed to let Frances go home to prepare the children for church. Completed toxicology reports would require a few days and, until then, police would continue to gather evidence.

On Monday, October 7, 1935, Frances and John Creighton were brought back to police headquarters for further questioning. By then, District Attorney Littleton had the results of all the autopsy reports. They showed massive arsenic ingestion killed Ada Appelgate. Throughout the afternoon and into the night, the interrogation continued. Eventually, Frances began to make admissions. She told police that she was very upset with Ada over the rumors she was spreading about her daughter, Ruth. "I told her I thought it was an awful thing to do . . . if she had a girl of her own I would not pass any remark about her youngster, and she should not do it to Ruth . . . I felt she allowed herself to do an awful lot of talking with her mouth."[28] Littleton dispatched police psychologist Dr. Richard Hoffman and Inspector King with her to the Baldwin Place home for the purpose of interviewing Ruth Creighton.

As soon as he arrived at the home, Inspector King noticed the teenager. "I saw at once that Ruth Creighton was developed beyond her years. Her body more closely resembled that of a girl of twenty-one. She had on only a nightgown and a thin dressing robe." While Frances prepared breakfast, Dr. Hoffman questioned Ruth about her relationship with Appy. Within minutes, Ruth not only admitted having sexual intercourse with Everett, but said the relations continued to that very day. She said it began the previous June and that her mother knew all about it because she had caught her in the act several times. "In fact, Ruth avowed, she and Appelgate often warmly embraced each other in the presence of the mother and the latter said or did nothing about it!"[29] When Frances heard this, she objected and claimed she knew nothing about the relationship. But Ruth was insistent. "Why Mother, you knew!" she said in front of Inspector King and Dr. Hoffman. "You've been watching my periods for four months."[30] After securing Ruth's statements describing the affair, Inspector King brought everyone back to headquarters. There Everett was confronted with the new information. He admitted that he had been having sex with the girl since she was fourteen. "It's no use trying to hide it," he said. "I'll just have to take my medicine."[31]

Late that night, Frances broke down and admitted giving Ada the poison. She gave the first of three confessions, each of which conflicted with the other. She also claimed that Everett had driven her to the drugstore on the night she bought the Rough on Rats poison. She told Inspector King that she was upset with Ada for talking about her daughter.

"It was under the spur of the impulse which I generally regret I decided to do an injustice to Mrs. Appelgate," she said.

"When you say you decided to do an injustice to Mrs. Appelgate, tell me what you mean?"

"Give her the poison."

"By what means did you intend to give her this poison?"

"Through her food."[32]

But as far as Everett's involvement in the murder, Frances kept changing her story. At first she said that he knew that she intended to murder Ada. At other times, she denied that he knew anything about the plot. In her second confession, she told police she only wanted to hurt Everett by swearing that he was part of the plot to kill his wife.

"In that statement, you implicated Mr. Everett Appelgate?" asked Inspector King.

"Yes," replied Frances.

"Your reason for doing that was because you felt that he had gravely mistreated your daughter Ruth?"

"Yes."

"And you wish to punish him as greatly as you possibly could?"

"Yes," she said. Nevertheless, Appelgate was quickly arrested and charged with second degree assault for having sexual relations with the underage Ruth. Frances was charged with murder and the following morning, the defendants were arraigned in Nassau County Court.

On October 8, District Attorney Littleton held a press conference where he outlined the details of the murder plot for reporters. In an article titled "Woman Confesses Arsenic Slaying, Clears Appelgate," the *Times* reported, "Mrs. Creighton told the prosecutor that she was downstairs with Appelgate when the latter mentioned to him that Mrs. Appelgate needed a drink of eggnog and that he was going to prepare a drink for her. Mrs. Creighton volunteered to make the eggnog herself . . . when Appelgate's back was turned for a moment . . . she mixed an extra heavy dose of arsenic with the eggnog."[33] Littleton, basking in the media spotlight for having solved a difficult murder case, described Mrs. Creighton's demeanor during her confessions. "She hasn't expressed any nervousness, confusion, unhappiness nor indicated emotional upset of any kind," he said. "Her tenacity and ability to speak incessantly is the most amazing quality I have ever seen in my life."[34] This description of Frances Creighton as a cold and heartless woman was a theme other reporters quickly picked up; it became the dominant one whenever her name was mentioned in the press. Like Ruth Synder, Mrs. Creighton's failure as a mother and her lack of compassion became part and parcel of nearly every tabloid story that was written about her after her arrest.

Though her confessions offered several different versions of the events leading up to the murder of Ada, Littleton had little trouble convincing a Nassau County Grand Jury to indict both her and Everett Appelgate for the murder. "Mrs. Creighton's indictment was expected, since she had confessed giving poison to Mrs. Applegate," said the *Times* in a story on October 12. "But her statement was said to have exonerated Applegate, so that his indictment on the murder charge was surprise." Appelgate was also indicted for felony assault in connection with his sexual relationship with Ruth.

At his arraignment, he was defiant. "I plead guilty to this charge," he said. "I wish to marry this girl!"[35] Local attorney Elvin N. Edwards was appointed by the court to defend Frances. Charles R. Weeks was chosen to defend Appelgate. Littleton announced that he was ready to try the case within the week, but decided to give the defense team time to prepare their case. Since Littleton also decided to hold John Creighton as a material witness, Ruth and Agnes were turned over to Nassau County's Children's Society until a permanent place could be found for them.

Edwards, who was also a former district attorney, made a motion in court to have a separate trial for his client. He knew that no benefit could be achieved from Mrs. Creighton and Everett sitting at the same table during the trial. It would surely appear as if they plotted the murder together. Other than Frances's statements, there was no corroborating or independent evidence against Appelgate. Judge Cortland A. Johnson tended to agree, but Littleton was ready. He was aware that little evidence existed against Appelgate and that if a separate trial were granted, there was a good chance that the defendant would be acquitted. Littleton argued forcefully for a joint trial. He said that the act was committed in concert and therefore, legally, both defendants participated in the murder. Judge Johnson eventually agreed, and during the week of January 5, 1936, he ruled a single trial would be held for both defendants.[36]

The public soon learned of the sinful sex–love triangle inside the Creighton home. Frances became the target of much hate mail, which emphasized her failure as a mother for allowing her daughter to have sex with the married and much older Appelgate. Many letter writers saw Frances as a predator and a pervert. "Do you call yourself a mother?" one writer asked.

"Some mother! You are a lousy prostitute that's what you are. You are no damn good . . . and your husband, he is a skunk, he's worse than a snake . . . you are the worst kind of people and the sooner the electric chair gets you the better."[37] In a letter to District Attorney Littleton, another writer said that Mrs. Creighton "is an immoral woman who has a mania for degeneracy for women as well as men." Another note said "such people are a menace in this world, she was inclined to like fat women for her maniacal desires."[38]

A pool of 160 men was summoned to the county court during the first week of January as the process of choosing a jury began. Since the case had already generated a great deal of publicity, it was difficult to find people who had not heard of the murder and who could remain impartial. By January 14, after twenty-five were examined, just three men were chosen to serve. While the selection process continued, a motive for the murder of Ada Appelgate appeared for the first time in the New York press. In an article titled "Juror No. 5 Ousted in Creighton Case," the *Sun* reported that "the motive was to free Applegate in order that he might marry Mrs. Creighton's sixteen-year-old daughter, Ruth."[39] Two days later, on January 16, the jury was chosen and the trial was ready to begin.

The first witness was Dr. Alexander O. Gettler, the toxicologist who was now on the staff of the Medical Examiner's Office in New York City. Gettler, who also testified at Frances's Newark trial in 1923, told the court of his autopsy findings. He said he "found varying quantities of white arsenic, which caused him to estimate that the entire body contained eleven grains of the poison. Authorities conceded that three grains of arsenic constituted a lethal dose."[40] John Creighton was called to the stand to tell the court about the rather curious living conditions inside the Bryant Place home prior to the murder. Under questioning, he said that he didn't believe his wife had anything to do with Ada's murder. He also recalled the anger that Everett felt toward his wife after he lost an election for a higher post in the American Legion. For that loss, John Creighton said, Everett blamed Ada. When he stepped off the stand, Creighton smiled at Frances causing her to sob quietly as he left the room.

Following Creighton to the stand was Inspector Harold King, Chief of Detectives for Nassau County Police Department. When prosecutors asked King whether he heard John Creighton say anything on the morning Ada died, he replied that Creighton asked his wife, "Have you given her anything, Frances? You know I've been through this thing with you before and if you've given her anything, I want to know?"[41] Upon hearing that response, defense attorney Charles Weeks immediately objected and asked for a mistrial. In chambers, Judge Johnson denied the motion. But he ruled that there was to be no mention that Frances had been arrested and tried for two previous murders. After Inspector King testified, the judge admitted Frances's first written statement in which she implicated Everett. Though the defense objected and said the statement was obtained by coercion, the ruling stood, and the statement was read for the jury.

Judge Johnson also admitted her later confessions as well, all of which contradicted her earlier statements. In one statement, she claimed that Everett helped her in the murder; in others, she said that he knew nothing about it. "She also desired to punish Applegate for relations with her daughter and so she named him as an accomplice. In the statement read in court today, she said she did not think Applegate even knew of the administration of arsenic."[42] As jumbled and disjointed as they were, the lengthy confessions were powerful evidence against Frances. She admitted buying the Rough on Rats arsenic and told police where she purchased it. The store salesman identified her and Frances later admitted giving Ada the poison.

When prosecutor Littleton rested the people's case, the first witness called by Weeks was Ruth Creighton. The young girl, obviously terrified, walked to the stand, shaking noticeably. She tried not to look at her mother, seated only a few away from her. "Gone were the slave bracelet, the flippant manner in which she had previously spoken of 'Uncle Ev.' She was white-faced and trembling, but still an unusually pretty girl. And as she told her story, she was an unwilling partner in the sex acts—a victim of seduction and rape."[43] After she was sworn in, Ruth folded her hands on her lap while she fielded the questions.

"How old are you?" Weeks asked.

"Sixteen."

"Before the Applegates came to your home, did you know the Applegates' daughter?"

"Yes."

"Was Agnes a visitor at your house?"

"Yes."

"Was that before Applegate came to live with you?"

"Before."

"You were good friends?"

"Yes."

"And you remember me first calling on you?"

"Yes."

"You told me about relations you had with Mr. Applegate?"

"Yes."

"When did you first have something to do with him . . . improper relations?"

"It was at his home." Ruth began to cry. She wiped the tears from her face with the sleeve of her blouse.

"After this thing occurred, did you tell your mother about it?"

"No, I didn't."

"Did the relationship occur again?'

"Yes." But Ruth again denied that her mother knew anything of the relationship. She also denied ever having told the police that her mother knew which was in direct conflict with Inspector King's assertion that her mother was fully aware that Everett was having sex with Ruth.

"Did Mr. Appelgate have improper relations with you after they came to the house?" asked Weeks.

"Yes."

"How long after?"

"Soon after."

"Where in the house?"

"It happened outside the house, in his automobile."

"Did Appelgate have relations with you in your own home?"

"Yes."

"More than once?"

"Yes."

"Did Appelgate have relations with you in his own room?"

"Yes, he did."

"How often?"

"Oh, many times."

"Did Appelgate ever say he wanted to marry you?"

"No, he did not."

"Did Appelgate tell you he would like you better under any certain conditions?"

"Yes, he did. He often told me he would like me better if he were single."[44] In between her answers, Ruth sobbed continuously, glancing over at her mother who avoided eye contact and stared down at the table in front of her. As Ruth told her story of sex with Everett, Frances wept and frequently placed her hands over her face. Some of the women in the pews behind her could be heard crying as well.

It would be up to Frances herself to clarify matters for the court. On the morning of January 21, she walked to the stand. The court saw a very calm and proper woman as she settled into the witness chair. "She pulled her brown skirt down and composed herself in the big chair. She folded her hands in her lap, sighed deeply and managed a weak smile."[45] Her attorney, Elvin Edwards, took her through her explanation of the death of Mrs. Appelgate.

"Did you give arsenic or any other poison to Mrs. Appelgate?"

"No, I did not."

"Did you know of any wrongdoing on the part of Mr. Appelgate?"

"No, not actually. I had no positive knowledge," she said quietly. Her testimony, at first, repudiated some of her previous statements in the confessions she gave to police when she was arrested. "In all of these the motive for the killing was given as the illicit relations between Ruth Creighton and Appelgate. They also contained alleged admissions that Appelgate was Mrs. Creighton's lover as well as her daughter's."[46]

"Did you know of your daughter's intimacy with Mr. Appelgate?" asked Edwards.

"I did not."

"Did you ever see any act of intimacy between them?"

"I did not."

"Did Mr. Appelgate say anything about his own attitude toward Ruth?"

"He said he had a fatherly love for her, the same as he had for his own daughter."

"Did you believe him?"

"I did."

But when Littleton began his cross-examination, things became decidedly worse for Frances. She shifted uneasily in the wooden chair and wiped her forehead repeatedly with a paper napkin. Her eyes darted around the courtroom and they frequently welled with tears. Littleton turned his questioning to the night of September 26 when Frances prepared the eggnog for Ada Appelgate. "Earlier in the day, in answer to questions by her own attorney, the defendant had repeatedly denied that she gave the poison. She admitted giving a "gray powder" at the request of Appelgate."[47]

"When you took the milk to Mrs. Appelgate and waited for her to drink it, you knew then there was arsenic in it, did you not?" asked Littleton.

"Yes, I did," she answered. "Appelgate told me."

"Knowing that, you took it to her to drink?"

"Yes."

"You stood by and watched this woman, who was your best friend, die?"

"Yes."

"When the empty glass came into the kitchen you knew she had drunk poison?"

"Yes."

"But you didn't tell the doctor or anyone else?"

"No."

"You didn't tell the police that you were being forced by Appelgate to do this?'

"No."[48]

It was a fatal admission. For the first time, Frances may have realized that the end was near. Her attorney tried to resurrect her with some pointless

questions concerning her previous admissions but her testimony seemed evasive and self-serving. When asked why she admitted to crimes that she says
she didn't commit, Frances said that she was intimidated by the police. "I said
whatever was suggested by them," she said. "They were my words but at their
suggestion." None of it sounded true and the press reported the new development in the next day's editions. "The poison murder trial of Mrs. Mary
Frances Creighton reached a dramatic climax today with the admission of
Mrs. Creighton under cross-examination that she had given arsenic to
Mrs. Ada Appelgate, wife of a former American Legion official," reported the
Times in a story on page one. The *Herald Tribune* carried the story on its second page and wrote that "Mrs. Creighton was a haggard woman . . . Littleton
reduced her to tears and hopeless stuttering in less than three-quarters of an
hour and broke down a defense she painstakingly had built up."[49]

The Daily News, ever the leader in negative and sensational stories, put its
coverage on the front page. "Mrs. Mary Creighton admitted to all the world
that she murdered Mrs. Ada Appelgate. Her confessions of arsenic poisoning,
wrung from her lips in tortured frantic phrases, was one of the most melo-
dramatic scenes in an American courtroom in decades." The reporter for the
Daily News was Grace Robinson, the same writer who covered the Eva Coo
case. Her stories contained the same type of opinionated coverage she provided during the Oneonta trial. "The fat unloved Ada was Appelgate's
wife . . . the jury also learned of the plump housewife's astounding poison
past . . . when Mrs. Creighton made her astonishing blunder, in quiet lady-
like tones, she didn't forget to drag Appelgate into the confession."[50] The
News also pointed out that Frances lost her composure on the stand under the
relentless questioning of Littleton. "The prosecutor's words fell like whips about
the tearful, beleaguered woman. She knew it was arsenic, didn't she? She knew
arsenic was a poison? Well, she replied, she only knew what 'Appy' told her."[51]

But there was one more witness that the jury hadn't heard from yet.
Throughout the proceedings, Everett Appelgate sat at the defense table next
to Frances. He rarely showed interest in the proceedings. Occasionally, he
whispered in the ear of his attorney or scribbled notes on a paper pad. After
Frances left the stand, it was Appelgate's turn. His cocky attitude, smug
demeanor, and effeminate physical appearance did not help his case.
Reporter Dorothy Kilgallen later wrote, "I was doing my best to be objective
about the man, but when he took the stand I must admit that his round, wet-
lipped, pallid face repelled me as few others have since . . . and his testimony
was hardly expected to win him any friends."[52]

"Appelgate, when did you first begin to have acts of sexual intercourse
with Ruth Creighton?" asked Littleton.

"Sometime in the summer of 1935."

"What part of the summer was it?'

"Probably around June or July."

"And from that time on your sexual relations with Ruth became a matter of constant practice?"

"Well, the occurrences were not frequent."

"That was a practice that occurred almost every other day without exception?" asked Littleton.

"Yes, it occurred quite frequently."

"That is true isn't it?"

"Yes."

"And did there come a time when Ruth slept in the bed with you and your deceased wife?"

"Yes, she did it on five different occasions."

"You recall five. On those occasions . . . some of them or all of them . . . did you have acts of sexual intercourse in the bed, with your wife present?"

"On one occasion," came the reply.

"You had intercourse with Ruth in the very bed where your wife lay?" Littleton's voice rose in tone and expressed incredulity.

"Yes."

"You all slept nude in the bed?"

"Not entirely."

"You were nude?"

"Yes."

"That is true of the five occasions?"

"It is not."

"Did you ever use pajamas when she slept there with you?

"Yes."

"Was your wife nude?"

"Yes."

"And Ruth slept nude?

"She came in clothed."

"But she soon stripped?"

"Yes."

"So we have this picture of your wife and Ruth and you in this bed, nude?"

"That is right."

"So that in fact, on a bed fifty-seven inches wide, on five occasions, with your wife present, Ruth slept with you at the time when you were nude and on two of them . . . you had intercourse with her?"

"Yes."

"What did your wife say to that?"

"She didn't know anything about the intercourse."

"Do you want this court and jury to believe that on a bed of those dimensions, you had an act of sexual intercourse with this girl without your wife knowing about it?"

"Certainly."

"So far as your wife is concerned, you think she never knew of these associations?"

"Not so far as I know."

"She permitted this child to come into her bed naked?"

"Yes."

"The girl naked and you naked?"

"We slept that way."

"Now, this one occasion . . . where was your wife sleeping? On the wall side?"

"No, my wife was on the outside."

"Ruth didn't have to climb over her to get in back with you?'

"No."

"You were in between them?"

"Yes."

"Ruth on one side and your wife on the other?"

"Yes."

"Where was Agnes?"

"On the cot on the floor."

"In the same room?"

"Yes."

"Was Agnes in the nude too?"

"No."

"Did you take any precautions?"

"I did."

"What measures did you use?"

"Do you wish me to state them?"

"Yes, I want to know."

"Withdrawal."

"You didn't care if she became pregnant, I suppose?"

"If she did, she wouldn't through me."

Throughout the remainder of his testimony, Appelgate denied that he ever gave Ada any poison and told the court that he had no idea that there was poison in the eggnog. "Whether I got the liquor or not, I don't know," he told the court. "I have frankly admitted I was confused about that. I recall going through the icebox and then taking a spoon handed to me by Mrs. Creighton. I had put in a larger amount of liquor then usual because Ada was feeling so badly and I tasted it then. Mrs. Creighton asked me,

'How does it taste Appy?' I said, 'It tastes alright to me. She ought to get a good sleep after it!'"[53]

But Littleton focused a great deal of his questions on Applegate's relationship with Ruth and Frances, making the self-absorbed defendant recite every detail of the sordid affair inside the house on Bryant Place. The jury was thoroughly repulsed by Applegate and his sexual activity with underage Ruth. The fact that he was having sex with her mother at the same time incensed the court and spectators as well. Self-absorbed, arrogant, and cocky to the point of being obnoxious, Applegate's own testimony sealed his fate. "In the end, he emerged an object of ridicule as well as loathing. As guards led him back to his cell, the crowd booed him and a woman broke through the police escort to claw at his face. The papers had whipped up a hysteria of hatred."[54]

Following Everett to the stand was his uncle Joseph Applegate, from Ridgewood, New Jersey. He testified that he visited his nephew a few months before the murder and had a chance to talk with Mrs. Creighton. He told the court that the conversation drifted to the subject of Ada's treatment of Everett, of which she strongly disapproved. During this same talk, Joe Applegate said that Mrs. Creighton remarked, "Ada is a real nuisance! I'd like to drop her some rat poison!"[55]

Closing arguments began on January 24. Charles Weeks, counsel for Applegate, went first. "He bitterly attacked Mrs. Creighton's testimony today in summing up his case for the jury after both sides had rested. He stated that he had never seen a witness so crushed as she was crushed by the District Attorney."[56] Weeks said that he was aware of the revulsion that the jury must feel for his client. Having sex with a fifteen-year-old girl is crime in the State of New York, he told the jury, but that didn't make Applegate guilty of murder. He pointed out that in Mrs. Creighton's first statement, she exonerated his client and said he'd had nothing to do with the poison plot. "I think it took a monumental gall to get on the stand and repudiate this statement and a greater gall to expect you to believe it. Mrs. Creighton said that she put rat poison in Mrs. Appelgate's eggnog and she also said that Applegate didn't know anything about it!"[57] But Weeks emphasized the sinful relationship with Ruth as the real reason Applegate was charged in the murder case. He said that the district attorney knew if the rape of Ruth was put before the jury, it would sway them to a guilty verdict. "Why was the girl brought here?" he asked the jury. "She testified to nothing on the murder charge. She was brought here without the usual rouge on her lips to prejudice you against Appelgate." Then he walked to the defense table and pointed to Mrs. Creighton. "Are you going to believe her?" he shouted. "Are you going to believe a woman who admittedly told as many lies as she did? With no evidence except her word, how can you decide when she told the truth? What is the evidence? . . . If you believe my man did it, don't hesitate . . . but don't believe it on the word of this woman. . . . I ask you not to punish him for something he didn't do."[58]

Once Weeks finished his impassioned defense of Appelgate, it was Elvin Edwards's turn to try to defend Mrs. Creighton, who seemingly had little in her favor. "In his final address, Edwards characterized the plump, confessed Borgia as 'a woman of putty manipulated by a man of steel.' Applegate, he declared, dominated her in all that transpired in the curious joint household. He begged the jurors, if they must convict, not to condemn the woman and set the man free."[59] Edwards pointed out to the court that Mrs. Creighton was helpless while under the control of her lover and that the murder was committed at the command of Appelgate. "I say she was a good wife and mother, and you can't put your finger on anything she did until she came under the influence of Appelgate," Edwards said. "They say she is an evil, ferocious Borgia. If she is, she must be crazy . . . but Appelgate is clever. He is smart. He fooled others. He is clever . . . gentlemen, this woman was a victim of domination, a victim of circumstance—or she's crazy!"[60] It was a curious summation, given the fact that the jury knew full well of Mrs. Creighton's previous murder trials. Newspapers repeated the story of the 1923 Newark trials over and over until most readers must have felt that Mrs. Creighton escaped punishment for the murders of her brother and in-laws.

Martin Littleton had the advantage of presenting his summation last, leaving the final impression on the jury. He detailed the evidence against Mrs. Creighton, including her own words on the witness stand. But he reserved special condemnation for Appelgate. "Look at him! Look at him!" he shouted to the jury as he held his finger close to the head of the defendant. "Appelgate, the poseur [pretender]! See him walking down the street, strutting the uniform that he wore but three weeks. Parading under the banner he'd never seen float anyway, except here at Mitchell Field, to reserve plaudits and approval of all [with] whom he came into contact."[61] Littleton repeated descriptions of the love-sex relationships inside the Bryant Place home, and suggested it was a breeding ground for betrayal and murder. "Littleton demanded death in the electric chair for both. Reviewing the amazing welter of lust, fear, hate, and jealousy in which the Creighton and Appelgate families lived in their joint Baldwin bungalow, he asserted that nothing short of capital punishment could atone for the murder of fat, unloved Ada Appelgate."[62]

The jury received the case for deliberation at 9 p.m. on Friday night, January 24. Less than four hours later, at 12:47 a.m., the jury foreman announced a unanimous verdict had been reached. The defendants were escorted back into the courtroom that, even at that late hour, held several hundred spectators. "In the courtroom were about two hundred persons, half of them women. Many of the men were members of the Baldwin post of the American Legion, of which Appelgate formerly had been the commander."[63] When Mrs. Creighton was brought in, she looked despondent. "She was chalky white and two deputy sheriffs waited for her expected collapse," wrote the *Daily News*. "But the plump, brown-gowned Borgia gave no outward sign of dismay."[64] On the same day, the *Post* wrote that "Mrs. Creighton's face was ghastly as she was led in, though only her pallor betrayed her. She seemed already to have resigned herself to a verdict of guilty."[65] Appelgate followed her to the defense table, where he slouched down into his seat and waited for Judge Johnson to enter.

In the meantime, the Nassau County Police weren't taking any chances. The hostility among the spectators toward Everett Appelgate had reached critical levels. Each day when he was brought into the court, he was bombarded by insults and threats. Judge Johnson warned the court on several occasions to refrain from aggressive behavior or emotional outbursts. But still the display continued. "When word that the jury reached a verdict spread from the courtroom, twenty county policemen marched in behind Sgt. William Reaper and lined up across the middle of the courtroom, taking [the] place of a railing to separate spectators from the defendants."[66] Once the judge declared the court in session, he turned to the jurors and asked if they had reached a verdict.

"Yes, your honor!" replied the foreman.

"And how do you find the defendant Mary Frances Creighton of the charge of murder in the first degree?"

"Guilty, your honor!"

"And how do you find the defendant Everett Appelgate of the charge of Murder in the First Degree?"

"Guilty, your honor!"

Mrs. Creighton stood motionless next to her attorney. "Her eyes rolled wildly and if possible . . . her skin became of an even more unearthly pallor," wrote the *Daily News*. The *Herald Tribune* reported, "This morning when the jury foreman . . . announced the verdict, she showed no change of expression, nor did Appelgate." *Daily News* reporter Grace Robinson, who attended the trial every day, told her readers what she saw in court. "Appelgate, a few feet from her, was equally composed, although he was obviously more surprised. His pudgy face flushed a strange purple color . . . the plumpish, bullet-headed Legionnaire, who seemed a dashing Lothario to his child mistress, preserved his reputation for self-assurance throughout the solemn hour."[67] But the *Post* saw the scene differently. "In Appelgate's expression, there was shock and apprehension as if he had really believed those confident, flippant words he had said . . . but was beginning to feel a crawling fear that the incredible would happen to him."[68] The next edition of the *Daily News* dedicated its entire front page to the verdict using the words "BORGIA, LOVER GUILTY" printed in bold type.

As reporters shouted questions, the defendants supplied their pedigree to the court clerk, who recorded the information into the record. "The jury made a mistake!" said Frances. "They were misled by the district attorney. I feel sure that the verdict will be set aside on appeal."[69] Elvin Edwards immediately notified the court that he intended to appeal the case because the jury should never have learned of Mrs. Creighton's previous history concerning the death of her brother and in-laws. "As she lay dazed on her cot in jail today, this tragedy out of the past offered her her only hope of escaping the electric chair."[70] Appelgate's attorney, Charles Weeks, also stated he intended to appeal because his client should have received a separate trial. Once the defendants were removed from the courtroom, Edwards left the building and began his journey over to the Children's Shelter. "There slept Ruth Creighton, who publicly bared the shame of her intimate relations with the married Appelgate, and bared other shocking indiscretions, in a gallant effort to save her mother. There, too, unconscious of the momentous turn of events in his life, was 12-year-old Jackie Creighton. His appearance in court brought the only complete collapse the low-voiced, sphinx-like woman suffered during the trial."[71]

Later that same day, hiding under a heavy coat and slipping into the Nassau County Jail through a rear entrance, John Creighton visited his wife. "John Creighton, the condemned woman's husband, did not learn of the verdict until noon . . . he broke down completely and fell sobbing . . . on his knees and told her he still believed in her."[72] It was the first visit since she had been arrested in October the previous year. "As they embraced in the presence of Elvin N. Edwards . . . the convicted woman wept profusely and inquired between sobs about their children. She asked her husband to take care of the children and gave him detailed instructions about their future."[73] The *Post*, however, reported that Mrs. Creighton was fine and maintained her composure throughout the meeting. "Mrs. Creighton did not shed a tear," the article pointed out. "Her calm was unbelievable . . . one thing she told him was he would have to get new license plates for their car because the present plates were in her name."[74]

On the cloudy morning of January 30, Appelgate and Creighton were brought back to the same courtroom to receive their sentence. Judge Courtland Johnson, as required by the existing statutes, sentenced both defendants to death in the electric chair during the week of March 9, 1936. Elvin Edwards made a motion to set aside the verdict for Mrs. Creighton on the grounds that introduction of previous murder trials prejudiced the jury and turned the court against her. The judge denied that motion and both defense attorneys formally announced their intentions to appeal the verdict. On January 25, 1936, the *Daily News* ran a photo of Frances on its front page. The caption read, "Still dazed by the verdict that doomed her to death, Mrs. Mary Creighton is escorted by deputy sheriffs . . . the verdict branded Mrs. Creighton as a modern Borgia who handed the poison potions to the wife of her paramour."[75]

On the following morning, Frances and Everett were removed from the Nassau County Jail and driven up to Sing Sing prison in separate cars. Before leaving the county jail, Frances wrote a note to her daughter. "Mother is going away," it read. "No matter what has happened to you in your life, be a good girl and look after the best man you will ever have, your father . . . you and Jackie are all that Daddy has. Make every effort to help in this trying situation. I love you all. Please pray for me. Lovingly, Mother."[76] Enterprising reporters from the *News* and the *Mirror* followed the procession out of Queens and all the way up to the village of Ossining on the banks of the Hudson. Unable to get an interview with the convicted couple, they parked outside the prison gates and settled for interviews with prison employees.

Some people seriously doubted the guilt of Everett Appelgate in his wife's murder. It seemed clear that only the words of Mrs. Creighton damned him to the electric chair. There was no hard evidence at all that he either knew about the murder of his wife or participated in it. The American Legion on Long Island tried to raise funds to help Appelgate and used whatever influence they had to lobby for a new trial. Charles Weeks appealed directly to Governor Herbert H. Lehman, and requested commutation of the death sentence. The governor surely had his doubts about Appelgate's guilt, but was reluctant to act on behalf of an admitted child molester.

In the meantime, Elvin Edwards submitted a letter to the court that was written to him by Ruth Creighton in which the girl said that Everett had said they would marry if Ada was out of the way. "He would do away with Aunt Ada and have me for himself and that he could talk Dad into letting us be married," she wrote. "He also said no one would be able to blame him after she died." After reviewing the letter and the motion, Judge Courtland Johnson denied Edwards's request. "I cannot for the life of me see how what you say would change the verdict of the jury,"[77] said Judge Johnson. He noted that Mrs. Creighton had admitted poisoning Ada during cross-examination and was therefore guilty beyond any reasonable doubt.

While Frances waited on Death Row, she became friends with the only other female in the cell block, Dorothy Sherwood, an upstate mother who was convicted of drowning her two-year-old son in a creek to "save him from starvation." Sherwood and Frances frequently prayed together for new trials. Though it would not happen for Frances, Sherwood's request was granted during the summer of 1936. The Court of Appeals set aside her first conviction when it ruled that the trial judge had misled the jury during his charge. For Sherwood, it meant salvation. She was taken off Death Row and sent back to Orange County Court, leaving Frances alone in the cell block. But on the male side of Death Row, the cells were packed.

The year of 1936 was a special one for Sing Sing. More inmates were executed that year than in any other in its history. Twenty-one men and woman went to their deaths in the electric chair, an average of one every eighteen days. The executions began on January 9, before Frances went to trial in Nassau County Court. On that night four men—Amerigo Angelini, Raymond Newman, Raymond Orlikowski, and Thomas Rooney, all under the age of twenty two—went to their deaths for the murder of a policeman during one of their dozens of armed robberies. During the same month, Albert Fish, age sixty-six and the oldest man executed in New York State history, went to his death for the vicious murder and dismemberment of twelve-year-old Grace Budd. Fish was an extreme sexual degenerate, a cannibal, and a repetitive child molester. By the end of April, another five men were executed without much fanfare. On May 28, for the second time that year, four young men were executed on the same night. One of them had shot and killed an innocent bystander during a saloon robbery in Brooklyn and a jury had decided that all were equally guilty of murder.[78] After two more prisoners were executed in June, Frances and Everett would be the next inmates scheduled to die.

With her execution set for July 16, Frances's mental and physical health deteriorated. She became despondent, refused to talk to anyone, and laid in bed throughout the day and night. Her condition became so severe, that Warden Lawes requested she be examined by a panel of doctors in order to determine her fitness for execution. On July 14, the medical team arrived at Sing Sing, where they were allowed to examine Frances. "Mrs. Creighton has been in state of collapse for eight weeks," reported the *Times*. "For the last week, her hysteria has been such that she has been unable to leave her bed. Both legs appear to be paralyzed and she can retain hardly any food."[79] When District Attorney Littleton heard of the exam, he saw it as a ruse to either delay or prevent the execution. He told reporters that Mrs. Creighton "has been and is a menace to society."

The following day, a report was completed by the medical team and submitted to Governor Lehman. They concluded that Mrs. Creighton was of sound mind and did not appear to be suffering from any physical disease. The report stated that the doctors "found no evidence of organic disease of the central nervous system or of the body as a whole. Mrs. Creighton is well developed, well nourished and if she has lost weight, it is not apparent . . . she is suffering from a type of disability which would improve rapidly if she were encouraged and get worse if she is discouraged. Her condition is the reaction to the situation in which she finds herself." Once the report was submitted to the governor's office, there was no doubt that the execution would go forward. "In view of this, it was believed that Governor Lehman would not interfere with her execution. Mrs. Creighton has no other hope for life. For a while, it had been believed that her condition might prompt a postponement if it should be proven that she was really ill."[80]

During the first few weeks of her imprisonment on Death Row, Frances held up fairly well. She was convinced that she would be granted a new trial and later, that the governor would spare her. But after the Court of Appeals turned her down, her mental health grew progressively worse; she was overcome by fear and hysteria. "Those weeks immediately preceding Mrs. Creighton's execution were torturous ones for her," said executioner Robert Elliot. "She ate almost nothing . . . just ice cream. She refused to exercise. When not weeping, she was moaning or praying. Many a night she never closed her eyes, staring up at the ceiling from her cell cot. She often dreamed of the fate that awaited her and would wake up screaming, 'I can't stand it! I can't stand it!'"[81]

On the morning of July 16, John Creighton visited his wife for the last time. Frances asked him to take care of the children and try to provide them with a good home. When her attorney met with Frances, she lay on her bed and did not get up. "I have done many wrong things," she said. "But I know God will forgive me. I am not afraid so much to die because of myself but mostly because of John and the kiddies . . . I do not know what my husband and children will do without me, I was always their counsel and guide. I fear for them after I'm gone."[82] She then tried to get up out of the bed and collapsed onto the floor. The matrons lifted her back onto the bed and summoned the prison physician. In the meantime, her attorney asked her to clear Everett if he had nothing to do with the murder.

"Tell him I have no change to make in my story," she said.

For her last meal, Frances ordered bread, fruit, and water. Everett ordered roast chicken, baked potato, lettuce-and-tomato salad, bread, ice cream, coffee, and candy. When the food arrived at her cell a little past 5 p.m., it remained on the metal tray untouched while Frances lay in the bed unable, she said, to sit up. "Refusing food and professing to be unable to stand, Mrs. Frances Creighton lay in her cot in the death house at Sing Sing today . . . all hope of her escaping the chair seemed lost today after a commission reported to Governor Lehman that her paralysis was caused by hysteria and malingering," wrote the *Sun*.[83] As the hour of death grew near,

Everett began to lose nerve but said he did not murder his wife. "I'll insist to the end that I am innocent!" he told prison guards.

Warden Lawes permitted John Creighton to remain with his wife on Death Row for most of the evening. They held hands through the bars and talked with one another while her lawyer, Elvin Edwards, waited nearby for a possible phone call from the Governor. Frances would not permit her children to visit while she was in the death house. "I wouldn't care to have them see me in here," she told the matrons. "It would only upset them. I'm worried about what may happen to them."[84] Agnes Appelgate, however, did visit her father and remained with him for an hour during the later afternoon. His father, step-mother, and sister were allowed to visit as well, and said their emotional farewells while guards kept them at a respectable distance apart.

By 10:50 p.m. that night, preparations for the double execution were complete. Elliott had tested the machinery and everything appeared to be in fine working order. It had already been decided that Frances would go first. But by then, she was in a semi-coma and unable to get out of bed, let alone walk. Warden Lawes ordered a wheelchair and a few minutes later, it was rolled inside her cell. Guards lifted her into the chair and wheeled her into the corridor. Father John McCaffrey, the prison's Catholic chaplain, prayed nearby as the procession headed toward the execution room. "Mrs. Creighton, an old and broken woman at thirty-eight, was wheeled into the death chamber and carried to the electric chair, a strange caricature of the Borgia she had been called," wrote the *New York Post*.[85]

When she was pushed into the death chamber, the witnesses got their first look at the unconscious Frances. She was motionless and seemed to be in a comatose trance. Unknown to the press at that time, Frances had been given an injection of morphine by the prison doctor. It was decided that it would be better to have her sedated than take a chance she might struggle against the matrons as they placed her into the chair. No one, including Warden Lawes, wanted to face the gruesome scenario of an all-out battle with Frances while guards strapped her into the chair. "Due to her pathetic state, she was wearing the pink crepe nightgown and black satin kimono which had been her attire earlier in the day. Black bedroom slippers were on her feet. As the wheelchair was placed alongside the electric chair, I glanced at the woman. Her head drooped limply. Her dark hair, which had become streaked with gray during her imprisonment, was disheveled. Her face was a sickening yellow; her eyes were closed."[86]

After she was lifted and placed into the seat of the electric chair, nervous matrons quickly strapped her into place. Frances never moved nor gave any indication she was conscious. A set of rosary beads, which she carried on her lap, fell to the floor. They were retrieved by one of the matrons and placed into her pocket. In a truly bizarre coincidence, the name of the matron who picked up the beads was Mary Creighton. However, she was not related to Frances, nor did they know each other before they met on Death Row.

As soon as Frances was secure in the chair, the matrons and several guards then closed ranks around her, preventing any of the witnesses to see her clearly. This action was ordered by the warden to prevent a reoccurrence of the infamous incident in 1927 when Ruth Snyder was photographed at the moment of death by a reporter who had smuggled in a camera. As soon as the wall of matrons lined up in front of the chair, Warden Lawes gave the signal to the executioner. The current slammed into Frances with a loud hum that permeated the room. The dreadful sound continued for two long minutes. Then, Elliott shut it down for a moment and, as he had done more than three hundred times before, turned on the voltage again. When the current was switched off for the second time, the prison doctor stepped forward, examined Frances and declared, "I pronounce this woman dead!" The body was removed from the chair, placed on a gurney and taken into the adjoining room for an immediate autopsy. "To say that it was a distasteful task to execute a woman in Mrs. Creighton's condition is an understatement," Elliott later wrote. "But it would have been more revolting—certainly more difficult for me—had she been conscious and created an unpleasant scene."[87] A *Daily News* reporter told readers, "Her mouth was agape, her face ashen blue, but there was no evidence of a wasted body, though she has spurned food for days. When she went into the death house nearly six months ago, she weighed 165; last night she was down to less than 135. But she appeared a well-built woman, even when dead."[88]

Once her body was taken out of the death chamber, Everett Appelgate was escorted in. He was wearing a blue shirt and dark pants and was steady on his feet. The moment he entered the room, he looked the witnesses in the eye and spoke in a loud and clear voice. "Gentlemen," he said, "I want to say something. Before God, I'm absolutely innocent of this crime and I hope the good God will have mercy on the soul of Martin W. Littleton!" Even as he spoke, the guards moved quickly. He was placed in the chair and the leather straps were tightened around his chest, arms, and legs. The black leather mask was placed over his face while the witnesses could hear a faint murmur of prayer escape his lips. "The odor of seared flesh still clung to the execution chamber when the 38-year-old Appelgate, walking straight as a ramrod, stepped into the seat still warm from her body."[89] Within minutes, Everett Appelgate was dead. After guards removed his corpse from the chair, he joined Frances, for the last time, in the autopsy room.

In her last hours, Frances converted to Catholicism in the belief it would be easier for her to face death. In her final note to her daughter, who waited at the prison while Frances was executed, she wrote, "I have done many wrong things but I know God will forgive me. John knows that I was a good wife and mother and whatever I did, I did for him and the children. I hope they will have a better life than I did."

In Queens, District Attorney Littleton issued a statement to the press: "A prosecution for murder is not a pleasant duty for anyone connected with it . . . but in this instance I believe that every man whose duty it was to see that the laws were justly and firmly and impartially enforced has done his utmost to discharge that duty . . . the law has taken its course."[90]

Several years later, Ruth Creighton wrote an article for a national magazine in which she detailed her unhappy childhood, her sexual relationship with Appelgate, and the murder of Aunt Ada. In the same article, she told of a chance meeting with executioner Robert Elliot some time after her mother's execution. At first, she did not know who he was. But once they were introduced, they shook hands and exchanged pleasantries. She called it a "macabre touch of irony." But according to Elliott, the meeting never happened. "I have never seen or talked to the girl," he later said. "Neither have I met a relative of any other person who I have executed. Once, following an electrocution, I waited inside the prison for some time just to avoid the possibility of such a meeting."[91] Elliott was a considerate man in that way.

A Nuisance to Society:
Helen Fowler

Please! I'll live for God from now on if spared . . . for when children try
to have your life taken just to be free, it's a shame! I did wrong but please
for God's sake, give me a chance to prove these things!
        —Helen Fowler on Death Row, two hours before
                her execution on November 16, 1944.

In almost every way, the story of Helen Fowler is the antithesis of the Ruth
Snyder case. While Ruth was fashionable, financially secure, and white,
Fowler was unglamorous, poor, and black. Her story took place in a city
where the media did not wield much power and there were no feral tabloids
like the *Daily News* or the *Daily Mirror* to debate the psychological meaning
behind thin lips, a sharp chin, or narrow eyes, which had appeared in the
New York print media during the Snyder-Gray circus. Helen Fowler's alleged
crime was ugly and judged not very newsworthy. It did not entail any periph-
eral moralizing, as did the 1927 Leopold and Loeb case in Chicago, or any
important political overtones as did the Sacco-Vanzetti epic, which dragged
on for nearly six years. No one cried over Fowler's conviction; no one filled
endless pages of newsprint with stories on the significance of her case; nor was
her accomplice an "affable and friendly fellow" like Henry Judd Gray. Yet,
Helen Fowler was an historic figure. At the age of thirty-three, she became the
only black woman to be executed in New York during the twentieth century,
and only the second since the colony became part of the United States in
1787. Why then, did her case receive so little media attention? Why did the

tabloids and mainstream press practically ignore her execution, an event that—by any measure—was at least as newsworthy as the execution of Anna Antonio?[1]

To find another black woman who faced the death penalty in New York before Helen Fowler, one must go back to 1829, when Catherine Cashiere, a nineteen-year-old barmaid from Manhattan, got into a brawl with customer Susan Anthony. Cashiere stabbed Anthony to death in full view of other bar patrons. After a brief trial, she was sentenced to death by hanging on notorious Blackwell's Island, a small patch of land in the middle of the East River between Queens and Manhattan. During the eighteenth and nineteenth century, Blackwell's was used as a penal colony and a convenient location for executions.[2] Cashiere was hanged there on July 5, 1829. The tiny island was also a former safe haven for river pirates. Today, it is better known as Roosevelt Island. Helen Fowler's story took place in the city of Niagara Falls, which is about as far from Blackwell's Island one can go without leaving New York. This may be one reason why, of all of the women executed in the state during the twentieth century, Fowler received the least amount of press coverage despite the historical significance of who she was. Another contributing factor to explain the scant press coverage of Fowler's trial and execution may have been the dominance of World War II and the editorial attention paid to the ongoing military conflict.

Even though much of the nation's attention was focused on the conflict during the war years 1941 to 1945, there was no interruption in the execution process in New York. Records show that during those five years, sixty-five men went to their deaths at Sing Sing, an average of about one inmate every twenty-eight days. But it wasn't Elliott who pulled the switch. His long career as America's most self-indulgent executioner had come to an end on February 23, 1939. By then, Elliott had sent to their death 387 men and women, including some of the most famous criminals of the time. Ruth Snyder, Judd Gray, Sacco and Vanzetti, and Bruno Hauptmann all fell under the steady hand of Robert G. Elliott. Before he left his post, Elliott trained a replacement, Joseph Francel of Cairo, New York, who would have his own tenure as New York's official executioner.[3]

Helen Fowler's journey to death began on the night of October 30, 1943, when George William Fowler, a sixty-three-year-old Ransomville gas station owner, closed up his shop at noon to go out for a few drinks in the nearby city of Niagara Falls. Though they shared the same last name, Helen and Bill Fowler had no blood relation whatever. That day, Bill Fowler called his cousin, Lee Clark, who agreed to meet him at the station after he locked up.

Fowler, who had been married for thirty-six years, was a successful business owner who had profited from the war-time defense contractors who moved to the Niagara area in the early 1940s. He was a slightly built man who wore glasses and weighed less than 150 pounds. His wife, Mary, had recently left Ransomville for a trip to Ohio to visit relatives and was not expected back for several days. When Fowler closed for the day, he was carrying approximately $1,000 in cash and a few hundred dollars more in checks. With his cousin Clark in tow, Fowler stopped at several local bars before making his way to the city of Niagara Falls. There, the two men continued drinking into the evening hours. Since Clark lived in the Falls, he knew his way around town. During the night, he ran into a number of friends in the saloons and hotels along Buffalo Street and drank with them all.

Though Fowler was not a boisterous man when sober, after a few drinks he became somewhat of a braggart. At several of the saloons, Fowler flashed a thick wad of bills for everyone to see and bought drinks for Clark's friends. Though Clark cautioned his cousin not to display his cash, especially in front of strangers, Fowler remained boastful and unaffected. During their tour of the downtown area, they sometimes returned to the same bar twice, buying drinks for customers each time. Late that evening, Fowler decided to cross the railroad tracks to the other side of town, into the "black section." He told Clark that he felt like being with a woman, and he knew of a bar where lots of women could be had for a few dollars.

They arrived at a tavern on Memorial Parkway called Andrew's. It was crowded with drinkers, including several unattached women. Clark knew some of the people and began to drink with these acquaintances while Fowler picked up a woman who was at the bar alone. Together they drifted off to a corner where they found an empty booth. After an hour had passed, Clark met up with a young white girl; soon they were groping and kissing each other in a corner of the room.

As they sipped their drinks in the dark alcove of the bar, a loud commotion broke out a few yards away. Two women began to push and shove each other. One of the women, noticeably older than the other, punched the younger one in the face, sending her backward into a table. A powerfully built black man moved between them and tried to calm them down. Other customers yelled at the man to let the women fight. "George, let's see which one wins!" someone yelled from a bar stool. Lee Clark knew the shorter, older woman in the fight. He recognized her from the neighborhood and knew that most people called her "Black Helen." While the women battled each other, the bartender decided to intervene. He jumped into the fight and soon managed to toss both the combatants out into the street. After a few minutes, the bar calmed down and things returned to normal.

At about 8:00 p.m., Clark and his lady friend left the bar. They walked down the street to a house on Memorial Parkway known around the neighborhood as "Sugar's Place." They entered the building and walked to a back room. But before he entered, Clark saw the door of another room open, and to his surprise, Bill Fowler walked out with the same woman who had been with him at Andrew's earlier that night. She was later identified as Katie Brown. Clark had not even noticed that his cousin had left the bar. Though the men exchanged greetings, they did not stop to talk. Clark continued on his way to the room while Fowler exited through the front door. It would be the last time Clark saw his cousin alive.

Later that night, Clark returned to the bar and looked for Bill Fowler, but he was nowhere to be found. After a while, he assumed that his cousin had bedded down for the night with the girl. Clark returned to his home. The next morning, he tried to call Fowler but there was no answer. Clark then drove over to Fowler's gas station, but he was not there, either. Clark decided to wait until Monday morning, when the business would open. When he visited the station on Monday, Clark found it closed and his cousin nowhere in sight. He drove over to Niagara Falls where he asked friends if they had seen Bill Fowler. No one had seen him since their drinking tour on Saturday night. In the meantime, Mary Fowler had returned home from Ohio and became frantic when she found that her husband had been missing since Saturday. Together, Clark and Mrs. Fowler went to the police.

Investigators discovered that Bill Fowler was last seen at the house on Memorial Parkway where Clark passed him in the hallway. People reported seeing him leave the premise and walk down Buffalo Street toward the bar, but no one saw him go inside. To complicate matters, some patrons at Andrew's told police that Fowler never returned to the bar after he left with Katie Brown. The investigation came to a standstill. A few detectives believed Fowler had run away from his wife, but friends denied he was having any trouble at home. Clark told police that Bill had no reason to leave because his business was successful and there were no problems with Mrs. Fowler. Within a week, police discovered that a check that Fowler was carrying the day he disappeared had been cashed. "One of the checks was cashed by the Power City Trust Company but employees of the bank were unable to identify a suspect questioned by police as the man who cashed the check," the *Niagara Falls Gazette* reported.[4] For the next five weeks, despite numerous witnesses who had seen Fowler on the night he disappeared, police could not determine what happened. Most investigators were convinced that the victim was mugged somewhere along Buffalo Street, but they couldn't find a cooperative witness. "Practically all of the persons questioned in connection with Fowler's disappearance, with the exception of the man from Ransomville who had come to this city with him, were Negroes and included several men and women."[5]

Several weeks later, on the frigid morning of December 8, a tugboat captain guiding his vessel through the ice-filled waters of the Niagara River noticed an unusual object caught in the driftwood near the shore. He anchored his boat near the Niagara Power Company to investigate. When he gaffed the object and pulled it closer, he saw that it was a human corpse. The captain notified the Coast Guard, who in turn summoned the police. The body was badly decomposed and could not be visually identified. It was also covered with a thick, black coating of river muck. There were no identification papers present and no jewelry. An autopsy indicated that the person had a severely fractured skull and the coroner classified the death as a homicide. Captain Robert Fitzsimmons of the Niagara Falls Police Department was placed in charge of the investigation. He immediately suspected that the body was that of Bill Fowler, and asked the coroner to compare an X-ray of the body with an X-ray of Fowler taken when he had broken his arm some years before. It was a match. "Captain Fitzsimmons said today that there was no doubt that Fowler had been robbed and murdered. His body was completely nude when recovered from the river yesterday."[6]

Fitzsimmons had his detectives canvass the area where the body was found. A witness was located near River Road, which runs along the Tonawanda Channel. He provided a description of a car that he had observed on the North Grand Island Bridge some weeks before. He said that the two people in the car were acting suspiciously and he thought that they had dropped something in the water. The witness was able to provide a partial license plate number. By the process of elimination, police traced the car to a soldier who was stationed in nearby Fort Niagara. His name was Paul Blackwell, age twenty-three. He had been on a weekend pass the day that Fowler disappeared. When police interviewed him, Blackwell said he was not using his car on October 30 because he had loaned it to friends who lived on Memorial Highway in Niagara Falls. He identified these friends as George Knight and Helen Fowler. At first, police thought there was some mistake. But they quickly ascertained that there was no family or blood relationship between Helen Fowler and William Fowler.

Once the details of the case were brought to the attention of District Attorney John Marsh, he called in Captain Fitzsimmons, Lieutenant Merton Wager, and other members of the investigative team. It was decided that all the suspects in the William Fowler disappearance would be brought to police headquarters and questioned, even if this meant duplicate interviews. Early on the morning of December 10, detectives from the Niagara Falls Police Department raided the Memorial Parkway area. "Those held for questioning were booked on open charges at police headquarters as . . . George F. Knight, 25, 144 Memorial Parkway . . . Mrs. Helen Fowler, 36, Miss Genevieve Persons,

18, both of Memorial Parkway."[7] Genevieve Persons was Helen's daughter by a previous marriage. Police quickly discovered that Helen and her daughter had been arrested the week before in the nearby town of Lockport on assault charges. They were currently out on bail pending a court appearance and sentencing. As soon as the judge was informed they were in custody for a murder investigation, bail was revoked and Helen was remanded back to jail. The *Buffalo Evening News* reported that "police continued their investigation today of the slaying of George William Fowler . . . after five suspects had been questioned for several hours Sunday by District Attorney John S. Marsh, Detective Capt. Robert Fitzsimmons and deputies of Sheriff Fred Bigelow's office in Lockport."[8]

Helen Fowler was originally from Danville, Illinois. She moved to Niagara Falls when she was a teenager and continued to live there until her arrest for murder. Married three times and the mother of five children by an assortment of men, she was a tough woman raised in a tough time. She had only a seventh-grade education and had become pregnant at age sixteen. Helen stood five foot two and weighed more than 200 pounds. She lived in a run-down wood-frame house at 144 Memorial Parkway that was used as something of a flophouse for neighborhood derelicts and the unemployed. Helen had been arrested on several occasions, but did not do jail time. It was never determined what happened to her previous husbands though she was last divorced in 1938. Sometime during 1942, she met George Knight, who at age twenty-five was eleven years her junior.

Knight was born and raised in King William City, Virginia. He worked mostly as a laborer until 1941 when he was arrested for a robbery committed with a boyhood friend. He was later sentenced to two years for the crime. In late 1942, he was awarded an early release for good behavior. Knight then moved to Niagara Falls to live with a cousin. There, he met Helen Fowler and soon they were living together in Helen's house, along with her five children. Big and handsome, he had a volatile temper. Knight was a familiar sight in neighborhood bars where he frequently drank all night and brawled with other young toughs.

At police headquarters, Helen initially denied having any knowledge of Bill Fowler's disappearance and said she did not know the man. She said that she was home during the night of his drinking tour with Lee Clark and never saw the two men. She also denied having a knock-down drag-out fight with Knight and Willie Lee at Andrew's. Police decided to administer lie detector tests to all of the suspects. They were taken to the Buffalo Police department where a polygraph was waiting. While a police expert supervised the tests, questioning continued. Investigators soon realized that the statements of George Knight and Helen Fowler were inconsistent with each other and that someone was lying. Eventually, Knight admitted robbing and assaulting Bill Fowler. He also said that Helen helped him do it. When she heard that Knight had implicated her, Helen tried to explain to the police what happened. "I'm not guilty of any murder or robbery," she later said. "But I did help to get the man out of the house or he'd [Knight would] have left him there in the trunk because he was drunk for over a week after and a couple of days before."[9]

Knight said that on the night of October 30, he was in a bar on Memorial Parkway with his friends. He drank for the better part of the evening until he ran into a former girlfriend, Willie Lee Harris. Though Knight lived with Helen Fowler just a few doors down from the tavern, he frequently drank till late hours. While Knight cuddled with Willie Lee at the end of the bar, Helen suddenly appeared at the door. A loud argument erupted between the two women which quickly descended into a physical battle. But the bar's owner managed to throw Helen out into the street. A few minutes later, she returned with a knife in her hand. Again, a battle ensued and eventually spilled out onto the sidewalk. Willie Lee fled the scene while Helen then made her way back to her home at 144 Memorial Parkway. Inside the bar during this melee was Bill Fowler, who had been observing the drama from his seat at the bar. As he watched Helen walk away, Fowler exited the saloon and followed her home. A short time later, he passed his cousin, Lee Clark, in the hallway of Helen's house. In the meantime, at Andrew's, Knight decided to go home to make peace with Helen. It was all confusing to investigators because time sequences were wrong and others who were in the bar had different recollections about that night.

When Knight arrived at the house, he said, he found the drunken Bill Fowler already there with Helen. A fight soon began and Knight, who was much bigger and stronger, quickly knocked Fowler to the floor. He was no match for the younger man. Knight kicked Fowler into unconsciousness while Helen helped him, Knight said. He went through Fowler's pockets and took all his cash and a number of checks. They carried him into a back room of the house, where the injured man regained his senses. Another fight began and this time, according to Knight, Helen joined in beating Fowler into a bloody pulp. Knight then counted up the money and handed Helen a portion of the proceeds. At that very moment, Genevieve Persons arrived home and peeked into the room to see what was going on. Helen shouted at her to leave and Genevieve closed the door. Knight said that Helen checked Fowler's pulse and discovered that he was dead. They carried the body out into the rear yard where they tried to get it over a fence. But this required too much effort, so Knight decided to go back to the bar for more drinking. He told police he left the body and Helen in the yard behind their house. When he later returned, he found that Helen had placed the corpse in a large trunk. Together, they pushed it closer to the house where it remained overnight. The following day, Knight borrowed a car and loaded the trunk into the back seat. Then he and Helen drove to the North Grand Island Bridge where it crosses the Tonawanda Channel. Knight said they lifted the body over the railing and dumped it into the icy Niagara River. They placed the trunk back in the car and drove off. Knight's oral statements were transcribed to paper and, in the presence of several police officers, he later signed it.

When police questioned Helen again, she admitted that Bill Flower followed her home and propositioned her for sex. While he was in her living room, Knight suddenly arrived and the two men began to fight. She said that Knight beat Fowler to death without her help and she had no idea that Knight was going to rob the man. She said that Knight dragged the body into her yard and then left to go back to his drinking binge. She said that she later helped Knight load the body into a car and dump it into the river. But she did it because she was scared Knight would hurt her and was afraid that if police found the body at her house, she would be charged with his murder.

Captain Fitzsimmons filed charges against the two suspects on the morning of December 16. Helen Fowler and George Knight were brought into court where, in front of Judge Ernest Curto, they were arraigned for Murder in the First Degree. "A man and a woman, both Negroes, were arraigned today . . . on charges of Murder First degree," reported the *Buffalo Evening News*, "in connection with the death of George Fowler, a Ransomville service-station proprietor, whose nude body was taken from the upper Niagara River after he had been struck on the head and his skull fractured."[10] They both entered pleas of "not guilty." The judge remanded the pair to the county jail pending their next court appearance. "Although she appeared cool and collected when she faced the acting police justice during her formal arraignment and blandly stated that she wished the case adjourned so she could get witnesses, she broke down after being placed in the women's detention room in police headquarters and hysterically demanded to see Captain Fitzsimmons."[11]

The district attorney's office already announced that the prosecution would aggressively seek a conviction of Murder in the First Degree, which carried a mandatory death sentence under state law. Helen realized she would be fighting for her life at her trial. Capital punishment cases in Niagara County were rare. The last person to receive a death penalty was David Lucas, age twenty-nine, a resident of Lockport who was convicted in the robbery and killing of a local liquor store owner. Lucas was executed at Sing Sing on January 5, 1939.[12]

While detectives interviewed witnesses from Memorial Parkway and Andrew's tavern, Fitzsimmons told the press that he was satisfied that Helen

Fowler and George Knight were responsible for the murder. Though their statements were different in certain details, both defendants implicated each other in the killing. "The two suspects arraigned today and other witnesses in the investigation have been held by police since December 10 and have been subjected to almost continuous questioning," reported one local newspaper. "All the investigators today expressed themselves as satisfied that Fowler was killed in the home of Mrs. Fowler."[13]

In the meantime, the court appointed local attorneys to represent the two defendants. One of these attorneys was Earl W. Brydges, a well-known attorney in Niagara County who later went on to become a state senator. As police continued to build the case against Helen Fowler and George Knight, the defense team met with Helen at the county jail and prepared for trial. During the first week of January 1944, a grand jury heard testimony from witnesses and reviewed evidence presented by District Attorney John Marsh. On January 6, they announced their decision. " The Grand Jury of the County of Niagara, by this indictment, accuse the defendants, Helen Fowler and George F. Knight, of the crime of Murder in the First Degree . . . in the City of Niagara Falls . . . on or about the 30th day of October 1943, willfully, feloniously and of malice aforethought, struck and killed G. William Fowler with a blunt instrument."[14]

The following week, on January 14, Brydges submitted a motion to the court requesting that Helen be granted a separate trial, apart from co-defendant George Knight. The dangers of both defendants being tried together were obvious to the defense, for it was very likely that each would attempt to blame the other for the killing. "In the event of a joint trial," wrote Brydges, "the defendant's constitutional right not to be required to be a witness against herself will be infringed because of the effect of her co-defendant's statement . . . may compel the deponent to testify."[15] Brydges also felt it necessary to remind the court that his client was black and, therefore, the court had an obligation to ensure that her rights were protected. "Deponent feels that because of her race she is at a disadvantage in all events and for this reason alone she asks the Court to be scrupulous in its attempt to see that she receives substantial justice."[16]

District Attorney Marsh responded by pointing out that it cannot be assumed that the defendant's rights would not be protected at a joint trial. He told the court that although Knight's statement would be used against Helen, her own oral statements to police would be offered to the court as well. Marsh said that no one should "speculate as to the type of evidence produced upon the trial nor should it be required to speculate upon the effect of such evidence on the rights of the parties to a fair trial."[17] He also told the court that separate trials would simply be too expensive and defense motions should be denied.

Before that response was even received, Brydges asked the court for a change in venue. He said that, since Bill Fowler was white and lived in nearby Ransomville, he "enjoyed a wide acquaintance in the rural areas of the county from which the bulk of our trial jurors are drawn." The defense also noted that both the accused are "negroes who made their residence in the City of Niagara Falls, which is the only section of the County having any sizable Negro population." He also complained about the local media coverage. Brydges submitted to the court "clippings from the *Niagara Falls Gazette* . . . which have tended to inflame and incite the people of the County against the defendants. The newspaper stories were published at about the same time as the list of jurors now serving was published." And finally, Brydges said, "it would be impossible to accord a fair and impartial trial in this action in the County of Niagara, by reason of the public passion, prejudice, and strong conviction in the minds of the people of the community of the guilt of the defendants . . . and therefore, asks that the aforesaid indictment be transferred for trial to some county other than the County of Niagara."[18]

Marsh responded by pointing out to the court that Brydges did not provide names of the people who he claimed were prejudiced by newspaper articles nor did he attempt to show where they resided or whether these people were even on the jurors list. As to the racial allegations, Marsh said that "no evidence is submitted to substantiate a claim of strong racial antagonisms or prejudices in the county" and "that the impressions and conclusions by the defendant's counsel do not form a factual basis for the granting by the court of the relief asked for."[19] Judge William Gold agreed and on January 27, he denied all defense motions with regard to change of venue and separate trials.

During the first week of February, one hundred twenty-five prospective jurors were summoned to the county courthouse in Lockport where the tedious process of questioning, acceptance, or denial began. Only sixty-three actually reported. On the first day, prosecutors used twenty-five challenges while the defense used twenty-seven. D.A. Marsh excused the very first applicant on the list when the man stated that he did not believe in capital punishment. Judge Gold used thirteen challenges to exempt those who he felt could not serve for a variety of reasons. By February 8, the process was complete and a panel of twelve jurors, which included five women, was chosen. "The first murder case to have been tried in Niagara County since women served on juries will open Monday at Lockport," reported the *Niagara Falls Gazette* on its first page. "Women have been permitted on Niagara County juries only since 1939."[20] Court convened again on the morning of February 9 when the prosecution delivered its opening statement.

Marsh told the court that he would prove that the defendants viciously beat Bill Fowler to death for the purpose of robbery. He said that on the night of October 30, Bill Fowler had flashed a great deal of money in several bars and everyone in the neighborhood knew that he was carrying a large amount of cash. Marsh also told the jury that it didn't matter who struck the final blow that killed Fowler. Because the killing took place during the commission of a felony, both parties were equally guilty of murder. Brydges rose to his feet to address the jury. "You will hear a lot of sordid stuff," he said. "But you will have to keep an open mind when you hear the other side of the story."[21] Brydges indicated that Helen might not take the stand during her trial. "If they do not take the stand," he said, "you are not allowed to take that into consideration. There are many reasons why a defendant may not testify. I have seen innocent persons go to the stand and appear like regular liars and I have seen guilty persons take the stand and appear innocent."[22]

J. William O'Brian, who had been appointed as Knight's attorney, told the court that a lot of people knew Fowler was carrying cash on the night of his death. "I don't think there's much quarrel about that," he said in a loud and booming voice. "He was up there drinking, going around from one place to the other, fooling around with women. He had some money on his person, bragging about it and there was plenty of opportunities to take that money away from him!"[23]

After opening statements were complete, the first witness took the stand. Dr. Harry Emes, County Coroner of Niagara, explained the injuries to Bill Fowler that caused his death. Dr. Emes said that all the wounds will never be known due to the advanced decomposition of the body when it was found in the Niagara River. The cause of death was determined to be a severely fractured skull, apparently caused by some type of heavy instrument, Dr. Emes said. The nature and severity of the injuries indicated that Fowler was already dead by the time his body entered the water. Dr. Emes added that the victim had suffered a terrible beating before he died. Following the coroner's testimony, Mary Fowler, wife of the deceased, took the stand. She had nothing to offer as far as evidence was concerned, but she told the jury that her husband was a good man and worked hard. Her testimony was brief and seemed designed to win sympathy from the jury.

Marsh then put Lee Clark on the stand. Guided by the prosecution, Clark described his drinking tour with his cousin on the night of October 30, which began with a stopover at Andrew's. Clark testified that they had been drinking since noon and visited several bars in the Falls area. Telling the court that he met numerous friends that afternoon, Clark said that his cousin showed off a thick wad of cash and spent it freely at each stop along the way. But when it came time for Clark to relate how he and Bill Fowler picked up women in the bar, he became vague and claimed some failings of memory. Lee Clark was married and his wife was present during testimony. He had to admit to the court that the last moment he saw the deceased, it was under embarrassing circumstances. As reported in the *Gazette*, "Lee Clark said he last saw Fowler early in the evening of October 30 coming out of a room at Sugar's with a Negro woman as he [Clark] was entering with a white woman."[24]

Next to take the stand was Mrs. Katie Brown, the woman who was with Fowler at Sugar's Place. She said that she was at Andrew's earlier that evening when Bill Fowler and Lee came into the bar. Brown said that when the pair entered Andrew's, Fowler tried to buy her drink but she declined. But she admitted that she left the bar to go to "Sugar's Place" with him. She also told the court that she saw Helen Fowler a few minutes earlier standing outside Andrew's.

Following Brown's testimony, Judge Munson ordered a dinner break. At 7 p.m., court convened again. District Attorney Marsh called Helen Fowler's oldest daughter, Genevieve Persons, to the stand. She told the jury that on the day of the murder, she returned home from work to find her mother and George Knight in the kitchen having a conversation about a white man at Andrew's who had a lot of cash in his pocket. Later that same night, Genevieve witnessed the assault on Bill Fowler. "I saw George hit this white man with a hammer twice on the side of the head." she said.[25] Genevieve went on to say that she saw her mother in the same room while the fight was going on and that her mother sat on the victim while he was unconscious on the floor. Though her testimony was confusing at times, Genevieve's description of what occurred that evening must have made an impression on the jury. She said that when Knight moved the man's body, her mother helped. "Miss Genevieve Persons, daughter of Mrs. Fowler by a previous marriage, declared on the stand she saw the Ransomville man, begging for mercy, beaten to death with a hammer by Knight in her mother's apartment. She said her mother knelt beside the victim and once sat on him during the assault."[26]

During cross-examination, Brydges was able to bring out Genevieve's recent arrest and implied that she cut a deal with the district attorney's office in exchange for her testimony. It was also revealed that Genevieve was caught attempting to cash two checks that were stolen from the victim's body. She told the court that she and her boyfriend had taken the check from George Knight's pockets when he fell asleep later that same day. But, she said, there was no doubt who killed Bill Fowler. "Knight would just lift the man off the floor a little and then punch him in the face," Genevieve said. "He did it six or seven times. Then he kicked him. Kicked him all over his body."[27] When she was asked why she didn't immediately tell the police what she saw, Genevieve said she was afraid of Knight. "George told me if I mentioned anything about it, I would turn up missing!"[28]

When it was time for the defense to put on its case, it was not much of an effort. In response to the prosecution, which put on seventeen witnesses and introduced dozens of pieces of evidence, Brydges could only provide two witnesses. They were Helen's children, June Tucker, age fifteen, and her brother George, age nine, who because of his age could not be sworn in. June told the court that on the day Bill Fowler was in their house, she saw George Knight beating him over the head with a vase. She said that her mother was standing close by and telling Knight to stop what he was doing. In response, June said, Knight hit Helen with the same vase. Both children told the court that they saw Knight go through Bill Fowler's pockets and remove a large amount of money. "Then, according to the children, Knight kicked the prostrate, groaning figure until it became still. Later, he carried it to the rear of the building they said."[29] June also told the court that she watched as her mother and Knight tried to throw the body over the fence.

Summations followed the testimony of the Tucker children. Brydges's closing statement was not supportive of his client. "It is hard to make an argument for Helen Fowler," he told the jury. "She is guilty of any number of crimes . . . she has been handed from man to man; has had children by them all. She has lied; she has cheated; she has sold herself. Perhaps it would be better for her children if she were put out of the way."[30] Prosecutor Marsh told the jury that "the crime of which she is accused is one of the most brutal and atrocious crimes ever perpetrated in the history of Niagara County."[31] He asked the jurors to set aside their feelings of sympathy for Helen as a mother and rely on the testimony of witnesses and the evidence that proved "that both defendants committed a murder and that both were equally guilty. He said that even the testimony of Mrs. Fowler's two youngest children had established this."[32]

After closing statements were complete, the jury retired for deliberations at 3:10 p.m. Just two hours later, jury foreman William Wendt, from the nearby Town of Cambria, indicated that he wished to clarify a legal issue with Judge Munson. When the jury was brought back into the courtroom, the defense asked whether the panel could consider a sentence of life imprisonment for one defendant. Or, in the event of a guilty verdict, would the same punishment have to be applied to both? Judge Munson was emphatic. He told the jury that since both participated in the robbery, both defendants are equally guilty of the murder. Judge Munson also added that for the purposes of the trial, Knight and Fowler have to be treated as one. "If they are engaged in a felony they can not be separated," he said.[33] By 8:10 p.m., the jury had reached a verdict.

Both defendants were found guilty of Murder in the First Degree. Helen cried uncontrollably while Knight was unmoved. Brydges, who was unhappy with the judge's charge to the jury, wanted to know whether the jurors had considered leniency for his client. "If the court please," he said, "I ask that the jurors be polled on the question of recommendation for leniency for the defendant, Helen Fowler."

"May it please the court," Marsh objected. "There is only one verdict. I mean it is all-inclusive and the jury brought it in."

Judge Munson agreed and said the jury had already decided; the verdict applied to both defendants. But, to satisfy the defense, he inquired about the leniency issue.

"The jury took into consideration the question of leniency—did you?"

"We did," replied jury foreman Wendt.

"And the verdict is guilty as charged?"

"That is correct," said the foreman.[34]

Munson then polled the jurors who each answered individually with a guilty verdict. He set sentencing for February 19 and remanded both defendants back to the county jail. The *Buffalo Evening News* published a brief seventy-word article on the verdict on page four. "Mrs. Helen Fowler, 36, and George Knight, 25, of Niagara Falls, were convicted tonight of First Degree Murder in the robbery slaying of George W. Fowler. The verdict was returned by a Supreme Court jury of seven men and five women after five hours of deliberations."[35] In the meantime, defense attorneys Brydges and O'Brian notified the court of their intention to appeal. The following week, Helen and Knight were brought back to the same courtroom where Judge Munson unceremoniously sentenced both to death. The execution was set for the week of April 3 at Sing Sing. Defendants were told to prepare for the move and to say goodbye to their families. Once again, Helen became hysterical and protested that she never killed anyone.

Later that day, while the defendants prepared for the long train ride to Sing Sing, defense attorneys Brydges and Rotella submitted a request to the court for payment of their fees. The amount agreed upon prior to trial was $500 for each attorney. The defense team also submitted additional expenses of seven lunches at $0.75 each, two dinners at $1.50 each, and ten trips to Lockport for attendance at the trial and interviews of the defendants. The total amount for each of Helen's attorney's was $523.25. Judge Munson approved the fees and recommended payment.

Though Helen Fowler was the only black woman to face execution in New York during the twentieth century, media coverage was sparse. The first newspaper article on the Fowler case to appear in New York City was printed in the *Times* on February 22, 1944: "Mrs. Helen Fowler, 36 years old, was admitted to Sing Sing prison here this afternoon, the first woman committed to the death house since the execution on July 16, 1936 of Mrs. Frances

Creighton."[36] Warden Snyder directed the hiring of three matrons to care for Fowler and ordered them to report to the female cell block. On the day Fowler arrived at Sing Sing, there were twenty-one men waiting for execution in the male cellblock. Despite the war, little had changed on the nation's best-known death row. During the nine-month period that Helen Fowler and George Knight were in Sing Sing, fourteen men went to their deaths. This period was especially difficult for Knight since each one of those fourteen had to pass his cell on the way to the execution chamber.

The most notorious of the condemned who passed Knight on the way to execution—and one of the most famous ever to be executed at Sing Sing—was Louis Buchalter, the overseer of drugs, extortion, and labor racketeering, and the undisputed "King of Crime" in metropolitan New York. He was the brains and money behind Murder Inc. and better known to the public as Louis Lepke.[37] When he went to the electric chair on March 4, 1944, there was a sense of disbelief that a man of his legendary stature could actually be dead. "Symbol of an orgy of crime that had its origin in the easy violence of the Prohibition Twenties . . . Lepke's execution brought to a close a murderous era in the underworld annals of the city . . . he was said to have directed the cold-blooded murder of eighty men."[38] Lepke's death was an ominous development for all fourteen men on death row, each of whom hoped for a commutation of their sentence or a new trial. If someone as famous as Lepke was denied mercy, what, they asked themselves, could they ever hope for?

In the meantime, Defense Attorney Brydges filed a motion with the Niagara County Court for a new trial. He alleged there were three points of contention that, when addressed by the court, would establish the basis for retrial. Though there was evidence introduced at trial that Helen did assist in the moving of the body of Bill Fowler, there was no direct evidence that she participated in the robbery. "The only evidence connecting the defendant, Helen Fowler, with the alleged robbery seems to be contained in the testimony of June Tucker and George Tucker," said Brydges in his seven-page affidavit. "They testified that George Knight handed Helen Fowler a five dollar bill while the decedent was lying on the floor as a result of an injury inflicted by the defendant Knight."[39] Brydges also pointed out that according to testimony, the victim was still alive at this point and therefore the crime of murder had not been committed as yet.

And finally, Brydges argued that the court made a grievous error during deliberations that strongly supports the argument for a new trial. "The jury was misdirected by the court in a matter of law and decided the case by means other than a fair expression of opinion." When the jury temporarily returned from deliberations to ask Judge Munson whether they could consider life imprisonment for one defendant, they were instructed by the judge that the defendants could not be separated, which was inaccurate. The jurors, said Brydges, understood this to mean that, if they recommended life imprisonment for one, they would have to recommend the same for both—a decision that most of the jurors opposed. Therefore, according to Brydges, the jury's deliberations were tainted by the instructions from Judge Munson. "Under the statute, it is the duty of the trial jury to determine the question of recommendation under proper instructions from the court in the same manner [in] which they determine the question of guilt or innocence. In this case they were not permitted to decide the question through a fair expression of opinion because of the no doubt inadvertent misdirection from the court."[40] How could the jury deliberate fairly if they received incorrect instructions, asked Brydges: "In fairness to this defendant, who in many respects did not have a fair trial, the least this court can do is to examine into the question herein raised by producing the trial jurors in open court for examination and cross-examination."[41]

District Attorney Marsh responded with his own seven-page affidavit attacking all the points raised by Brydges. Marsh said that the issue of incorrect instructions was already addressed in a previous court and it had been rejected. "The point now urged by defendant's counsel was argued at great length on appeal before the Court of Appeals," he said.[42] Furthermore, Marsh pointed out, Helen's participation in the crime was beyond question. "The defendant's own statement, testimony of three eyewitnesses, all children of the defendant, and the other evidence in the case, all establish her presence on the premise while the murder took place, her participation in the crime . . . in the disposing of the body . . . her efforts to remove all traces of the crime and her sharing of the loot."[43] Even if she were granted a new trial, said Marsh, it would be extremely doubtful that a different verdict could be reached, taking into consideration the volume of evidence and quality of testimony.

After a review of both affidavits, Judge Alonzo Hinckley of Buffalo issued the court's opinion on September 7. The application for a new trial for Helen Fowler was denied. "The court could not grant a new trial upon this ground because of the unanimous affirmance of the conviction of the defendant Helen Fowler by the Court of Appeals," wrote Judge Hinckley. "Counsel for that defendant raised the identical question in a separate point in his brief. And the affidavit of counsel upon this motion only emphasizes a point already determined by the highest court in the State."[44]

For the next two months, Helen simply waited in her cell. Mercifully, no other executions took place during September and October. Though her children had permission to visit her, none did. Edison Tucker, a former husband of Helen's and father of two of her children, applied for and received permission to visit her at Sing Sing. He was her only visitor during her time on Death Row. The date of execution was moved back to October 2 for final legal arguments to be decided. Those issues, which included alleged discrimination by the court in the selection of the jury, were later rejected. Helen received another respite until the week of November 13. It would be her last postponement.

Time finally ran out for Helen on November 16, 1944. During her last night, she prayed in her cell with the Catholic chaplain, Father Bernard Martin. She still hoped she could be saved. "Mrs. Helen Fowler, 37, Negro of Niagara Falls, the first woman scheduled to be executed in Sing Sing Prison in the past eight years, hoped today that a last-minute reprieve would save her from the electric chair tonight," reported one newspaper.[45] Desperate for anything that would help, Helen wrote out a letter to Acting Governor Joseph Hanley—appointed to the post while Governor Thomas Dewey campaigned for the presidency—to plead for her life.

Helen told the governor that her daughter Genevieve had lied at the trial because she hated her. Helen wrote that Genevieve and another daughter, Ruth, had tried to poison her. She said that Ruth lied about her just to get her freedom, and that her daughters were glad to be rid of their mother.

> I did wrong, but please for God's sake, give me a chance to prove these things and you'll see the things just like I do and not lying for my life and begging a chance to prove these things. I can. Please, I now you can if you please would. I never told my lawyer these things to bring out. Besides I could not hear through the trial hardly anything that was said. I was deaf on one side. There was a lot of things that were said that I never knew until I read the court minutes. I kept asking the court matron what was said . . . I could not understand what the judge said. I know this is a late time to ask for this but I'm telling the truth and it can be proved so please help me. A life is a life and I'm framed through my own daughters just to be rid of me but as far as Knight he was afraid I'd tell on him because I threatened to. Please don't take my life until I have a chance to prove these things . . . if you'll please let my life be spared I'll tell you just how and where I can prove these things and through my lawyer. Please help me, please don't let me down for sticking to my children you see it's true or I'd have brought this out before now . . . Please I'll live for God from now on if spared for when children try to have your life taken just to be free, it's a shame![46]

Helen dictated her plea while a stenographer wrote it down. It was then typewritten onto two pages and signed in the presence of a notary. By the time it was finished, it was almost 9:00 p.m., less than two hours before the scheduled execution. Warden Snyder took the letter to his office and called Acting Governor Hanley. Snyder then read the letter over the phone word by word. Hanley said that he would consider it and then hung up. It was 9:40 p.m. There was nothing left to do but wait.

George Knight chain-smoked cigarettes and made small talk with the other men in their cells. Knight knew his chances for a commutation were slim. After Lepke went to the chair back in March, hope for the men on Death Row evaporated. After Lepke's execution, nine of Knight's cellmates made the final walk to the death chamber, each one a torturous reminder of what the future held for him. There was a sense of resignation and despair that even the clergy, with all their prayers and uplifting sermons, could not alleviate. Knight refused to eat a last meal; instead, he spent his time praying on his knees. Like Helen, he had no visitors on his final day.

At 10:55 p.m., with no word from the governor's office, Warden Snyder ordered the guards to escort Helen to the death chamber. Two matrons went to her cell and told her that it was time. Helen rose to her feet without saying a word and walked steadily down the short corridor. There are no eyewitness accounts of Helen Fowler's execution. Unlike previous executions at which numerous reporters in attendance, there was not one single representative from the press at Helen's execution. The official witness list shows twenty-four names, none of who are identified as press. "We, the undersigned," it reads, "certify that we were present and witnessed the execution of the judgment and sentence of Helen Fowler #102-981 as set forth in the foregoing certificate and we do hereby, pursuant to the statute, at Sing Sing Prison, Ossining, New York subscribe to the same on 16th day of November 1944."[47] At 11:17 p.m., she was pronounced dead by prison physician Dr. Charles Sweet and removed from the chamber for autopsy.

A few minutes later, George Knight entered the same room. Just before he sat in the chair, he motioned to the warden.

"Can I talk?" he asked. Snyder nodded. "I just want to thank you all for being nice to me."[48] Guards immediately strapped him into the chair and moved away. A few minutes later, Dr. Sweet pronounced him dead at 11:26 p.m.

The only New York City paper to mention the double execution was the *Times*. Buried in a small article on page thirteen, under the heading, "Woman Goes to Chair," the story consisted of two paragraphs. "Mrs. Helen Fowler, Negro, of Niagara Falls, went to the electric chair tonight for a holdup murder in Niagara County on October 30, 1943. Also put to death was her accomplice, George F. Knight, Negro."[49] The story pointed out that Mrs. Fowler was the first woman to be executed in New York in eight years and gave a brief description of the crime. Curiously, the article ended with details of her last meals. "Each chose to eat the regular prison fare at the last two meals rather than make special food selections."[50] It was an amazing lack of press coverage for a female execution. Most people were not aware of the historical event that took place at Sing Sing on the night of November 16, 1944. Perhaps one newspaper editor summed it up best: "Why should we have run the story?" he asked author Wenzell Brown. "Why waste space on the last words of a woman like her? It wouldn't have been worthwhile. There just aren't enough people who care what happens to a woman like Helen Fowler."[51] Of course, during these years, the nation's newspapers were filled with stories of the war with Germany and Japan. Executions of convicted murderers barely made it into print, especially in large metropolitan areas, like New York.

After the death chamber was secured for the night and the matrons went home, Francel packed away his electrodes. He picked up his $300 check from the warden's office and walked out into the parking lot where his car was waiting. He drove through the front gate of the prison, which was strangely deserted. There were no reporters, no photographers, and no unruly crowds gathered along the road. This was in dramatic contrast to the nights when Ruth Snyder and Anna Antonio were executed. Francel drove north on Broadway through the serene and picturesque village of Ossining toward the Bear Mountain Bridge where it crosses the Hudson River. It would be the last trip he would make to Sing Sing until 1946. For the first time since the electric chair replaced hanging as method of execution in 1890, there would be no executions for an entire year.

Though Helen Fowler's trial moved quickly, it was not as fast as some others. Helen Fowler experienced justice in a manner that was fairly typical of America's courts at that time. Issues raised in her appeal were serious, but were later rejected by the court. Whether there was enough evidence presented at trial for Fowler's murder conviction is doubtful. Like Everett Applegate, who was convicted of murder almost solely on the testimony of one person, Helen Fowler faced a similar situation. In Fowler's case, the ambiguity was worse. "Fowler's conviction resulted from conflicting testimony, none of which depicted her as responsible for the death of a Ransomville gas station owner . . . each witness at her trial described George Knight as the culprit. Even Knight himself recanted his initial story portraying Fowler as the murderer."[52]

Curiously, this issue was never raised by the defense at trial. The jury seemed to accept testimony at face value with the assurances by District Attorney Marsh that, as long as Helen participated in the robbery, she was equally guilty of the murder. Brydges touched on the point in his appeal but chose to emphasize a new statement given by Genevieve Persons after the trial had concluded. That effort was rejected by the court when it decided that Genevieve's statement was made too late and was probably untruthful. "Genevieve Persons, in her affidavit, simply contradicted her testimony at the trial," wrote Supreme Court Justice Hinckley. Post-trial statements supplied by witnesses who recant their own sworn testimony are viewed with suspicion by courts. However, the fact remains that no one ever testified that Helen Fowler killed Bill Fowler, not even Knight.

In her emotional plea to the governor on her last day of life, Helen accused her daughters of lying for reasons of their own. She told the governor that her daughters, Ruth and Genevieve, would not even sign the petition to save her from execution. "Ruth said I'd make a nice fat crackling in the chair! Please spare my life! I've been no nuisance to society . . . I was never around a thing like this . . . I made a mistake by not calling the police because I knew I'd be held and kept from the children . . . It's a mother's love and it's been so much disgrace but this is the truth of why I am here . . . Please spare my life!"[53] Governor Thomas E. Dewey, who ran for President of the United States that year and lost to Franklin D. Roosevelt, made the final decision in the case. He chose to ignore Helen's request and to allow the execution to go forward.

The Lonely Heart: Martha Beck

Something I got into. I had no control.
—Martha Beck at Sing Sing on August 22, 1949,
in response to a question she was
asked about her crimes.

The post–World War II mood in the United States was a poignant mixture of relief, pride, optimism, and overwhelming grief. Millions of families were affected by the carnage of war in ways that would transcend generations. By the late 1940s, the nation had barely started the long and precarious road to recovery, a journey whose direction could not be charted and whose destination was impossible to predict. There was no going back to the pre-war years, no return to the life that existed before the attack on Pearl Harbor on December 7, 1941. That would be impossible. Ironically, the world for which the American soldier fought—the symbolic, uncomplicated life that was the idealistic mirage of the average G.I.—was gone forever. Instead, that myth was replaced by a hard-edged realism, an acknowledgment that something drastic had happened to the America portrayed in the films of Frank Capra and the stories of Mark Twain and Horatio Alger. Soldiers who displayed incredible courage on the battlefield, the same heroes who conquered the terrifying Bliztkrieg and survived the living hell of Iwo Jima, trembled at the thought of returning home to face their loved ones. They were aware something had changed, even if they couldn't articulate it. But they also knew they could never be the same again. Many veterans suffered deep psychological scars, punctuated by recurrent depression and suicidal thoughts. They wondered about their sanity and their ability to fit back into a normal, peacetime environment. Those feelings of abandonment, their emotional destabilization, and the nagging fear of an uncertain future eventually found their way into Hollywood.

The gangster-film era of the 1930s, fueled by newspaper headlines of the age, was long gone. By war's end, infatuation with the gangster image had faded into history, obliterated by the shock of Pearl Harbor. A new style of filmmaking, whose fundamental tenets were the direct opposite of traditional American values, began to evolve. It was called *film noir*, or literally "black film." Directors like Billy Wilder, Fritz Lang, and John Houston utilized the themes of corruption, betrayal, and especially cynicism to tell their stories. Many scripts during that era reflected the post-war uneasiness and feelings of paranoia experienced by returning veterans, most of who were emotionally wounded by the horrors of a brutal war. Audiences found it difficult to watch the inane, romantic comedies of the 1930s when Buchenwald, Auschwitz, and the Bataan Death March were still fresh in the nation's collective memory. It was against this cultural tapestry, which was shifting painfully toward a new age of anxiety and trepidation, that the case of the Lonely Hearts Killers unfolded in the spring of 1949.

Martha Jule Seabrook was born on May 6, 1920, in Milton, a small town located in the northwest corner of Florida. She was one of five children from two different fathers. Her mother, Julia, divorced her first husband after having a daughter named Vera. A short time later, Julia married Holland Seabrook, a local man who seemed to have no real interest in family and was frequently unemployed. Together, they managed to have four more children over the years. Martha arrived late in life, when her mother was forty-four years old. She was an unwanted child and her conception was an accident, a fact which her mother never failed to remind her. As a child in the Seabrook home, Martha never fit in. She was constantly reminded that her birth was not a happy event and that her presence placed additional stress on a family that couldn't bear it. Her oldest sister was twenty when Martha was born and, as a result, had little contact with her. Her other sisters had no time for their youngest sibling, a fact that probably intensified her feelings of loneliness and isolation. In the town where they lived, rumors circulated that Holland Seabrook was not Martha's real father. This humiliated Martha and generated a lasting sense of insecurity at a very early age. She became indifferent toward her father and convinced that he had no love for her. When he left home one day and never returned, Martha barely noticed.

Her mother was, at times, overbearing and contemptuous toward her as well. Whenever her mother displayed affection to her sisters, Martha experienced internal jealousy and rage. Though she tried to please her mother, it never happened and she was often punished for her efforts. This ongoing tension between mother and daughter, which began when Martha was a small girl, continued into adulthood. That anxiety became resentment and the resentment eventually turned into hate. "Life was not worth living," she later said. "I'd rather be dead than to continue arguing with my mother each day of my life."[1] To make matters worse, Martha had a tendency to be overweight, even as a child. Classmates and friends ridiculed her at school. The ridicule alienated the young girl and made her formative years extremely difficult.

By the time she was ten years old, Martha had developed a glandular condition that caused her body to physically mature at an accelerated rate. She began to menstruate and her breasts developed like those of a much older woman. She felt ashamed but didn't exactly know why. Martha did not understand these changes and her mother never offered even a rudimentary explanation of what was happening to the girl. It wasn't long before the young boys in her neighborhood began to notice Martha's body. She couldn't walk down the street without someone uttering suggestive remarks about her or tease her about her breasts. Girls her own age would not associate with her. Others considered Martha some sort of freak. As a result, she had no friends her own age and felt ostracized by her peers.

When she was thirteen years old, Martha suffered a traumatic experience that would haunt her for the rest of her life. According to her court testimony, she was sexually assaulted by her older brother. "My only brother forced his attentions upon me by telling me he learned a new game and would try it out on me."[2] But the abuse did not end with one attack. "The following months had the quality of a nightmare for Martha. There was no place to go, no one to whom she could turn for advice."[3] Frightened out of her mind and under the belief that she could be pregnant, Martha decided to tell her mother of the attacks. When she did, her mother's response may have been worse than the attack itself. She whipped Martha and said it was all her fault. Her mother told her she was a slut and a whore and would never amount to anything in life. At the same time, Martha's brother was not punished in any way. These attacks, she later said, "were preying on my mind ever since."[4] After that summer, her mother followed her wherever she went. If a boy showed any interest in Martha, her mother was sure to chase him away with a barrage of insults and threats. "I had to give her a day by day story of whom I was with and what I did," she later said.[5] For years, this pattern continued and Martha was unable to cultivate any sort of normal relationship with a boy her own age.

Despite her emotional problems at home, Martha was a good student and did well in high school. After graduation, she entered the Pensacola School of Nursing. In her application, she wrote, "I chose this profession without thought of self . . . not for material gains but for the purpose of aiding humanity and rendering services to others."[6] She finished her training at the top of her class. Though she was later called for interviews, she was never offered employment. Martha noticed that other women, much less qualified than her, were getting the jobs. She attributed this to her physical appearance. She was grossly overweight at the time, weighing more than two hundred pounds. She was sure that men were repulsed by her and resigned herself to rejection and despair. As a result of these deeply entrenched feelings of inadequacy, Martha invoked a psychological shield to protect her ego from further pain. Whenever she felt threatened, Martha used this shell of indifference which was frequently interpreted as defiance by those around her. Later, both in court and in public, that aura of coldness would work against her. Others perceived her as unfeeling, superior, and arrogant. But nothing could be further from the truth. Inside the adult Martha was a sensitive, emotional child that knew nothing but repudiation in life and an unsatisfied hunger for love.

After months of idleness and the nagging possibility that she would never work in the nursing profession, Martha was forced to accept employment in a somewhat different field. She took a job with a mortician in a local funeral home preparing bodies for burial. It was a surreal environment for a woman who already felt excluded from human contact. She worked at night, alone with the corpses in the basement of the funeral home. Though she found it disgusting, Martha forced herself to perform her duties. She hardened herself to the gruesome sights and blocked the disturbing images out of her mind. As she tended to the bodies of the dead in the silence of the funeral home, Martha may have found true solace in the company of those who could not ridicule her. In a sense, she experienced a more comfortable life with the dead. That realization must have generated a psychological tremor within her, the final straw that crushed whatever fragile mental stability that remained.

During her free time away from the funeral home, she read magazines like *True Love* and *True Confessions* and romance novels in which the literary "knight in shining armor" would always rescue the young girl in distress. She immersed herself in the world of pulp magazines and phony romance stories. There she was transported her into a fantasy world where daydreaming was everything and love conquered all. Her modest apartment was filled with these publications which she read over and over, never tiring of the identical plots and the inevitable triumph of the handsome hero. When she wasn't reading such novels, Martha was in the local movie theater watching the light-hearted films of the day, films that featured leading men like the athletic

Errol Flynn and the sophisticated Charles Boyer, her personal favorite. She watched him dozens of times in films like *All This and Heaven Too* (1940) and *Appointment for Love* (1941). She loved Boyer, worshiped him and prayed that someday she would meet someone as dashing and attractive as he, someone who would take her away from a grotesque existence among the dead.

By 1942, Martha decided that she had to try something to change her life. Desperate for a man and eager to get away from her domineering mother, she used all her savings to move to California, which was about as far away as she could get from Florida. She managed to get a job as a nurse at a San Francisco Army hospital treating combat victims from the battlegrounds of the Second World War. She labored long hours at her job, feeling some satisfaction that she was working in her chosen field. At night, Martha would frequent the bars on the waterfront and pick up soldiers on leave. Sometimes she would have sex with them. Soon, she found herself pregnant. The father was a G.I. who had no real interest in her. When confronted by Martha, he responded in dramatic fashion. He tried to kill himself by jumping off a nearby dock into the San Francisco Bay. Unable to convince the man to marry her and deeply ashamed that he would rather die than marry her, Martha decided to return to Florida.

In Milton, she soon realized that she had to explain her pregnancy. She secretly bought a wedding ring and placed it on her finger. Then, she carefully invented a story that while she was in California, she married a naval officer on leave from the war. She told friends and neighbors that her husband would soon return from the Pacific and everyone would get to meet him. Of course, Martha knew she could not continue the farce indefinitely. She arranged to have a telegram sent to herself that said that her husband was killed in action and his body could not be recovered. When she "received" the telegram, Martha went into phony hysterics. A doctor was summoned and she had to be sedated. Because Milton was not a large city, everyone soon learned about the "tragic news." The town grieved for her and the heart-breaking story appeared in the local newspapers. For the first time in her life, Martha received genuine sympathy from people. Even strangers were nice to her. She reveled in the attention. In late 1943, she gave birth to her first child, Willa Dean. By January 1944, she had been hired as a nurse at Pensacola Hospital.

For a time, she was contented and happy in her job. The public sympathized with the "war widow" and she even enjoyed some measure of respect. A few months later, Martha met a man at a bus depot named Alfred Beck. They became attracted to each other and soon, they were living together. But rumors spread that she was inviting more than one man to stay at her apartment and her employers did not like the idea. The hospital felt these activities reflected badly on the institution; she was fired. Again, Martha found herself with no job and diminishing prospects. She pressured Beck to marry her and, after months of persuasion and marathon crying spells, they wed in December, 1944. The marriage did not too last long. On their wedding night, a woman who claimed to be Alfred's wife showed up at her door with four children. "You have taken my husband," she said. "You can have my children too!" Martha was stunned. "I was dumbfounded," she later told the court. "When Mr. Beck stepped into view, the kids ran all around yelling 'Daddy! Daddy'!"[7] Just six months later, Martha asked for and received a divorce. She said her husband was unfaithful to her and, in effect, had abandoned her and her child. Unfortunately, Martha was pregnant again and in December 1945, her second child, Anthony, was born.

For years, she had buried her feelings of hostility toward life in the mirage of pulp magazines and movie theaters, where for a time she could escape from perennial depression and fear. In February 1946, she saw some glimmer of hope when she was hired for a job at the Pensacola Crippled Children's Home. She immediately gained a reputation as a conscientious worker who performed her duties with enthusiasm and care. Over the next few months, Martha continued to work at the home. She made friends with other workers and even attended several parties where she felt uncomfortable but determined to promote her friendships.

As the result of a practical joke by a coworker, Martha received an advertisement from a "lonely hearts club." These clubs, which advertised in newspapers and magazines, were popular during the 1940s. They were the modern-day equivalent of computer match-maker firms that arranged for couples to meet based on criteria provided upon sign-up. When Martha opened the mail and read the brochure, she was deeply embarrassed. "How could I ever forget that day?" she later said in court. The advertisement was from a company called *Mother Dinene's Friendly Club for Lonely Hearts*. It included an application for membership and a promise that applicants would fulfill all their romantic dreams and aspirations. "She flung herself face down on the bed and burst into hysterical tears."[8] After she recovered from the humiliation, Martha began to think about the club and its claims of success. She read the testimonials and assurances by previous clients. How could they say such wonderful things if they weren't true, she thought. She decided to fill out the form and submit it to *Mother Dinene's Club*. After she mailed the application, she returned home and fantasized about who would answer her plea for a romantic soul mate. For several weeks, she anxiously checked her mail box for a letter from *Mother Dinene's Club*. Each day, she hurried home expecting to find a message from her own Prince Charming, her new lover, the man who would rescue her from her life of anguish and heartbreak. Instead, she received a letter from Raymond Fernandez.

His full name was Ramon Martinez-Fernandez, born in Hawaii in December 1914 of Spanish parents. As a child, Raymond was frail and underdeveloped. His father, a proud man who worked for everything he had achieved in his life, was ashamed of his sickly son. In 1917, when Raymond was three years old, the family left Hawaii and moved to Bridgeport, Connecticut. His father purchased a farm and the entire family worked every day to make it a success. It was hard for the boy but he was determined to please his father and contribute whatever he could to the family's success. By the time he was eighteen, Fernandez decided to travel to Spain to work on an uncle's farm. He felt comfortable there, away from his father and, for a time, he imagined he would stay in Spain for the rest of his life. At the age of twenty, he met and later married a local girl named Encarnacion Robles. By then, he was a handsome, well-built young man who was known to have a calm and gentle nature. Everyone in the village knew and liked Fernandez and considered Encarnacion a lucky girl to marry such a fine man who seemed destined for success.

When the Second World War began, Fernandez joined the Spanish Merchant Marine where he worked on ships transporting war materials to and from his country. "Raymond Martinez Fernandez was entirely loyal to the Allied cause and carried out his duties, which were sometimes difficult and dangerous extremely well."[9] After hostilities were over, Fernandez decided to return to the United States. He left Encarnacion in Spain and promised her that as soon as he made enough money, he would send for her. He got a job on a freighter sailing out of Gibraltar to the island of Curacao, located in the Netherland Antilles off the coast of Venezuela. From there, he hoped to secure passage to America. It was during this voyage that Fernandez suffered a life-changing event that altered the course of his behavior in such ways that even his family believed he had become a different person.

Just two days from port, Fernandez attempted to come up to the deck after his work shift. It was something that he had done many times before. Weather was clear and the sea was relatively calm. But just as he emerged from below deck, a shift in the waves occurred. A heavy metal hatch suddenly closed and fell directly on the top of his head. Fernandez was knocked unconscious with a severe skull fracture. He remained in a coma for several days as the ship continued its journey to Curacao. Upon arrival at the island, Fernandez was removed from the ship's infirmary and taken to the local hospital. When he awoke several days later, he experienced memory loss and violent mood changes. Doctors told him that X-rays showed a deep indentation on his skull and it could not be determined what effect it would have on his future health. But it was evident that something peculiar had happened to Ramon Fernandez.

Before the injury, he was friendly, outgoing and considerate toward others. Afterward, Fernandez became extremely moody and displayed a quick temper. During conversation, he would frequently ramble incoherently and say things that were not relevant to the matter at hand. From the day he left the hospital until the day he died, he suffered from sudden, intense headaches that no amount of aspirin could alleviate. There was no doubt; the accident had forever changed him in ways that even he could not articulate.

In March 1946, Fernandez was released from the hospital. He got a job on a ship headed for Alabama where he decided he should go to New York City to visit with his sister, Lena. In the port of Mobile, Fernandez stole a large quantity of ship linens. When he passed through customs, police discovered the items which were clearly marked with the ship's name. Fernandez was arrested for the theft and later convicted. When the judge asked him why he committed the crime, Fernandez had no answer. "I don't know," he said. "I can't think. I can't say why I did it."[10] He was sentenced to twelve months in the Tallahassee Federal prison.

While he was a prisoner, his cellmate was a Haitian native. This man, a follower of the ancient religion *Vodun*, introduced Fernandez to voodoo, a corrupted version of *Vodun* that was adopted by many people in the rural areas of Haiti. Fernandez became fascinated with the religion and plunged into the world of the occult, inhabited by the undead, zombies, bizarre rituals, and holy priests called houngans. He studied Caribbean literature, including *The Black Republic*, written in 1884 and the perennial source for erroneous details on voodoo. Filled with vivid descriptions of human sacrifices, tortures and sacred rituals, the volume later attracted the attention of Hollywood film producers whose films reflected those misunderstandings and perpetuated distorted views of Haitian religions. Fernandez became convinced that he possessed special powers that enabled him to control women at his whim. He read Seabrook's *The Magic Island*, the recognized bible of voodoo and practiced the secret rituals described in its pages. He was sure that he was blessed with a mystical power derived from the supernatural spirits of voodoo. He told friends he could make love to women over vast distances and bring them to orgasm.

Using addresses that he accumulated from newspapers and "lonely hearts clubs," he sent letters to women all over the United States, hoping to gain their trust and affection. Once he made contact and developed a relationship, he frequently asked for a lock of hair or some other item that he could use in a voodoo ritual to enhance his control over the victim. The more time went on, the more he became fixated on the idea that he had become a houngan, a holy man whose powers were limitless. One by one, women were destined to fall under his charms, he believed, helpless to resist the mystical powers of the high priest of voodoo magic, Ramon Martinez-Fernandez.

In 1946, he was released from prison. He immediately returned to Brooklyn and moved in with his older sister. When he arrived, his family was shocked by his appearance. He had lost most of his dark, thick hair and was now partially bald with a receding hairline. On the top of his skull, a wide, long scar was plainly visible. But it was not only his looks that had changed. His personality had undergone a startling transformation. Fernandez was argumentative and abrupt when before the accident he was agreeable and easy to be with. At his sister's apartment, he locked himself in his room for long periods of time and complained of vicious headaches. But unknown to his family, Fernandez continued writing love letters to women he never met. After a few weeks of correspondence, he would arrange a face-to-face meeting. Then, under the guise of affection or the promise of marriage, he stole their money, checks, jewelry or anything else he could get his hands on. Most times, the women would not report the matter to the police out of fear of embarrassment and ridicule. As long as no one got hurt, Fernandez learned that he could get away with this scam indefinitely. He thought he had discovered his path to success.

In 1947, he met a woman named Jane Lucilla Thompson through the mail. After several weeks of exchanged letters, they agreed to meet. They carried on a romantic relationship until October of that year when Fernandez invited her to accompany him on a trip to Spain, for which Thompson paid. They traveled as man and wife, registered at hotels under his name and took sight-seeing trips across the Spanish countryside. Even though he was still legally married to Encarnacion, Fernandez returned to the village of La Linea where his wife lived with his two children. He even arranged a meeting between the two women during which he led Thompson to believe that he would soon divorce Encarnacion to marry her. However, on the night of November 7, there was an argument between Fernandez and Thompson in their hotel room. He was later observed running out of the hotel and never returned.

The next morning, hotel workers found the body of Jane Thompson in the hotel room. Because the cause of death could not be conclusively determined, Thompson was buried in a local cemetery without an autopsy. When police searched for Fernandez, he could not be found. He had already boarded a ship to the United States, leaving Encarnacion and the children behind. In New York City, he moved into Jane Thompson's apartment and took possession of her property. He produced a forged will for her mother and claimed ownership of her estate, despite the fact that her mother was already living in the apartment. Jane's mother was elderly and powerless to resist.

Throughout this period, as he traveled through Spain, touring with Jane Thompson, visiting with his wife, and returning to America, Fernandez carried on written correspondence with several other women. One of these other women was Martha Beck.

In Pensacola, Martha continued to work in the Children's Home. She enjoyed the praise of her colleagues for the performance of her duties. She soon received a promotion and her career seemed to be moving ahead. Though she yearned for a romantic relationship with a man, Martha was at last satisfied in her job. She had met new friends and even had a social life outside her workplace. A few days before Christmas, she received a reply from *Mother Dinene's Club*. The letter was neatly hand written on fine stationary and was obviously from an educated and apparently sincere writer. When she sat down to read it, her hands shook with anticipation and excitement.

"I hope you'll allow me the liberty of addressing you by your Christian name," it began. "To tell you the truth I don't know how to begin this letter to you because, I must confess, this is the first letter of this sort I have ever written."[11] He said his name was Raymond Fernandez, that he was thirty-four years old, not "a bad-looking fellow" and was in the importing business. He told Martha he lived in New York in a large apartment which he hoped to share with a wife some day. He said that he chose her, "because you are a nurse and therefore I know you have a full heart with a great capacity for comfort and love."[12]

Love-starved Martha was overwhelmed. Wherever she went, she carried the letter with her and read it dozens of times. Within the week, Martha wrote another letter and the correspondence began in earnest. Fernandez requested a photograph of her. This was a problem to Martha because she was painfully aware of her obese appearance and was ashamed of her weight. She temporarily solved this issue by sending a group photograph of her co-workers in which her image was partially obscured by others. On the back of the photo, she wrote, "it doesn't do me justice!" Of course, Martha did not know that Fernandez couldn't care less about the way she looked. By then, he had already victimized dozens of women across the country. He learned that it was better if his victims were of ordinary appearance since their insecurity worked to his advantage. They were more susceptible to his charms and grateful that a man like him would pay them any attention. Plain women were also much less likely to report the matter to the police since they would not want their reputation dragged though painful publicity if the man were ever caught. The self-possessed Fernandez was convinced that the women were satisfied with his sexual prowess and their losses were just the price to pay for a few blissful weeks with a wonderful man like himself.

When he felt the time was right, Fernandez asked for a lock of Martha's hair. Thrilled beyond words that a man would want a piece of her hair, she quickly responded. Once he received it, Fernandez performed his voodoo ritual in the safety of Jane Thompson's stolen apartment. The ceremonies he had learned from *The Magic Island* and the Haitian houngan in prison had served him well, he thought. Once the spell was invoked, it was time for a meeting. Fernandez was thrilled that since Martha's last name was the same as his favorite author, William Seabrook, it had to be an omen from the voodoo spirits.

After he had exchanged a number of letters with Martha, Fernandez arranged for a meeting. He boarded a train to Florida where she was to pick him up at the Pensacola depot. Martha, aware that she told many lies in her letters, realized she had a lot of explaining to do, especially about her over-weight appearance. But the excitement overcame all her fears as she drove over to the station to pick up her new Latin boyfriend. She couldn't wait to introduce him to her friends. When they finally met for the first time, Fernandez must have been shocked at what he saw. He had no clue that Martha was a rather large woman. But, as in the past, he had learned to overlook such details when money and profit were at stake.

They soon returned to her apartment where she had prepared a three-course meal for him. He met her children and her mother who was immediately suspicious of Martha's new boyfriend. His conversation was flamboyant, courteous, and seemingly sincere. Martha was impressed beyond words. She couldn't believe her good luck. Not only was her pen-pal good-looking and personable, he even resembled her favorite actor, Charles Boyer. Once she put the children to sleep and drugged her mother with sleeping pills, Martha immediately gave in to Fernandez and they made love in her bedroom. For the first time in her life, Martha enjoyed sex with a man. Even with her husband, she never had a good sexual relationship. "All sex relations were due to the fact that I felt it my duty as a wife to permit them," she later said.[13] She never knew sex could be so pleasurable. She swore her undying love to him and promised she would never leave him. Fernandez, of course, did not feel the same. Instead, he was fixated on her financial assets and where they were kept. After a few days of sex and food, and unable to make real progress on his plans, Fernandez decided to return to New York. Martha was devastated. But he soothed her hurt feelings by promising to send for her once he settled some business. Reluctantly, she finally agreed and Fernandez left Pensacola, never to return.

Several weeks later, Martha received a letter from Fernandez in which he told her that things could not work out between them and he didn't want to see her again. Martha was devastated. She attempted suicide by turning on all the gas outlets in her apartment. However, a neighbor smelled the gas and rescued her. When he discovered that Martha almost killed herself, Fernandez agreed to let her visit him in New York. She lived with him for a glorious two weeks in Jane Thompson's apartment. When she returned to Florida, Martha packed up her belongings, took the kids out of school, and said good-bye to her mother. She headed back to New York with her two kids in tow.

On the morning of January 18, 1948, Fernandez answered the doorbell of his apartment and found an elated Martha, with her two youngsters, standing on the threshold. But Fernandez told her that he could never be a father to her children and if she wanted to be with him, the kids had to go. Martha, already committed to Fernandez and sure that he was the only man for her, made a fateful decision. On January 25, 1948, she took her two children over to the Salvation Army office on Manhattan's First Avenue and abandoned them on the doorstep. For the next three years, she had no physical contact with them whatsoever. She never knew what happened to them until she asked her attorney during her stay on Death Row.

After the children were gone, Fernandez decided to tell Martha what he did for a living. He told her about the lonely hearts clubs, the endless parade of women, the scams and frauds he committed over the years. He told her that he was married several times to different women and that the police in many cities were probably looking for him. Martha was not put off because, to her, it was just another situation that she had to deal with. Fernandez was her man and, if this is how he made money, then it was simply her duty to support him. Fernandez showed her the dozens of letters that he had sent out recently and the responses he received. Soon they were making plans together to find his next victim. He told her that there was a woman, a Mrs. Esther Henne, in southern Pennsylvania that was ready for a personal meeting. Fernandez had been corresponding with her for several weeks and the time was right, he said, for him to take the next step.

They traveled to her home in Pennsylvania where Fernandez introduced Martha as his sister-in-law. A whirlwind courtship followed and within a few days, Fernandez married Esther and brought her back to New York. They moved into his apartment where they lived as man and wife, with Martha sleeping in the second bedroom. "He described her to me as her brother-in-laws sister-in-law, but they acted too loving to be relatives," Esther later said.[14] But Martha could not control her jealousy. She stole $4,000 from Esther and, during a heated argument, threw her out of the apartment. Esther threatened to go to the police, but she never did. "He was courteous for the first four days of our married life," she later told reporters. "Then he became irritable and gave me tongue lashings because I wouldn't sign over my insurance policies and my teacher's pension fund."[15] A succession of similar scenarios with different women followed; each ended the same way. The victim was cheated or robbed and was too humiliated to report it to the police. One of these victims was a middle-aged woman named Myrtle Young.

Myrtle was from Arkansas and after an intensive letter writing campaign, Fernandez proposed marriage. Myrtle agreed and arrangements were made for the couple to meet in Chicago. Again, Fernandez brought Martha along and introduced her as his sister-in-law. Within days, Fernandez married her on August 14, 1948 in Cook County, Illinois. But Martha would not go along with his plans. She insisted on sleeping in the same bed as Myrtle and took care not to leave the newlyweds alone for very long. Myrtle grew increasingly hostile until the days were filled with bitter arguments between the two women. One day, Martha arrived back at their rooming house unexpectedly and found Myrtle and Fernandez in bed together. She became enraged. She drugged Myrtle's food and placed her on a bus to her home town of Little Rock, Arkansas. When Myrtle arrived, she was in a state of semiconsciousness and had to be carried off the bus. Police were summoned and they immediately took her to the local hospital, where she died the following day. At the time, police did not suspect that she may have been the victim of a homicide. Only after Beck and Fernandez were arrested months later, and their activities became public, was Myrtle's case reopened.

After Myrtle's death, Fernandez and Martha began their trip back to New York. Along the way, they stopped in several towns to meet women who had been corresponding with Fernandez. Though they managed to steal some money, by the time they returned home, they were broke again. Immediately, Fernandez began to search through the "lonely hearts" ads looking for the next victim. After several attempts to initiate a new victim failed, Fernandez was at his wits end. As he went through additional prospects, he settled upon one who lived a lot closer than Arkansas and therefore would not require a great deal of travel.

Her name was Janet Fay, sixty-six years old and living in Albany, New York. She was a slightly overweight, religious-minded woman who had a habit of writing letters to lonely hearts clubs. Her family knew about her compulsion and tried to stop her from writing such letters, but Janet persisted. She had met men before through correspondence and the relationships never turned out well. But that did not stop her. After several weeks of exchanging letters with Fernandez, who was using the name Charles Martin, she agreed to let him visit her. On December 30, Martha and Fernandez arrived in Albany and checked into a downtown hotel. Fernandez left Martha in her room and went to meet with Fay. He brought flowers and candy and turned on the charm. After a few days of dinners and lunches with the lonely widow, he showed up with Martha and introduced her as his sister. Shortly afterward, he proposed marriage to Fay. She quickly accepted. They made plans to move to Long Island where Martha, unknown to Fay, had already rented a house at 15 Adeline Street in the village of Valley Stream. Fernandez convinced Fay that it would be best if she switched banks from Albany to Queens. She agreed and together, they withdrew over $6,000 in cash from her accounts without her family's knowledge. When he was sure that she had no additional funds, Fernandez said it was time to leave.

On the night of January 4, 1949, they settled into their Adeline Street home and prepared for bed. What exactly happened that night will never be known with certainty. Martha told several different versions of what transpired between them and she later claimed that she suffered from some type of hysterical amnesia and could not remember all the details. One thing is sure. Martha and Janet Fay became involved in an argument over Fernandez. Fay carried on to such a degree that Martha was afraid the neighbors would hear her screaming. In the living room, where the two women were engaged in heated words, a large hammer rested on the table. According to Martha, she blacked out during this period and could not remember what happened. But within minutes, Janet Fay lay at her feet, her head crushed by repeated blows from the hammer. Blood flowed from her wounds and covered the floor. Fernandez came into the room and yelled at Martha, "For God's sake, Martha! What did you do?" She checked Fay's pulse and found none. "Blood began to stream from her head," said Martha later. "I suggested to Fernandez to get a scarf, tie it around her neck to form a tourniquet to stop the blood."[16] They cleaned up the living room with rags and a mop and then dumped the items in the garbage cans outside. They placed Fay's body in a large wooden trunk. The next morning, they began searching for another rental house. Eleven days later, Fernandez located a two-story home in nearby South Ozone Park. Together, they buried the decomposing body in the basement of the new rental house and covered the grave with concrete.

The following day, Martha and Fernandez left New York and headed west to Michigan, the home of his next victim. While Fernandez was married to Mrs. Fay, he had made contact with Mrs. Delphine Downing, a forty-one-year-old widow who was living in Byron Center, a small community south of Grand Rapids. Delphine also had a two- year-old child, Rainelle. Fernandez introduced himself in his letters as "Charles Martin," a successful business-man engaged in the exporting trade. When Fernandez wrote to say that he would be visiting Byron Center, Delphine was thrilled, even though he said that he would be bringing his sister with him.

In January 1949, Fernandez met with Delphine for the first time. She was happy with his appearance and his good manners. They soon developed a romantic relationship and Delphine began to imagine Fernandez as her husband. Martha, ever jealous of every woman who wanted her lover, was enraged at the sleeping arrangements and seethed with resentment at the thought of the impending marriage.

One morning, Delphine arose early and stumbled upon Fernandez without his hairpiece. She was stunned. She accused him of fraud and deception. They argued all day while Fernandez tried to appease her. Nothing worked. In an effort to calm her down, Martha gave Delphine an overdose of sleeping pills. When Rainelle saw her mother stumbling around the house as if drunk, she began to cry. Martha panicked and choked the little girl into unconsciousness causing bruises around her neck. Fernandez began to worry that, if Delphine saw the injury, she would report it to the police.

"Do something, Ray!" screamed Martha. He searched the bedroom until he found a handgun that once belonged to Delphine's dead husband. He wrapped the pistol in a bed sheet and stood next to Delphine who was lying on the couch. Fernandez placed the barrel up against her head and pulled the trigger. The bullet crashed into her brain and killed Delphine instantly. Rainelle, who was still crying, watched the murder of her mother from a few feet away. Martha wrapped the body in the bed sheets and carried it into the basement. Together, Martha and Fernandez dug a deep hole in the dirt floor and dumped the corpse in. They then mixed up a quantity of concrete and—just as they had in the Fay murder—covered the grave with cement.

For the next two days, they discussed their plans for the future. First, they had to decide what to do with Rainelle. The little girl could not stop crying and Fernandez was very worried that neighbors would soon notice. He told Martha to get rid of her. At first, she refused but Fernandez insisted. Martha took Rainelle into the basement where there was a large vat of water. Then in an act of inexplicable cruelty, she plunged the screaming child into the tub and held her under the water until she drowned. Afterward, Martha dug another grave and buried Rainelle near her mother.

Later that same day, Martha and Fernandez went to a local movie theater where they ate popcorn and made plans to leave Michigan. In the meantime, however, neighbors had become suspicious of the new visitors at Delphine's house; they called police. Just a few minutes after Martha arrived back at the house, two detectives showed up at the door. After some pointed questioning, and a search of the basement, Martha and Fernandez were arrested.

The first newspaper report on the case in New York appeared on March 2, 1949, in the *New York Times*. Under the title "3 Lonely Hearts Murders Trap Pair; Body Dug Up Here," reporter Kalman Seigel provided the details of their arrest in Michigan for the murders of Delphine Downing and her daughter. "A thin thread of crime, spun by a 200 pound divorcee and her balding partner around lonely widows seeking companionship, broke yesterday when the pair confessed to Michigan and New York police that they had murdered three persons."[17] The same article pointed out that Martha had already confessed to the killings and Fernandez had told New York police where they had hidden the body of Janet Fay. "Queens and Nassau police, following specific directions telephoned by Fernandez, found the body of a woman in the wrapping paper in which the prisoners said they had put it on January 4, the day of the murder."[18] The *Times* told its readers that the murderous pair had traveled through the eastern United States searching for victims through lonely hearts club lists. Martha was usually introduced as Fernandez' sister, said the *Times*, and together the pair cheated lonely women out of their money and valuables.

In 1949, there were only seven major daily newspapers in operation in the nation's largest city. The *Sun* had shut down its presses that December after forty years in publication causing most of its readers to switch to the *News*. Not that the *Daily News* needed readers. By then, it was a publishing juggernaut, a media colossus, selling over two million copies a day, the highest daily circulation of any paper in the world. It was known as, "a snappily written, cleverly edited digest emphasizing the seamy side of life."[19] Its formula for success, which included on-the-scene photography and detailed crime reporting, appealed to a working-class readership who had neither the time nor desire to read more intense, information-filled papers like the *Times* or the *Herald Tribune*, which was selling only 300,000 copies a day. The *Daily News* was easy to read. It had a simple format and utilized a vocabulary that everyone understood. Most of its columnists were indigenous to New York, spoke the language of the city, and empathized with its long-suffering working class.

In the meantime, New York prosecutors appealed to Michigan authorities not to contest extradition requests to bring the accused pair back to Nassau County. Though two murders were committed in Kent County and confessions of Martha and Fernandez made their convictions a certainty, there was a general feeling that justice would be better served if the pair were prosecuted in New York. The reason was obvious; Michigan had no death penalty. "Nassau County District Attorney explained in Mineola that the purpose of the hearing was to settle legal questions, such as the right of Michigan to get the suspects back in their custody if Nassau County failed to get a conviction."[20] On March 8, a hearing was held in Grand Rapids to determine the course of action. Martha and Fernandez were brought to the courtroom in chains and without an attorney. Michigan Governor C. Mennen Williams said through a representative that "consideration should be given to the fact that the crime committed in New York State was the first in a series of three and that as a matter of logic the first crime should be the first one tried."[21] In a questionable decision—one that was not contested by the defendants—arrangements were made for the suspects to be sent back to New York. As she was taken out of the courtroom, Martha told reporters, "the only thing is, I would prefer to remain in Michigan."[22]

Upon arrival in Nassau County, the court assigned Herbert E. Rosenberg to represent both defendants, a development that would have fatal consequences for Martha and Fernandez. Rosenberg, already a well-known lawyer in the Manhattan legal community, immediately asked the judge for a change in venue. He said that his clients could not get a fair trial in Nassau County due to adverse press coverage which had the defendants guilty before a trial. Supreme Court Justice Thomas J. Cuff agreed and ordered the trial to be held in Bronx County Court. "He said his decision was not to be construed as criticism of the press but maintained that handling of the stories was such as to prejudice readers against the defendants."[23] Over the next few days, the press adopted the label that was to stick to the defendants for the duration of their trial and beyond. They were called the "Lonely Hearts Killers."

Jury selection began in the Bronx in early June. Newspaper coverage, which emphasized the sexual aspects of the case, was filled with references to Martha's insatiable appetite for Fernandez. "From beginning to end, the trial was fiasco," writes author Wenzell Brown in *Introduction to Murder*. "Everyone got into the act. Lawyers on both sides used flowery, over dramatic language. Witnesses seemed determined to steal the show with startling revelations. Psychiatrists issued statements bound to make newspaper headlines . . . even the defendants seemed to be playing for the grandstand."[24] After ten grueling days of picking a jury, opening statements began on June 27. "For the first time," the *Daily News* said, "the simpering Martha became serious and Fernandez lost his gold-toothed smile."[25] Even the *Times* described the defendants as, "swarthy Raymond Fernandez and plump Martha J. Beck."[26] But court spectators listened intently when defense attorney Rosenberg told the jury during his opening statement that the defendants "became so involved sexually that it was impossible for them to act as normal individuals."[27]

During the first two days, the prosecution, led by Edward Robinson Jr., put fourteen witnesses on the stand. Some of these witnesses testified that Janet Fay was seen in the company of Martha and Fernandez as they went around Albany cleaning out her bank accounts. "Just before and after the hammer-scarf murder of trusting Mrs. Janet Fay, the Lonely Hearts suspects were lovingly absorbed in details of the widow's $5,918 savings."[28] Kent County District Attorney Roger McMahon was called to the stand and told the court that Martha had provided a confession after her right to a lawyer had been explained to her.[29] The judge took the unusual step of having Martha read her own confession to the court. "The fat but well groomed Mrs. Beck, frequently described by her own attorney as a mentally unstable sex victim, read her own alleged confession during yesterday's session," said the *Daily News*. "She showed no emotion except when she gazed with loving eyes on Fernandez and carried on a rapid fire conversation in undertones with him. She does not seem the least bit worried."[30] After strenuous arguments that lasted several days between Defense Attorney Rosenberg and prosecutors, Fernandez' confession was admitted into evidence as well. Martha, whenever she heard testimony to which she disagreed, would frequently talk out loud causing the judge to admonish her and her defense attorney. When prosecutors tried to introduce the hammer, which was allegedly used in the attack on Mrs. Fay, a witness said that an inventory was taken of Mr. Fernandez' car.

"No, it wasn't!" yelled Martha from her seat. "Well, I was sitting right there, your honor. I heard it!"

"Madam, let your attorney talk for you!" said Judge Pecora.

But Rosenberg continued to pound away at his client's confessions which he knew were at the core of the prosecutor's case. He tried to show the court that when Martha confessed in Michigan, she was promised her admissions would not be used against her in New York and that police would not testify against her.

Grand Rapids Detective John Vander Band was called to the stand to explain the circumstances under which the confession was obtained and exactly what was said to the defendant on the day of her arrest. However, Vander Band's testimony was a repetition of answers such as "I don't recall" and "I can't remember." According to one estimate, Vander Band provided those responses over one hundred times during his five hours of testimony. Judge Pecora instructed the witness to be more specific, but it was to no avail. "The evasive answers to even the most simple questions finally brought laughter to Mrs. Beck and Fernandez which spread to the spectators and several of the jurors as well," reported the *Post*. "The two defendants finally resorted to covering their faces with handkerchiefs to conceal their amusement."[31] The detective's testimony was so evasive, it prompted Robinson to ask the witness about his mental state. "As a matter of fact," said Robinson, "you've been confused throughout your testimony haven't you?" That question caused Rosenberg to jump to his feet and respond, "I will concede the witness is confused."[32] The spectators convulsed in laughter as Judge Pecora called for order.

But the mood changed when Raymond Fernandez took the stand. Confident, smug, appearing dapper and unconcerned, Fernandez spoke of his love for Martha and tried to explain his persistent habit of bilking lonely women out of their possessions. But the prosecution fired away at the defendant, exposing his career of thefts and deception for the jury. "Robinson forced Fernandez to admit he had married two women in 1948 and entered into evidence a will of a third . . . turning all possessions over to Fernandez upon her death. Two of the women are now dead."[33] Robinson also questioned him about Esther Henne, the woman in Pennsylvania he met through a lonely hearts club.

"Did you have any sex relations with her?" he asked.

"No, she wouldn't allow such a thing. She told me she was through with men sexually," Fernandez said.[34]

To explain his confession to the Downing murders, Fernandez claimed that he was awake for twenty-four hours at that time and he only made those admissions because he was mistreated by police. He was given no water, he said, and served food that was eaten by rats and mice in his cell. When Robinson started to challenge Fernandez on these statements, Martha stood up to object.

"Mr. Fernandez is not deaf, Mr. Robinson!" she shouted. Again, the judge warned Rosenberg about Martha's outbursts. But Fernandez simply smiled back from the stand. He told the court that he made up the story he told Michigan police and that he did so because he wanted to protect Martha.

"All my statements were made for the purpose of helping Martha," he said.

"Did you love her?" asked Rosenberg.

"Definitely. I love her. It couldn't be anything else." For three days, Fernandez remained on the stand. At times, he was charming, belligerent, and evasive. He frequently boasted of his sexual talents along with his ability to convince women to do his bidding. But when he was questioned about Delphine Downing, he admitted killing the widow while Martha watched. At that point in his testimony, Martha suddenly jumped up out of her seat and loudly declared, "I think at this time, your honor, I want to take the stand!"

"I have admonished you on more than one occasion, madam!" Judge Pecora said. "Please take your seat and speak with your attorney." Though Fernandez admitted he and Martha murdered Delphine and her daughter, he denied killing Janet Fay. He said that Martha was upset with Fay because the widow wanted to sleep with him and Martha disapproved. Fernandez said that Fay became argumentative and Martha wouldn't back down.

"I said to Martha, 'See how you can keep that woman quiet—no matter what!' and when I got back, she had kept her quiet by hitting her on the head with the hammer!"[35] Fernandez then found Mrs. Fay laying on the floor in the living room. "Mrs. Fay was crouched over the suitcase in the living room," he said in court. "Her head was splattered with blood. The suitcase was bloody, there was a great, big puddle."[36] Fernandez said he didn't know Martha was going to kill Fay. But once she was dead, he realized something had to be done about the body. He told the court how he and Martha bought a large trunk later the same day. They placed the body inside and stored it at the Adeline Street home. But over the next few days, the odor became too strong and they decided to bury it in the basement of a rented home in the nearby town of Valley Stream.

While he told the story of the murder, Fernandez frequently smiled at Martha who returned his attention with her own grins and winks. Fidgeting in her seat like a schoolgirl when testimony addressed descriptions of Fernandez' sexual habits, Martha sat up in her seat and nodded approvingly. "Three women jurors closed their eyes and shielded their faces with their hands and a woman spectator fled from the room during Fernandez' admissions of unusual love-making."[37] Robinson asked about a three-way strip poker game that Fernandez played with Esther Henne and Martha. The last hand was played for which woman would have the right to sleep with Fernandez that night. Martha won. When Robinson finished his cross examination, he obtained permission from Judge Pecora to read Fernandez' written statement into the record. "Mrs. Beck smiled serenely and Fernandez took frequent notes as his seventy-three page statement of March 3 was read, recounting the hammer and scarf murder of Mrs. Fay."[38]

Police from Michigan then took the stand to describe property that was found in Martha's possession that belonged to the Downings. Afterward, the New York police testified to letters and papers that she had at the time of her arrest which were addressed to Mrs. Fay. But anticipation was building for the day when Martha would testify. The tabloids were wondering if she would protect Fernandez or would the truth send him to the electric chair?

Outside the courtroom, huge crowds had gathered each morning waiting for the day's proceedings. The sexual aspects of the case were well publicized in the New York newspapers. As a result, the trial drew legions of curious women who couldn't wait to catch a glimpse of the Latino Lothario who had a mysterious power over women. Rumors were rampant. Fernandez was a voodoo priest, a magician, a hypnotist, a man who could make a woman do anything. After he described some of the "abnormal practices" he used on Martha, police could barely control the hundreds of spectators who lined the hallways and stairways of the Bronx County courthouse.

In the meantime, New York was experiencing a scorching heat wave that caused people to drop to the floor in the hot building that had no air conditioning and little ventilation. Those who couldn't get into the court flocked to nearby movie theaters where films like *Forbidden Street* with Dana Andrews and *Illegal Entry* with George Brent were running. The Lowe's Paradise on the fabled Grand Concourse was showing *The Barkleys of Broadway* with Fred Astaire while John Huston's epic film of greed and murder, *Treasure of Sierra Madre* starring Humphrey Bogart, was opening that very week. The theaters were air conditioned and offered a welcome relief from the heat. After the show, people returned to the court building and tried again to get a seat at New York's most salacious criminal trial. The case was reported nationwide and the entire country knew the trashy, yet irresistible story of the Lonely Hearts Killers.

When her name was called on the morning of July 25, 1949, Martha rose from the defense table and slowly brushed her hair. She wore a gray and white large polka dot summer dress, accentuated with a white pearl necklace and bright green wedge-heel shoes. The outfit made her appear even more overweight and, worse, was totally inappropriate for a courtroom. As she passed the table where Fernandez sat, Martha suddenly veered in his direction, grabbed him by the neck and planted kisses all over his face. When the court officers pulled Martha away, several large lipstick impressions could be seen on Fernandez' cheeks. He smiled, his gold-teeth sparkling for everyone to see.

Rosenberg asked the witness to tell the court where she was born and what her childhood was like. When Martha began her story to a hushed courtroom, no one knew what to expect. She recalled her experiences as an obese and unwanted child. She told of her problems with her mother and how she was continually ridiculed at school and home. When she was thirteen, Martha said, she was sexually assaulted by her brother and then, to make matters worse, blamed for the attack. Every time she began to develop a relationship with a boy, her mother would destroy it. Then later, as an adult, Martha had no luck with men. Her first marriage was a disaster, she told the court, leaving her pregnant and with no means of support. She broke down in tears several times during her testimony causing the judge to call a recess when she was unable to recover.

But her demeanor changed when she began to speak of Fernandez. She told the court how, through a friend's practical joke, she met the man who would change her life. Robinson objected to that testimony. But before the judge could answer, Martha interrupted him. "If it wasn't for that joke, Mr. Robinson, I wouldn't be in the courtroom now!" she said.[39] Even though she knew he was a murderer, she still loved him, she told the court. At times, she was condescending and sarcastic, especially when she had to talk about other women. "Raymond got quite a kick out of the photographs of some of the old hags who wrote to him and expected him to correspond with them," she said. Martha giggled whenever she recalled how simple it was for Fernandez to steal from his victims. When questioning turned to the night of Janet Fay's death, Martha claimed she suffered from amnesia and couldn't remember most details. But she remembered enough to describe how Mrs. Fay tried to get the attention of Fernandez. "Giggling profusely and covering her face with a handkerchief, Mrs. Beck mimicked Mrs. Fay's actions in attempting to entice her lover. 'Just think of that old lady resorting to baby talk!" she chuckled."[40]

Time and time again, Martha told the court of her utter devotion to Fernandez and how she forgave him for everything because of that love. "My love is so great for him," she told the court, "if he told me to hold my breath and stop breathing, I would have done so, if in the end, he and I could be married, I'd consent to anything."[41] The *Daily News* said Martha gave her testimony, "in a strange blend of tears and earthy humor . . . and told with giggles that almost choked off her words how her co-defendant had been harassed by the amorous old women he met in his romance-by-mail profession."[42]

As Prosecutor Robinson guided her testimony to the night Mrs. Fay was killed, Martha berated the Michigan authorities who tricked her into a statement by making promises that were never fulfilled. When Judge Pecora told her to answer only the question asked, Martha angrily responded. "Remember, your honor, it's my life I'm fighting for here and not yours!"[43] Martha went on to say that she was burning up with anger and jealousy on January 4 when Mrs. Fay was murdered. After a loud argument, the elderly widow slapped her face and Martha became enraged. The next thing she knew, she found herself standing over Mrs. Fay and blood was everywhere. "I dropped to my knees, tried to get her pulse . . . she was dead."[44] Martha told the court that there was so much blood that she and Fernandez had "to use a mop, dustpan and papers to clean up the place."[45] The *Times* report on the same testimony simply said, "the 29 year old divorcee, who weighs 200 pounds, corroborated previous testimony."[46] The *Daily News* described Martha as a "200 pound figure of wrathful emotion."[47] The *Post* most frequently used the term "pudgy defendant."[48]

But it was the sexual aspects of the case that enthralled spectators and enticed crowds to nearly riot outside the courtroom doors. Martha told the court that she often blacked out when she made love to Fernandez and would do anything that he asked. "That is something that took place because we loved each other and I consider it absolutely sacred . . . you referred to the love-making as abnormal, but for the love I had for Fernandez nothing is abnormal!"[49] The women in the courtroom swooned. After the lunch break, extra police had to be summoned to the Bronx County courthouse to control the unruly crowds. "The trial was disrupted yesterday afternoon by a near riot of would-be spectators outside the courtroom . . . a pushing, shouting crowd of 150 persons attempted to elbow past court attendants."[50] The

Post said that, "in the melee, one woman was injured and another had her dress nearly torn off."[51] Martha ended her testimony by admonishing the district attorney. "I am on trial for murder, not for lying," she shouted. "He's so determined to make me a liar, he's forgetting the lie he swore to!"[52] The *Daily News* reported that "some 300 persons, many of whom had stayed in line four hours tried to storm the courtroom . . . fourteen cops and several court attendants had such difficulty controlling the mob that the doors were locked and the public ordered out of the corridors."[53]

During the next week of testimony, a team of psychiatrists offered their diversified interpretation of Martha's mental condition. They struggled to explain how she could do such a thing as smash a hammer over the head of a sixty-six-year-old woman, and not remember it. As spectators dozed in their seats, the psychiatrists analyzed the defendant's motives amid a web of sophisticated terms that few people understood. One of the most respected psychologists in New York, Dr. Perry Lichenstein, provided a setback for the defense during his testimony. Asked about Martha's mental state at the time of the crime, Dr. Lichenstein said she knew what she was doing and therefore, was legally sane when she killed Mrs. Fay. He also told the court that Martha's sexual needs and desires were not necessarily abnormal. After his testimony, both sides gave lengthy closing statements. The *Post* said, "Judge Pecora will soon charge the jury . . . who will then consider the fate of the swarthy Fernandez and his paunchy paramour."[54]

Trial coverage by the *Daily News* was always opinionated and frequently sensationalized. It was the style of that newspaper and a goal to which the editorial staff aspired. Of course, a lurid and trashy story like the Lonely Hearts Killers was at home in a big-city tabloid like the *Daily News* which, more than any other New York publication, covered the trial on its first or second page. Reporters, including Grace Robinson, Edward Dillon, and Henry Lee, attended each day's proceedings at the Bronx County courthouse and were a familiar sight to attorneys and police. It was the *Daily News* that was most responsible for the public's lasting impression of Martha. Characterizations of her as, "plump," "fat," "emotional," or "obese," and the often-used "200-pound-Martha Beck," were repeated in almost every article written on the case during the forty-four-day trial.

On August 17, after ten long weeks of testimony, the case was handed to the jury for deliberations. "The 'lonely hearts' murder trial decision was in the hands of a Bronx jury at 7:56 o'clock last night, after a charge by Supreme Court Justice Ferdinand Pecora that lasted for five hours and twenty minutes."[55] The jury of ten men and two women debated the case through the night but were unable to come up with a decision. "The fate of swarthy Raymond Fernandez and his fat mistress, Mrs. Martha Beck, still remained in doubt today as the jury failed to reach a verdict after deliberating all night."[56] But at 8:30 a.m. the next morning, it was over. The jury sent word a verdict had been reached.

Martha and Fernandez were brought over to the courthouse from the nearby holding pen. Because of the early hour, the courtroom, for the first time in the trial, was almost empty. Only about a dozen people waited for the verdict. Both defendants were found guilty of Murder in the First Degree. The *Post* reported the verdict on its front page with the headline, "Hearts Pair Guilty; Get Chair." "The Lonely Hearts lovers, fat Martha Beck and Raymond Fernandez, were found guilty of murder in the first degree . . . the defendants were impassive as the jury foreman read the jury's findings."[57] The *Daily News* said, "the 28 year-old, 200 pound divorcee accepted the grim prospect with no particular show of emotion, although she gripped the edge of the defense table and glared at her attorney. Both defendants looked haggard from the all-night ordeal of waiting for a verdict."[58] After providing the court reporter with her pedigree, Martha was escorted out and returned to Bronx County jail. Rosenberg announced he would appeal the case and promptly posed for photographers who arrived at the close of the proceedings.

On August 22, both defendants were brought back before Judge Pecora for sentencing. "Mrs. Martha J. Beck and Raymond Fernandez were sentenced yesterday to die in the electric chair . . . the two stood impassively before the bar as the judge pronounced the sentence."[59] Within the hour, they were taken to Sing Sing in separate vehicles. At the prison gates, crowds of curious people gathered to watch the famous couple enter the facility. When processed at the admissions desk, Martha was asked the routine question.

"To what do you attribute your criminal act?" said the guard.

"Something I got into. I had no control," she replied. To the same question, Fernandez replied, "an accident." Afterward, they were escorted to their respective cell blocks. They could not have known that it would be the last time they would ever see each other. Martha was assigned the center cell in the female block. It was the identical cell once occupied by Ruth Snyder in 1928 and Eva Coo in 1936. Martha was the only female prisoner in the death house. When she filled out the approved visitors list, she included her children, Anthony, four years old, and Carmen, five, who she hadn't seen since she dropped them off at the Salvation Army office in January 1948.[60]

Martha and Fernandez' term on Death Row had to be one of the most trying experiences a Sing Sing warden ever had. From the day of their arrival, amid a surging crowd of reporters and spectators, the continuing drama of the love-sick Martha and her killer boyfriend never ended. Encouraged by periodic news stories that described Martha's complaints about the food, her trial, and prison life in general, the public never seemed to tire of the gossip about the "lonely hearts killers." In September 1950, rumors spread of a supposed sexual relationship between a prison guard and Martha whose sexual appetite was in high gear since being separated from Fernandez. "For several weeks, I have suffered in silence because of the rumors started by Mr. Fernandez," she wrote in a letter to the warden. "To print that or say that I am having an affair with a guard is one of the most asinine and ridiculous statements ever made!"[61] For those rumors, she blamed Fernandez who was trying to convince the court that he was innocent and Martha was capable of anything, including murder. As time passed, the strange couple carried on a love-hate relationship that fluctuated almost weekly. At times, Martha would profess her undying love for Fernandez and he would do the same. At other times, they would express revulsion for each other in letters written to their friends and family.

> How low can a skunk get? The papers are full of lies about me today . . . he says he is being subjected to mental torture beyond endurance by the "sadistic death house triangle" and that he wants to drop his appeal so he can go to the chair! What a character! He hasn't got the guts to commit suicide nor could he walk to the chair . . . he'd be dragged all the way . . . fighting and screaming! Oh yes, he's brave when it comes to hurting others, he can kill without batting an eyelash. But to hurt himself, he'd never do it. It takes a man to kill himself, not a sniveling, low down, double-crossing lying rat like him.[62]

As for Fernandez, he continued his habit of writing letters, even from Death Row. From the day of his arrest, and unknown to Martha, Fernandez maintained a letter correspondence with his first wife, Encarnacion, who was still living in Spain with their children. "Kisses and hugs for the children and the baby and for you from the one who will always love you."[63] Although Encarnacion knew that Fernandez was under a sentence of death, she was unaware of the extent of her husband's crimes. "What are we going to do?" she wrote in a letter to Fernandez. "God has not listened to our prayers . . . if you had done something to me I always pardoned you with my heart . . . the only pains I have is thinking of the situation in which you are in . . . have faith in God . . . love from the one who will never forget you. Your wife."

But it was Martha, the starry-eyed romantic, whose words and actions seem torn right out of the pages of a dime store novel, who fascinated the press and at the same time, inspired sympathy from legions of women. They could understand the irrational acts of a lonely woman who knew nothing but rejection because of a weight problem. They could feel for a woman sent to Death Row because she had the bad luck to fall for a man who betrayed her love. Many women, especially those who were single or suffered from the same type of loneliness, had empathy for Martha despite her crimes. Many female readers understood very well the condescension from the media, along with the derogatory references to Martha's physical appearance; they experienced similar reactions in their own lives. "I'm still human, feeling every blow inside, even though I have the ability to hide my feelings and laugh," Martha wrote in another letter to her sister. "But that doesn't say my heart isn't breaking from the insults and humiliation of being talked about as I am. O yes, I wear a cloak of laughter."[64]

Soon after the conviction, Rosenberg filed an appeal for both his clients. Ironically, one of the important points of the appeal—and the one upon which he rested his hopes for a new trial—was the issue of legal representation. Some experts, including other judges, felt that having one lawyer represent both defendants was a fundamental injustice to both. How could Rosenberg adequately serve Fernandez' interests if he were Martha's attorney as well, which forced him to blame Fernandez for the murder? That paradox existed for both clients. There seemed to be no fair way for any attorney to represent two defendants in such a situation. The New York Court of Appeals was aware of this dilemma and on July 11, 1950, they announced their decision.

The court first decided on the admissibility of Martha's statements in Michigan on the night of her arrest. Martha made admissions without the benefit of counsel and under assurances by police that the statements would not be used against her in New York. To this point, the court decided that all statements were legally obtained and therefore admissible in court. "No weight can be given to that argument when applied to the corrective statement made by Mrs. Beck on March 11, which was done at her own request . . . in which she stated she knew that it would be used against her in New York."[65] The judges pointed out that this issue had already been decided in a pretrial hearing where all the statements were reviewed and supported by witness testimony. Martha also made additional statements at a later time when she was represent by attorney in Michigan and at that time she was aware that any admissions could be used against her in New York.

On the second issue, the appeals court recognized the difficulties of defense counsel in representing both defendants, but strangely, blamed Fernandez himself for the error which was compounded by Rosenberg. The court pointed out that Fernandez, in a letter he wrote to Judge Pecora, asked for Rosenberg to represent him even after he knew the same attorney was defending Martha. Then later, when Fernandez was asked if he were satisfied with the defense, he replied, "I certainly am." He was asked again on July 28 in open court and again, Fernandez replied that he was. When the question of adequate representation arose to Rosenberg, he told the judge, "If your honor pleases, for the record may it be noted that both defendants are perfectly satisfied with counsel that is now representing them."[66] Judge Pecora then asked Rosenberg if he wanted additional counsel to assist him and he replied that he did not.

Appeals Court Justice J. Lewis said, "I feel equally certain that the defendants in this case have had the benefit of an exceedingly zealous and industrious and capable service rendered to them by their counsel . . . true it is that there developed in this long trial instances where the interests of the two defendants were in conflict."[67] Those instances were most notable when each of the defendants took the stand. During testimony of both Martha and Fernandez, there were many opportunities when opposing counsel should have raised an objection to statements that were made against the defendant who was not on the stand. But Rosenberg could not do that because he represented both defendants.

That problem was made very clear in the court's dissenting opinion written by Judge Conway. "We think the court should have exercised its own judgment and not been guided by defense counsel (who on the previous day had been of a contrary opinion) nor by the defendants themselves who were not competent to decide . . . a fair reading of the record indicates that . . . counsel failed to properly protect the interest of Fernandez but seems to have subconsciously placed Mrs. Beck in a preferred position in the defense." Judge Conway also took issue with the defendants' attitude toward each other. He pointed out they frequently expressed hostility toward each other and for one attorney to handle the defense of both, especially in a death penalty case, would be impossible. "The final complete abandonment of Fernandez by counsel and of his defense, will be found in his summation . . . when he asks for the mercy of life imprisonment for a client whose defense was that he was an accessory after the fact for which the penalty was five years."[68] Despite these arguments, Judge Conway was outvoted. The conviction was upheld.

As the prison staff prepared for their executions, which were scheduled for March 1951, Martha and Fernandez went through a period of reconciliation and they later exchanged love notes to each other. "The lustful lovers were reported calmly resigned to die in the electric chair tonight as the final payoff in their murder for profit partnership," said the *Citizen Register*. "But lawyers continued last minute efforts to save the condemned lonely hearts slayers—200-pound Mrs. Martha Beck and Raymond Fernandez, the balding Romeo."[69] Two other convicted killers were also scheduled to die on March 8. They were John Joseph King, twenty-one, and Richard Power, twenty-one, both convicted in Queens for a 1950 car-jacking murder.

According to prison records, at least fifty-two people were granted permission to witness the executions. The list contained an unusually high number of press reporters who were personally approved by the warden. They included representatives from the *Daily News, Daily Mirror, Journal American, World Telegram*, UPI, Associated Press, *Star Journal, El Diario, Detroit Times, Detroit News, New York Post*, and many others. Judge Pecora, who sentenced Martha to death, also agreed to witness the executions as well.

Martha slept during her last night, according to a death row inmate log, and on the morning of March 8, she "ate a good breakfast, ham, eggs, coffee and took a shower." Later that day, "Martha ate a fair dinner. Laundry sent out, returned and checked." But when Martha discovered that a matron, with whom she did not get along, was scheduled to work on her last day, she became angry and disappointed. She immediately fired off a letter to Warden Denno. "I do not appreciate it one bit, but I am glad that no member of my family will know how hurt and misled my last day was. It hurts me deeply to realize that I have been wrong in thinking there could be 'good' in a state paid employee. Martha Jule # 106594."[70]

For her last meal, Martha ordered fried chicken, French fries, and lettuce and tomato. She refused a dessert. Fernandez had a fried onion omelet, sliced tomatoes, almond ice cream, fruit, and coffee. During her entire fifteen-months on Death Row, no family member visited Martha; her last day was no exception. Fernandez had many visits from his sister who also waited with him until the last possible minute on his final day. Though Martha had hopes the governor might commute her sentence, she realized it was unlikely. Governor Thomas Dewey was a former prosecutor and, during his time in the governor's office, never commuted a death sentence. It was Dewey who also denied clemency to Helen Fowler—the last female to face execution—in 1944.

By 10 p.m., preparations were completed and witnesses began to congregate in the waiting room. The executioner, Joseph Francel, who would make $150 per execution that night, had checked on the equipment and reported to Warden Denno that the electrical apparatus was in fine working order. It would be the first quadruple execution at Sing Sing in almost four years. Reporters took notes while dozens of witnesses crowded into the room. With barely enough space to contain everyone, some of the judges and police personnel took it upon themselves to walk into the execution chamber. They took their seats in the front row nearest the electric chair, while Francel busied himself with last minute details behind the control panel.

After her hair was cropped short to accept the electrodes, Martha put on a gray dress and red sandals. As she finished dressing, Protestant chaplain Luther Hannum visited Martha and began his prayer vigil. By 10:55 p.m., the execution procedure was ready to begin. Guards responded to the cell of John King, who was terrified of the chair and needed help to walk down the corridor. According to one report, his face "was a study in terror." A few minutes later, the same guards returned to the cellblock to retrieve Richard Power. "He went quietly, his hands folded and his eyes closed. He seemed to be praying."[71] Once Power's body was removed, it was time for Fernandez.

He was wearing black pants, white shirt, and slippers. He carried a crucifix in his right hand and was accompanied by the Catholic chaplain, Tom Donovan. "Fernandez' brown eyes were sparkling when he entered the death chamber. His charms had been fatal bait for the love starved widows."[72] When they first saw Fernandez, the witnesses rose from their seats to get a better look. Reporters hastily jotted down their impressions on their paper pads while the guards hastily took Fernandez to the chair. Within seconds he was seated and the straps were fastened across his chest and arms. He stared straight ahead, appearing not to see the witnesses. A brief suggestion of a smile appeared on his lips. Less than three minutes after he entered the room, he was dead. Dr. Howard Kipp approached the lifeless body and listened for a heartbeat with his stethoscope. "I pronounce this man dead!" he said in a loud voice. Fernandez was removed from the chair and loaded onto the gurney. The room was quiet again.

Suddenly, the green door swung open and Martha appeared in her drab gray dress. She walked steadily, accompanied by the matrons. "She entered the high, bare death chamber unassisted . . . and smiled ever so faintly."[73] As she attempted to sit in the chair, she had to wriggle into the seat due to her girth. Making weird faces as she lowered herself down, the matrons held her arms. As they fastened the straps to her arms, tears rolled down their cheeks. Martha mouthed the words "good-bye and thank you!" but no sound escaped from her lips. Her eyes closed as the mask was lowered over her face. The matrons quickly moved away. Francel took a last look in the area of the chair and when he was sure it was clear, he turned the dial. The current hit Martha with the force of sledge hammer. In two minutes, she was gone.

The tale of the "lonely hearts killers" eventually found its way to the big screen. In 1970, a film was made of the case titled *The Honeymoon Killers*. It was directed by Leonard Kastle, apparently his only film, and met with limited success. The black-and-white production starred Tony LoBianco, who later went on to fame in *The Seven-Ups* (1973). Actress Shirley Stoler played Martha and later received acclaim as the Nazi guard in Lina Wertmuller's disturbing *Seven Beauties* (1976). Stoler bore an amazing resemblance to Martha Beck, which contributed to the film's sense of realism despite its inaccurate storyline. As a movie, *The Honeymoon Killers* was as bizarre as its principal characters. Disjointed, confusing, and lacking a coherent plot, the film was quickly forgotten, though it receives mention in Danny Peary's book *Cult Movies*. Critical opinion was almost universally negative. "It's such a terrible movie," said critic Pauline Kael. "I wouldn't recommend it to anyone."[74]

With all its inadequacies though, *The Honeymoon Killers* helped to ensure Martha Beck and Raymond Fernandez a place in the annals of criminal justice. Another film about the case, starring John Travolta and Salma Hayek and titled *Lonely Hearts*, was released in 2007.

Shortly before she was executed, Martha wrote her last statement for the press. "My story is a love story," she said. "But only those tortured by love can know what I mean. I am not unfeeling, stupid, or moronic. I am a woman who has had a great love and always will."[75] Her body was eventually claimed by her mother and brought back to Florida for burial.

Within a few days of their execution, Martha Beck and Raymond Fernandez were quickly forgotten. The world moved on, too fast, too complex, and much too busy to dwell on a murder whose roots seemed entrenched in the trash-filled pages of pulp fiction and detective magazines. Already, the eyes of America were focused on another criminal case, one that had much more frightening implications than a lovesick, overweight woman who killed for love. Just ten days later, Ethel Rosenberg and her husband Julius were convicted of one of the most notorious betrayals in American history, a crime for which she and her husband would pay for with their lives.

8

A Difficult Concept

The papers today are full of more lies about me. I want a stop put to this
crap—once and for all!
                    —Martha Beck on Death Row, September 22, 1950.

New York has not executed a female since Martha Beck in 1951. Though
Ethel Rosenberg was put to death at Sing Sing in 1953, she was prosecuted
and sentenced under U.S. federal authority and was not a state prisoner. In
line with the experience of other females executed before her, press reports on
Ethel Rosenberg's case were, at times, hysterical, inflammatory, and permeated with the type of bias which was made worse by the pressures of an anxious age. The crimes of which the Rosenbergs were accused, and eventually
convicted, had such far-reaching consequences that it was especially difficult
for the media to report on her case with a sense of balance and fairness. After
America had suffered so much during the war years, it must have been a bitter shock to discover that an American citizen would sell the secrets of the
atomic bomb to the Soviet Union, the one nation in the world that was perceived as a threat. In some ways, the Rosenberg case marked the beginning
of the Cold War, a nail-biting struggle with no physical battlefield, a war of
nerves that was to take place under the ominous threat of a possible nuclear
war. The crimes committed by the Rosenbergs brought a gut-wrenching fear
to the American psyche and, much like the murder of John F. Kennedy on
November 22, 1963, it altered the course of history and affected the lives of
millions of people. When Ethel and Julius Rosenberg were executed in 1953,

there was a sense that they deserved what they got, despite many demonstrations in their support.[1]

While most states have executed women, albeit at a much slower rate than men who were convicted of similar crimes, sixteen states have never executed a female. These states consist primarily of the northwest quadrant of America plus Alaska and Hawaii. Surprisingly, the tradition of not executing women extends back to the pre–Revolutionary War period. In fact, almost 98 percent of the prisoners executed in the history of the United States have been men. And, since 1900, only forty-seven of the nearly eight thousand executions that took place in the United States were of women. Is it then fair to say that some sort of bias exists in the application of capital punishment that favors women in the nation's courts?

Some experts agree with that assessment, while others say the data does not necessarily point to that conclusion. Professor Victor Streib, one of the nation's authorities on the death penalty, generally supports that theory. "On the way to finding sources of sex bias, this research has more clearly revealed the death penalty as a masculine sanctuary," Streib writes. "Typical macho posturing over the death penalty is disrupted and confused when the murderer is a murderess."[2] Streib sees the numerical disparity between death sentences given to men as opposed to women as being so dramatic, there can be no other way to explain it, except by gender bias in the courts. But others still do not agree. There may be fewer women on death row because they commit less crime. "The paucity of women on death row and in the death chamber may be explained by the simple facts that women commit only about one eighth of the nation's murders, that they are much less likely to have established criminal records and that they are quite unlikely to commit felony murders."[3]

However, according to the Supreme Court, statistics alone, no matter how one-sided they may be, are not enough to establish a case for bias or discrimination. In *McClesky v. Kemp* (1987), the plaintiff claimed that a black man was more than four times as likely to receive a death sentence in Georgia as a white man. Though the case addressed racial discrimination, its conclusions could be valid in gender discrimination as well. The court said that it didn't matter what the proportions were; plaintiff had to prove that discrimination was used in his particular case. The court's decision suggests that even when the numerical disparity between male and female executions is demonstrated, that fact alone can not be used as a basis for remedial court action unless it can be shown that the trial court erred in its sentencing strictly because the defendant was a woman. That could be a substantial hurdle for a plaintiff to prove.

Reluctance to send females to the death chamber is apparent in every state in America. Even in the states where women have been subject to execution, the numbers are exceedingly low when compared to men. Texas, despite a long history of executing male offenders, did not execute a female in 130 years, until Karla Faye Tucker in 1998. Curiously, public opinion immediately before Tucker's execution was sharply divided. A poll "conducted in Texas just weeks prior to her execution found that 61% supported the death penalty but only 48% thought Tucker should be executed."[4] That disapproval rating becomes more meaningful when Tucker's vicious crime is taken into account. She murdered two people with an ax and later claimed she enjoyed every moment of the killings. A leader in capital punishment since the Colonial Period, Virginia has not executed a female since 1912. When Oklahoma sent Wanda Jean Allen to her death in 2001, it was the state's first female execution since 1903. There can be no doubt that when a woman faces a death sentence anywhere in the United States, it is an unusual event and, therefore, becomes legitimate news.

But women do not usually receive balanced treatment from the media when accused of murder, especially when their story might take on symbolic meanings that become more important than the offense itself. Ruth Snyder, for reasons explained previously, was the target of much hostility by New York City's print media. The crime of which she was convicted pales in comparison to the symbolic threat she represented to the remnants of Victorian Age society.

Press stories about Snyder took on negative tones almost immediately and grew in intensity as her prosecution moved forward. "She listened to the district attorney's excoriation of her as an unbelievable fiend, a wicked, designing woman, a lustful wanton," said the *Daily News*. "It seemed incredible that such a devil could hide behind that pink mask."[5] Even the normally subdued *Herald-Tribune* joined in the chorus when it portrayed Snyder as a cold, calculating bitch. "She might have been sitting in her home sewing for all the emotion she showed."[6] Media coverage in her case became the benchmark by which all future female-killer stories would be measured.

News reports do not have to show disgust, promote lies, or indulge in exaggerations to be damaging to the defendant. Coverage can be frivolous and demeaning, as it was during the Eva Coo trial in 1935, and be just as damaging. The media was not kind to Eva, though not on the same scale experienced by Snyder, who became a magnet for every sort of contempt and cruelty. Eva was treated more in a condescending fashion, a sort of private joke among some Otsego County officials who may have thought that her conviction could be beneficial for their own reputations. Like Martha Beck in 1949, Coo's prosecution was rife with procedural errors during trial, errors almost totally ignored during appeal.

The local press never fairly analyzed these missteps. Instead, they praised the efficiency of the court. The *Freeman's Journal* said that, "District Attorney

Grant, while he tried the case carefully . . . conducted it in a most dignified manner, maintaining at all times, a calm and serene manner and showing no malice against the defendant at any stage of the procedure." On the other hand, *Journal* reporters withheld criticism when the district attorney referred to the defendant as the "tiger woman," and later, dismissed her claims of a coerced and inaccurate confession. The same publication also chose to ignore the bizarre interrogation on Crumhorn Mountain, orchestrated by Grant and Sheriff Mitchell, an event that would surely generate front page headlines and a monumental scandal if it happened in a different time and place. And it seems clear that Eva's conviction, which was largely based on the uncorroborated statement of an accomplice, would be unacceptable in today's courts since it was never firmly established who actually killed Harry Wright.

The Otsego County press, however, was outspoken when it came to criticism of other newspapers, especially the New York City media. "They took great pleasure in speaking of Mrs. Coo, a poor, degraded woman of somewhat portly build, as "Little Eva," "Blond Eva," etc., not one of which appellations had any real application in fact and so on ad nauseam," said the *Freeman's Journal* in an editorial. "One of the tabloid stories even went so far as to claim that Mrs. Coo's place was something like a night club . . . these are but a few examples of how the tabloids played upon the susceptibilities of their readers, too simple to know how they were being fooled."[7] For some reason, the New York City press corps had difficulties reporting accurately on this case and were unable to keep the facts consistent throughout the trial. "Coo's story was confusing as reported and raises questions about the truth of the information used to send her to the electric chair."[8]

The trial of Martha Beck is another example of how a criminal prosecution can be manipulated by officials who harbor ulterior motives. Beck's case is filled with procedural irregularities and dubious legal maneuvering that contributed to her conviction and ultimately her execution. Her extradition from Michigan back to New York, pursuant to a less than truthful agreement between state authorities, was the first indication of how her prosecution would be carried out. Later, when Beck and Fernandez were assigned legal counsel and agreed to share the same attorney, their right to a fair trial was plainly compromised. No matter what their crimes—and there were many— the defendants were still entitled to constitutional protections and competent representation. How could one attorney represent both when it required him to blame his other client for the murder?

When this issue came under judicial review in 1950, the New York State Court of Appeals blamed the defendants themselves for the error. "We prefer to give the Trial Justice the benefit of the presumption that he did his duty, not only because he is entitled to that presumption but also because . . . as the trial progressed . . . the question was repeatedly brought to the attention of all concerned."[9] Of course, Martha Beck was not in the best position, nor did she have adequate legal experience to correctly assess the dangers of having one attorney represent two defendants, especially when her own life hung in the balance.

The New York City press, led by the powerful tabloids, whose financial success hinged on the element of sensationalism, had a long and less than honorable history of accurately reporting on criminal prosecutions. A review of the newspaper articles used in this book, which describe identical events, show amazing discrepancies in their reports. The same defendants were "morose" in the *Daily News*, "alert" in the *Post*, and "passive" in the *Herald*. They are "inattentive" in the *Times*, "tearful" in the *Sun* and "steady" in the *Times-Union*. Martha Beck was a "200 pound divorcee" in the *Times*, "a simpering paramour" in the *Daily News*, a "pudgy defendant" in the New York *Post* and simply, "the mother of two children" in the *Tribune*. It is remarkable how many different characterizations can be attributed to one person at the same moment.

In defense of reporters, however, they were up against deadlines which sometimes required a copious amount of print by the end of the day. The *New York Times* article on the Martha Place execution on August 7, 1890 was eight full columns, a total of at least fifteen-thousand words. During the Ruth Snyder trial, daily coverage sometimes exceeded that length and at least once, on May 3, 1927, a series of articles on her case was twenty-thousand words in length. Output of this magnitude must place a tremendous amount of pressure on the writing staff of any newspaper. In such cases, conversations with others and assurances from colleagues undoubtedly took the place of eyewitness observations and personal interviews. Ambiguous perceptions had to be made clear, incomplete information had to be coherent, and the story needed to be entertaining as well. In such a pressure cooker, accuracy and truthfulness must have suffered, even if it was unintentional. If the piece didn't turn out as well as planned, there was no time to fix it. And if a reporter allowed his or her personal feelings or resentments into the work, editors must have been reluctant to cut it, especially if they tended to agree with those viewpoints.

The Mary Frances Creighton case shows how the press can focus on a certain aspect of a story and then cling to that viewpoint throughout its follow-up reporting. Once the details of her criminal history were leaked by the police and the district attorney's office, Creighton never again experienced any sort of fair reporting by the media. Among all the newspaper stories that were written about her, there was not a single article that could be characterized as balanced or favorable. Some of the tabloids decided that her nickname should be "Borgia," a reference to the devious fifteenth century Italian Renaissance family who would do anything—including murder—to achieve political power. The headline on the day Creighton was convicted, which took up the entire first page of the *Daily News,* was "BORGIA TO DIE!" Every reader knew who the *Daily News* was talking about; there was no need to use the name of Mary Creighton.

In truth, it could have been far worse. When it comes to degrading women in circumstances such as these, some of the media know no bounds. It is axiomatic that the role of the press is not to convey a defendant's guilt—or even innocence—to its readers, but rather, to report on the news as accurately and truthfully as possible. Opinions are for editorials. Not that Mary Creighton deserved friendly press; because by the time she poisoned Ada Appelgate, Creighton may have already murdered four people, including her own nineteen-year-old brother. In reading the substantial case file, there is little doubt that Creighton was a deeply disturbed woman who had no mercy or compassion for her victims. However, that is not what is at issue.

To complicate matters even further, the blatant negativity in press reports was limited not only to media representations; it was prevalent in the political arena as well. Not only were women not permitted to vote until 1920, they were prohibited from serving on juries as well. It was a practice that had its origins in colonial times when contemporary mores dictated similar injustices, ones which would require generations to correct. America was never perfect. Even from the beginning, many compromises had to be made on the altar of progress. In time, many of those injustices were rectified, but it required Herculean efforts from dedicated people who worked long and hard to correct those inequities. When the Nineteenth Amendment gave women the right to vote, things began to change, though some authorities remained obstinate about women serving on jury panels. "To put women on juries meant that men had to rethink, to a degree, their notions of the nature and role of women . . . some men were fearful of disruption in the home."[10] Change moves slow in a democracy; it's the nature of the system. And the issue of women's equality was no exception.

So when Snyder, Antonio, Coo, and Creighton were convicted, no women sat on those juries. That exclusion immediately raises the question of fairness, since studies have shown that jury panels are more sympathetic to others with whom they can identify. In the Snyder case, men had a psychological stake in a guilty verdict and were less likely to give her any benefit of the doubt. Women, on the other hand, might have at least tempered some of that bias, though it is doubtful if Ruth Snyder could have been exonerated, or even deserved to escape punishment. But female presence on the Antonio and Coo jury panels could have affected those trials where testimony was ambiguous and the evidence was less convincing. In the Helen Fowler case, five women did serve on the jury, but no blacks. That is not to say that racial discrimination played a role in that decision, but an all-white jury surely could not have helped the defense.

It is a sad fact that, historically, blacks have received less than perfect treatment in the nation's courtrooms, especially in southern states. Research gathered from across the country in capital punishment cases, "shows that blacks are over-punished as defendants or undervalued as victims, or both."[11] And in the Fowler case, where pivotal issues of involvement and culpability could determine life or death of the defendant, it would have been best to avoid even the appearance of impropriety by the court.

Of course, it may be impossible to determine exactly which factors influence the perceptions of jurors in the courtroom and during deliberations. All people are different, and a jury's decision is ostensibly based on the testimony and evidence presented during trial. But even before the jury is selected for the panel, they carry with them a sort of psychological Pandora's Box, an unknown reservoir of personal beliefs, prejudices, and knowledge accumulated during ordinary life experiences. If a prospective juror is exposed to a continuous stream of negative media reports concerning the defendant, does it affect judgment during deliberations? Research indicates that jurors will frequently act independently, though usually make special efforts to be fair. If the evidence is clear and conclusive, a jury will most often act accordingly. But if the evidence is not convincing and eyewitness testimony is not firm, their personal bias creeps in. In such cases, jurors are much more likely to interpret the proceedings in line with their own beliefs and biases. A strong case, one with solid evidence and convincing testimony, better serves both prosecution and defense. The quality of the evidence seems to be more important than any other single trial factor and weighs more heavily on a jury's decision than personal prejudices.[12]

When the press decides early on that a defendant is guilty, it may have an irreversible effect on the trial. "When jurors are exposed to damaging pretrial publicity . . . in simulated trials, the judge's orders were sometimes followed, but often, especially when the judge's admonition came after an impression was made, they were not."[13] This may be bad news for the defense, especially in today's world where there is no real way to avoid pretrial publicity in high profile cases such as Scott Peterson or O. J. Simpson. Twenty-four-hour a day news cycles, all-news satellite TV channels, and the as yet uncharted universe of Internet blogs must have some effect on public opinion and, undoubtedly, touch upon the jury pool. To say that it does not have any effect is to deny reality; for the media's persuasive powers have been well documented. Why else would corporate America spend billions each year to advertise their products on the nation's television broadcasts?

Even during the earliest part of the twentieth century, there was concern over the media's intrusion in the criminal justice process. Dr. Amos Squire once wrote, "as I see it, newspapers that persist in the exploitation of crime news solely for profit, with little or no honest regard for civic welfare, are contributing to the increase of crime in three ways: by stimulating anti-social conduct in indiscriminating readers, by handicapping the forces of order through the premature and unwise publication of evidence, and by creating prejudicial opinions that make the impartial administration of justice difficult and often impossible."[14] Thanks to the media saturation of the Information Age, that statement may be even more valid today than when it was made in 1935.

Even the defendants themselves recognized the harmful effects of negative publicity. In 1951, while awaiting execution, Martha Beck was permitted to read about her case in the New York press. After one particularly critical newspaper story appeared, she wrote a letter to her sister in which she railed against the press. "Today's *Mirror* quotes his lawyer as saying Fernandez witnessed me and the guard's personal relationship! What evil lurks in the heart of men?" And later, after the negative press reports continued, she wrote, "but that doesn't say my heart isn't breaking from the insults and humiliation of being talked about as I am. O yes, I wear a cloak of laughter."[15]

There was one common theme that ran throughout the newspaper coverage of each of these death penalty cases: the belief in the concept of deterrence. The press, much like the police, the courts, judges, and the penal system, were convinced that crime prevention was related to a swift and efficient punishment. As far back as 1912, the *Times* touted the achievement of the courts when four death-penalty murder trials, from jury selection to verdict, were completed in less than thirty hours of court time. "It is believed that Westchester has established a new record for the quick disposal of murder trials in this state."[16]

In 1988, one of the most important studies on the deterrent value of capital punishment was completed in Texas. Researchers compared executions in that state since 1930 with homicide rates and found no correlation whatsoever. The study was significant because, during that fifty-eight-year period, Texas had executed over three hundred prisoners making its conclusions especially valid. Later research produced similar results. In one study in 1993, nearly 300 pairs of counties across America were analyzed and sorted by murder rates and whether they were located in a state that had a death penalty statute. The conclusion was that capital punishment had no visible effect on violent crimes.[17] But misgivings concerning the value of the deterrence factor are nothing new. Even those who were involved in the execution process and witnessed executions up close, had serious doubts concerning its effectiveness as a deterrent. As far back as 1923, prison physician and author Dr. Amos Squire wrote, "We cannot help but feel that capital punishment has not been the deterrent factor that its advocates hoped it would be."[18]

However, there is valid research which indicates a death penalty, despite its flaws, helps to save innocent life. In one of the most frequently quoted studies on the subject, criminologist Isaac Ehrlich examined murder and execution data from across the nation. He found that just the possibility of a death sentence was enough to deter some killings. "As a result of his analysis, Ehrlich concluded that each individual execution per year in the United States would save seven or eight people from being victims of murder."[19] Still, other experts say criminal behavior has many causal factors and is not so easily deterred by a faint abstract such as a death penalty whose implementation may be decades away. When Oklahoma executed Lois Nadean Smith in 2001, she had been on death row for over nineteen years.[20] And there are many female inmates on various death rows today who have waited more than ten years for the outcome of their appeals.

Having women in the execution chamber is a difficult concept for America, and always has been. Since Colonial ties, the nation's courts have displayed a spirited resistance to such a possibility. Statistics confirm that, for whatever reason, females are seldom convicted of murder, rarely sentenced to death, and almost never put to death. With that in mind, it may be more easily understood why almost every female execution is newsworthy, becomes subject to individual interpretations by the press, and if the circumstances are right, evolves into a media circus. When the notorious photograph of Ruth Snyder in the electric chair appeared in the *Daily News* on January 14, 1928, the image rocked the publishing world. Condemnation was received from every corner of society, including other newspaper editors, some of whom may have been suffering from professional jealousy. But was the outrage against the Snyder execution photograph the end result of all the male-inspired anger toward women, all the demeaning press reports, and all the pontifications of the press who worked overtime to achieve that end?

In many ways, the media has not changed much since then. The technology of print media, of course, is vastly improved, far beyond anything that could have been imagined during the Jazz Age. But the principles of journalism, what makes a story, what doesn't make a story, and the public's fascination with the drama of a murder trial, have remained the same. Carolyn Warmus, arrested for the murder of her lover's wife in 1990, experienced similar antagonisms from the New York tabloids. Her case was almost always referred to as "the Fatal Attraction Murder." And Pamela Smart, convicted in the killing of her husband in New Hampshire in 1992, was the target of virulent press coverage that was eerily reminiscent of Snyder's case.

Interestingly, most reporting seemed to follow a repetitive pattern, a format that remained consistent regardless which newspaper reported the story. It did not seem to matter if it was the traditional *Herald-Tribune*, the pensive *New York Times*, the tabloid king *Daily News,* or the sedate *New York Sun*. In order to convince society—and perhaps themselves—that the defendants deserved to die, reporters first called into question the value of the accused as a mother. As pointed out earlier, Martha Beck's abandonment of her children in New York City in 1949 was perceived as an unforgivable offense, one for which she was not entitled to mercy.

Second, if the defendant was married, as were five of the six executed at Sing Sing, she was held up to ridicule as a wife. A frequently repeated theme was "she betrayed her husband." Just as popular was, "she deserted her marriage bed." And finally, her reputation as a woman was attacked using quotes, often anonymous, from police, the district attorney, or other officials who had an interest in her conviction. The most common themes in this category were, "she is a cold and calculating vampire" or "she was always a slut." Once it was revealed what kind of woman was being accused, then society could be confident that the defendant was not only guilty of the crimes but worthless as a woman as well and, therefore, deserving of the death penalty. It only remained for reporters to cover the execution ritual, coupled with the inevitable, last-minute quote from the condemned while they trembled in the shadow of the electric chair. That scenario was always the final act in the media-created drama which most of the press strived to attain.

Without question, it is very difficult to examine a criminal case decades later and conclude that a defendant was deprived of a fair trial, wrongly convicted, or, in those rarest of cases, innocent of the charges. In some instances, transcripts are unavailable and official records are either incomplete or lost. In those cases, it is nearly impossible to second guess a jury who reviewed the evidence and listened to all the testimony during the original trial. However, three of the female defendants (Antonio, Coo, and Fowler) never admitted to their crimes. Antonio, until the time of her execution, denied having a hand in the murder of her husband. In Coo's case, there were always doubts which defendant killed Harry Wright. And, in Helen Fowler's case in 1944, she denied killing the victim, though she admitted to helping move the body. Surely, her situation was not improved by her reputation in the community and there may be lingering suspicions that racial prejudice may have played a role in her conviction. During Fowler's trial, her attorney told the court that, "on information and belief, there is only one colored person on the jury list of the county of Niagara," and the local press stories, "have tended to inflame and incite the people of the County against the defendants."[21] In his book on how newspapers cover female executions in America, Marlin Shipman concludes, "News coverage of women condemned to death has been mixed. For the most part, the press did not do an especially admirable job of protecting defendant's rights . . . press reports seemed more likely to produce unfairness than to guard against it."[22]

A review of the hundreds of newspaper articles utilized in this book shows an amazing tendency of the press to report negatively on all the women who were convicted of murder. Sometimes, this perceptible slant appeared on the very first day of coverage. The amount and intensity of that criticism varied with the defendant and the newspaper. Each defendant had a certain aspect of her case to which the media responded, often with a barely-hidden vehemence. For Ruth Snyder, it was betrayal. For Eva Coo, it was her reputation as a madam; for Mary Creighton, her criminal past; and for Helen Fowler, her lifestyle. For Martha Beck, it was her abdication as a mother and her physical appearance that stimulated media animosity. This systemic negative reporting becomes more compelling when you consider that twenty-four years passed between the Snyder and the Beck cases. That substantial time frame indicates more than just occasional institutional bias. It may be cultural as well, ingrained in the subconscious strata of a male-dominated media that cannot allow itself the possibility of female execution unless it is proven that the condemned are worthless beyond any doubt and have lost the protective shield of femininity they claim as a birthright.

Today, according to the best available statistics, there are fifty-four women on the nation's death rows awaiting execution.

Notes

PREFACE

1. Lewis E. Lawes, *20,000 Years in Sing Sing* (New York: Ray Long and Richard Smith, 1932).

2. Lewis E. Lawes, *Life and Death in Sing Sing* (New York: Garden City Publishing, 1928), 140.

3. Amos O Squire, MD, *Sing Sing Doctor, Formerly Chief Physician of Sing Sing Prison, Now Medical Examiner of Westchester County.* (New York: Doubleday, Doran & Company, Inc., 1935).

4. Squire, *Sing Sing Doctor*, 279.

5. Robert G. Elliott, *Agent of Death, The Memoirs of an Executioner* (New York: E. P. Dutton, 1940).

6. Elliott, *Agent of Death*, 299.

CHAPTER 1

1. As quoted on page 1 in Victor L. Streib, Gendering the Death Penalty: Countering Sex Bias in a Masculine Sanctuary. http//www.moritzlaw.osu.edu/lawjournal/streib.htm.

2. Patricia Pearson, *When She Was Bad, How and Why Women Get Away with Murder* (New York: Penguin Group, 1998), 153.

3. See Kelleher and Kelleher, *Murder Most Rare: The Female Serial Killer* (New York: Dell Publishing, 1998), xi, concerning female serial killers and the reasons why they are not recognized in the same way as males.

4. Helen Benedict. *Virgin or Vamp* (New York: Oxford, 1992), 23.

CHAPTER 2

1. Shipman, 133.

2. John Kobler, *The Trial of Ruth Snyder and Judd Gray* (New York: Doubleday, Doran & Company, 1938), 7.

3. Kobler, *The Trial of Ruth Snyder and Judd Gray,* p.127.

4. Leslie Margolin, *Murderess!* (New York: Pinnacle Books, Kensington Publishing Corp., 1999), 26.

5. *Crime and Punishment: The Illustrated Crime Encyclopedia* (Westport, CT: H. S. Stuttman, 1994), 2837.

6. Margolin, 27.

7. Gordon, 267.

8. Katz, 1409.

9. That quality of radio was later investigated by media analyst Marshall McLuhan in his landmark study, *Understanding Media* (1997). "Radio affects most people intimately, person to person, offering a world of unspoken communication between writer-speaker and the listener. That is the immediate aspect of radio. A private experience." (299) McLuhan likens radio to the beating of the primordial tribal drum, a sort of calling for the masses to participate in a collective experience initiated by a private message.

10. On September 22, 1927, at Soldier's Field in Chicago, a championship boxing match between Jack Dempsey and Gene Tunney was held. Billed as "The Battle of the Ages," it was a rematch of a fight that took place the year before, which Tunney had won by a knockout. The match generated so much interest that it was broadcast live nationwide over the radio. An astounding 50 million people listened in that night, making it the most widely "attended" sporting event in human history up to that time.

11. Goldman played a pivotal, yet unwanted, role in the assassination of President William McKinley in 1901. McKinley's assassin, Leon Czolgosz, was a deeply disturbed, yet dedicated anarchist who saw McKinley as an oppressor of the common people and used Goldman's words to justify his crime.

12. Diana Proper, *The Incomprehensible Crime of Leopold and Loeb: "Just an Experiment." Famous American Crimes and Trials*; Volume 3: 1913–1959 (Westport, CT: Praeger, 2004), 83.

13. Beautiful, tempestuous, and difficult to control, Pola Negri's origin is unclear. She may have been the daughter of a Polish gypsy or the unwanted child of a noble family; her birth record is vague. She was already a European star of the stage by the time she arrived in the United States in 1923. Once engaged to Charlie Chaplin, her off-screen romances and exploits kept the public entertained for many years. Negri's ongoing dispute with screen legend Gloria Swanson was well known by movie fans and her stormy love affair with Rudolph Valentino quickly became front page news. During the 1930s, Negri sued a movie magazine for reporting that she was the lover of Adolf Hitler. She won the case. Pola Negri died of pneumonia in 1987 at the age of 92.

14. Jessie Ramey, "The Bloody Blonde and the Marble Woman: Gender and Power in the Case of Ruth Snyder," *Journal of Social History* (Spring 2004), 5.

15. Ann Jones, *Women Who Kill* (Boston: Beacon Press, 1996), 256.

16. Bill Sloan, *I Watched a Wild Hog Eat My Baby! A Colorful History of the Tabloids and Their Cultural Impact* (Amherst, NY: Prometheus Books, 2001), 26.

17. Jack O'Brian, "Mrs. Snyder and Gray Confess," *Daily News,* March 24, 1927, 2.

18. *New York Times*, May 3, 1927, 20.

19. Kobler, 13.

20. Kobler, 14.

21. Kobler, 120.

22. Margolin, 28.

23. Lawrence M. Friedman, *Crime and Punishment in American History* (New York: BasicBooks, Perseus Books, 1993), 399.

24. For a brief interpretation of the Snyder-Gray case, see *The Iron Widow* in *Women Who Kill* (2002), edited by Richard Glyn Jones. Though factually correct, the article captures the stereotypical view of Judd Gray being the helpless puppet in the hands of the clever and manipulative Ruth Snyder. She was the "debonair pleasure-seeker, the iron woman who had played so determined a part in her husband's murder, the blue-eyed blonde who had been so frigidly composed in court." A review of trial testimony and other documents of the case, however, show a gentler, immature, even naive Ruth who felt abused, trapped, and neglected at the hands of an older and more refined Albert Snyder.

25. Kobler, 121.

26. Brown, *They Died in the Chair*, 30.

27. *New York Times*, April 27, 1927, 16.

28. Kobler, 285.

29. Kobler, 128.

30. Margolin, 56.

31. *New York Times*, May 6, 1927, 3.

32. *New York Times*, March 22, 1927, 2.

33. *New York Times*, May 6, 1927, 3.

34. *Crime and Punishment*, 2840.

35. *New York Times*, March 21, 1927, 3.

36. Kluger, 211.

37. *New York Times*, March 22, 1927, 3.

38. Kobler, 46.

39. *Crime and Punishment*, 2840.

40. March 22, 1927.

41. Robinson, 3.

42. *Times,* March 24, 1927, 1.

43. *Daily News*, March 22, 1927, 2.

44. March 24, 1927, 3.

45. *Ibid.*

46. *Daily News*, March 24, 1927, 3.

47. *Ibid.*

48. *New York Times*, March 24, 1927, 1.

49. *Daily News*, March 24, 1927, 2.

50. As quoted in Margolin, 79.

51. Peggy Hopkins-Joyce, *Daily Mirror*, quoted in Kobler, 55.

52. Kuhn, 3.

53. Ramey, 635.

54. This fictitious scene of the murderous couple who made love while the body of Albert Snyder lay in the bed a few feet away eventually made its way into literary fiction. Novelist James M. Cain, whose book *The Postman Always Rings Twice* is said to be modeled after the Snyder-Gray case, included a passage which resembles this scenario.

55. A. Jones, 255.

56. *New York Times,* March 24, 1927, 6.

57. *Ibid.*, 2.

58. *Ibid.*

59. *Ibid.*

60. Ramey, 634.

61. *Daily News*, March 23, 1927, 3.

62. April 26, 1927, 2.

63. *Ibid.*

64. Kobler, 118.

65. *Daily News*, April 27, 1927, 3.

66. *New York Times*, April 30, 1927, 1.

67. *Daily News*, April 30, 1927, 3.

68. *Daily News*, May 3, 1927, 4.

69. *New York Times*, May 3, 1927, 20.

70. *New York Times*, May 3, 1927, 21.

71. *Herald Tribune*, May 5, 1927, 1.

72. *Daily News*, May 4, 1927, 3.

73. *Herald Tribune*, May 6, 1927, 1.

74. As quoted in Margolin, 234–235.

75. As quoted in Kobler, 302.

76. *New York Times*, May 10, 1927, 1.

77. These three quotes are from the mentioned newspapers on May 10, 1927.

78. *Daily News*, May 10, 1927, 3.

79. Farmer was executed at upstate Auburn prison in 1909. All executions after 1916 were scheduled at Sing Sing.

80. His name was George Smith and the accident happened on the night of August 7, 1881, at the Brush Electric Light Company in Buffalo, New York. Smith died when he touched a generator and grounded himself on a metal railing. He may have been the first human being in history to be accidentally electrocuted.

81. The Chicago World's Fair of 1893, also known as The Columbian Exposition, was in many ways, the showcase for inventor Nikola Tesla, a Croatian genius

whose creations and discoveries were legendary even during his own time. Tesla was a direct competitor to Thomas Edison whom he disliked intensely after Edison cheated him and tried to discourage his rival from further research. Tesla was a true visionary, a man of almost supernatural talent. He had several university degrees and spoke five languages, exactly the kind of man Edison detested. Because Edison had no formal schooling and achieved what he did through hard work, he resented those who were different than he. Even though Edison recognized Tesla's genius, he remained envious and suspicious of Tesla for the rest of his life.

82. On December 5, 1888, in a bizarre demonstration attended by scientists and doctors, his representatives succeeded in electrocuting two calves and a horse that weighed over twelve hundred pounds. Photographs of this event still exist and can easily be found on the Internet using any of the major search engines.

83. Metzger, 112.

84. Squire, 202.

85. Drimmer, 51.

86. Within one hour of the scheduled executions of two men, Hulbert collapsed in the death chamber and was unable to continue. When prison physician Dr. Amos Squire responded, he found Hulbert almost catatonic. "I found him stretched out on one of the spectator's benches, colorless and his pulse scarcely perceptible," Squire later wrote. "I thought I might have to throw the switch myself. But after working over him and giving him stimulants, I brought him around, so he could go on with the executions" (Squire, 203). Dr. Squire's efforts proved to be only temporary. Hulbert became increasingly despondent as the years went by. His wife died suddenly in 1928 which added to the psychological pressure he must have experienced. In 1929, he was found dead in the basement of his Auburn home, apparently from self-inflicted gunshot wounds.

87. *Daily News*, January 13, 1927, 2.

88. Elliott, 34.

89. Elliott, 33.

90. Elliott, 104.

91. Elliot, Robert G., unpublished prison diary, 1926–1939, 1.

92. Lawes, 312.

93. Blumenthal, 161.

94. As quoted in Sloan, 27.

95. Elliott, 269–270.

96. Lawes, *Twenty-Thousand*, 311.

97. *Sun*, January 13, 1928, 1.

98. Dolan, 2.

99. January 13, 1927, 1.

100. *Sun*, January 13, 1928, 16.

101. *Sun*, January 13, 1928, 1.

102. *Citizen Register*, January 13, 1928, 1.

103. *Sun*, January 13, 1928, 16.

104. Elliott, 187–188.

105. Lewis E. Lawes was the most famous penal reformer of his time. He rose through the ranks of the correctional system. In 1920, he became the warden of Sing Sing, the most notorious prison in America. Though he spent his life in corrections, he was strongly opposed to capital punishment and lectured on that topic for many years. He also became a favorite of movie producers and wrote several books which later became successful films, including *20,000 Years at Sing Sing* (1933) starring Spencer Tracy. For a time, he was a favorite of the Hollywood crowd, acted as a consultant on prison films, and appeared at movie premieres.

106. Kilgallen, 1.

107. *Ibid.*

108. Elliott, 189.

109. Kilgallen, 36.

110. Elliott, 190.

111. *Ibid.*

112. *Sun*, January 14, 1928, 1.

113. Elliott, 221–222.

114. *New York Times*, February 1, 1928, 5.

115. Brown, 45.

116. *New York Times*, January 14, 1928, 8.

117. *Sun*, January 14, 1928, 1.

118. *New York Times,* February 22, 1928, 19.

119. This photograph, which appeared in the January 14, 1928 edition of the *News,* can be found on the Internet with little effort. However, in recent years, the *Daily News* tightly controls the use of the photo and it is illegal to reproduce it without permission and a fee. The photo can also be found in many textbooks, especially those published prior to 1960. The controversial image is on the front cover of Wenzell Brown's *They Died in the Chair* (1958) and Leslie Margolin's *Murderess!* (1999).

120. Sloan, 25.

121. A. Jones, 259.

122. As quoted in Jones, 265.

123. In *American Cinema/American Culture*, John Belton writes, "*film noir* deals with a uniquely American experience of wartime and postwar despair and alienation as a disorientated America readjusts to a new social and political reality." Snyder-Gray did not generate the birth of the *film noir* style, nor was it even indigenous to the same era. *Film noir* emerged out from the darkness of the Second World War and fears of the post-war era, when many sociological changes were taking place in a land wracked with grief and disillusionment. *Film noir* was decades in the making. Its roots were firmly embedded in the Great Depression, when all the basic tenets of American life were jeopardized amid a frightening economic landscape. And all of it—the shattered dreams, the erosion of the American ideal, and a generation raised under a cloud of deprivation—was something that seemed beyond the control of the ordinary man. That theme of helplessness, a core ingredient in *film noir*, was very much a reality of American life in the 1930s.

124. Leitch, 126–127.

125. Polito, 19.
126. Cain, 41.

CHAPTER 3

1. Robert G. Elliott, *Angel of Death, The Memoirs of an Executioner* (New York: E. P. Dutton, 1940), 214.

2. *Albany Evening News*, March 27, 1933, 4.

3. *Poughkeepsie Eagle News*, August 9, 1934, 5.

4. Brown, *They Died in the Chair*, 49

5. Brown, *They Died in the Chair*, 50.

6. *Ibid.*

7. *New York Times*, December 18, 1931, 1.

8. *New York Times*, December 19, 1931, 1.

9. *Albany Evening News*, March 27, 1933, 4.

10. *Albany Evening News,* March 29, 1933, 2.

11. *Ibid.*

12. *Times-Union*, April 11, 1933, 15.

13. *Times-Union*, April 12, 1933, 1.

14. *Albany Evening News,* April 13, 1933, 2.

15. *Albany Evening News*, April 13, 1933, 1.

16. *Albany Evening News*, April 16, 1933, 1

17. *Times-Union*, April 16, 1933, 1.

18. *Ibid.*

19. Squire, *Sing Sing Doctor*, 226–227.

20. *Times-Union,* June 8, 1934, 1.

21. *Daily Star*, June 21, 1934, 1.

22. *Ibid.*

23. *Times-Union*, June 26, 1934, 3.

24. *Times-Union*, June 26, 1934, 3.

25. *Ibid.*

26. Lawes, *Life and Death*, 168.

27. Lawes, *Twenty-Thousand*, 324.

28. *Times-Union*, June 26, 1934, 3.

29. *Times-Union*, June 28, 1934, 1.

30. *New York Times*, June 29, 1934, 3.

31. *New York Times*, June 30, 1934, 1.

32. *New York Times*, June 30, 1934, 3.

33. *Ibid.*

34. *Ibid.*

35. *Times-Union*, June 29, 1934, 1.

36. *Ibid.*

37. *Daily News*, July 3, 1934, 3.

38. *Times-Union*, June 29, 1934, 3.

39. *New York Times*, June 30, 1934, 1.

40. *New York Post*, July 5, 1934, 1.

41. Elliott, 138.

42. *Times-Union*, June 30, 1934, 3.

43. Herbert H. Lehman, *Public Papers of Governor Herbert H. Lehman* (1942), 671.

44. *Albany Times-Union,* June 30, 1934, 1.

45. *New York Times*, July 1, 1934, 6.

46. *New York Times*, July 2, 1934, 40.

47. Squire, *Sing Sing Doctor*, 201.

48. *Times-Union*, July 5, 1934, 1.

49. *Post*, July 5, 1934, 1.

50. *Post*, July 9, 1934, 6.

51. *Daily News*, July 9, 1934, 4.

52. *Ibid.*

53. *Daily News*, July 11, 1934, 3.

54. Lehman, 672.

55. *Times-Union*, July 7, 1934, 6.

56. Lehman, 673.

57. Elliot, unpublished diary, 253.

58. Lehman, 673–674.

59. August 8, 1934, 5.

60. *Herald Tribune*, July 9, 1934, 1.

61. *New York Times*, August 9, 1934, 1.

62. *Post*, August 8, 1934, 2.

63. *Citizen Register*, August 9, 1934, 1.

64. *Ibid.*

65. Squire, 244.

66. August 9, 1935, 4.

67. *Daily News*, August 10, 1934, 4.

68. *Post*, August 8, 1934, 2.

69. *Daily News*, August 10, 1934, 4.

70. *Post*, August 8, 1934, 2.

71. *Post*, August 10, 1934, 1.

72. *Citizen Register*, August 9, 1934, 1.

73. Elliott, unpublished diary, 214.

74. *Herald Tribune*, August 10, 1934, 1.

75. Blumenthal, Ralph, *Miracle at Sing Sing: How One Man Transformed the Lives of America's Most Dangerous Prisoners* (New York: St. Martin's Press, 2004), 219.

76. *Albany Evening News*, August 9, 1934, 4.

77. Elliott, unpublished diary, 216.

78. Elliott, unpublished diary, 144.

79. Squire, *Sing Sing Doctor*, 248–249.

80. *Herald Tribune*, August 10, 1934, 1.

81. *Poughkeepsie Eagle News*, August 10, 1934, 1.

82. *Post,* August 10, 1934, 1.

83. *Albany Evening News*, August 9, 1934, 4.

84. *Troy Record*, August 10, 1934, 5.

85. *New York Times*, August 10, 1934, 1.

86. *Citizen Register*, August 10, 1934, 1.

87. *Daily News*, August 10, 1934, 1.

88. *New York Times*, August 10, 1934, 11.

89. *Post*, August 11, 1934, 3.

90. *Poughkeepsie Eagle News*, August 10, 1934, 1.

91. *Troy Record*, August 10, 1934, 1.

92. *New York Times*, August 10, 1934, 11.

93. *Daily News*, August 11, 1934, 5.

94. *New York Times*, August 11, 1934, 16.

95. *Post*, August 10, 1934, 16.

96. *Post*, August 10, 1934, 1.

97. *Poughkeepsie Eagle News*, August 10, 1944, 1.

98. *Ibid.*

99. *Citizen Register*, August 11, 1934, 4.

100. *Albany Evening News*, August 11, 1934, 10.

CHAPTER 4

1. Richard Kluger, *The Paper: The Life and Death of the New York Herald Tribune* (New York: Alfred A. Knopf, 1986), 211.

2. Isidore Zimmerman and Francis Bond, *Punishment without Crime* (New York: Clarkson N. Potter, 1964), 128.

3. As author Jonathan Mumby points out in his book on crime films, *Public Enemies, Public Heroes*, the stars of these films had a great deal to do with their acceptance and success. The lead roles in *Little Caesar*, *Public Enemy*, and *Scarface* were played by Edward G. Robinson, James Cagney, and Paul Muni. All were, in real life, products of Manhattan's lower East Side, then acknowledged as America's fertile training ground for the traditional urban criminal.

4. Mumby, 84.

5. Jack Shadoian, *Dreams and Dead Ends: The American Gangster Film* (New York: Oxford University Press, 2003), 62.

6. Dorothy Kilgallen, *Murder One* (New York: Random House, 1967), 115.

7. Wenzell Brown, *They Died in the Chair* (Toronto: Popular Library, 1958), 65.

8. *Freeman's Journal* (Cooperstown, NY: June 27, 1934), 9.

9. Niles Eggleston, *Eva Coo, Murderess* (Utica, NY: North County Books, 1997), 45.

10. *Daily Star* (Oneonta, NY), June 20, 1934, 2.

11. Eggleston, 52.

12. *Daily Star*, June 18, 1934, 2.

13. *Albany Times Union*, June 22, 1934, 2.

14. Eva Coo, Statement of June 18, 1934, Oneonta Police Department. (From New York Historical Association, Cooperstown, NY), 2.

15. *Albany Times Union*, June 20, 1934, 3.

16. *Daily Star*, June 21, 1934, 12.

17. *Freeman's Journal*, June 27, 1934, 8.

18. *Daily Star*, June 23, 1934, 3.

19. *Daily Star*, June 21, 1934, 1.

20. *Daily Star,* June 22, 1934, 3.

21. *Daily Star*, June 25, 1934, 3.

22. Niles Eggleston, in his book on the case, *Eva Coo, Murderess*, writes as follows of this event: "Both Coo and Clift withstood this ghastly ordeal for four hours. During the trial, the State called this event a re-enactment of the crime, Byard (defense attorney) more accurately referred to it as "one of the most ghoulish third degrees in the history of any land" and asked, unsuccessfully of course, for the district attorney's arrest" (58).

23. *Times Union*, June 22, 1934, 2.

24. *Daily Star*, June 25, 1934, 3.

25. *Times Union*, Women Ran Over Man in Death Plot, June 24, 1936, 13.

26. *Times Union*, June 24, 1934, 3.

27. *Daily Star*, June 25, 1934, 3.

28. *Freeman's Journal*, June 22, 1934, 1.

29. *Daily Star*, June 26, 1934, 3.

30. *Times Union*, June 28, 1934, 1.

31. *Freeman's Journal*, July 4, 1934, 1.

32. *Times Union*, June 22, 1934, 1.

33. D. Kilgallen, 115.

34. *New York Times*, August 11, 1934, 25.

35. Eggleston, 64.

36. Brown, *They Died in the Chair*, 71.

37. *Daily News* (New York), August 15, 1934, 5.

38. *New York Times*, August 16, 1934, 5.

39. *Daily News*, August 16, 1934, 3.

40. This quote was from the *Freeman's Journal*, September 19, 1934, 12, but "sob sister journalism" is a term that was derived from a real criminal case that occurred in New York City in 1895. Italian immigrant Maria Barbieri murdered her boyfriend after he insulted her in front of friends. Though she was convicted of the killing, an avalanche of sympathy and support from the public and the press succeeded in forcing a new trial for Barbieri. After a tumultuous second trial in Manhattan's criminal court, attended by thousands, she was found not guilty. The press stories about her poor upbringing and abuse she suffered became known as "sob stories."

41. *Daily News*, August 14, 3–4.

42. *Ibid.*

43. *Freeman's Journal*, August 22, 1934, 1.

44. Nicknames for killers, assigned by the press, were nothing new. It was common practice for the media to "tag," or label, murderers during coverage of their crimes. Ruth Snyder was given many titles, including, "Granite Woman," and "Ice Maiden." Anna Antonio was most often called "Little Anna." But the difference between titles for male killers and female suspects is in their content. Male killers are often given names such as "The Night Stalker" (Richard Ramirez), "The Boston Strangler" (Albert DeSalvo), "The Red Light Bandit" (Caryl Chessman), or "The .44-Caliber Killer" (Berkowitz), which emphasize their crimes or instill fear in readers. Females are more likely to be given names that minimize or mock their crimes. In most cases, their nicknames will reflect their sex or have sexual undertones such as "Sugar Woman" (Helen Fowler), "Blonde Tiger" (Irene Schroeder), and the frequently used moniker, "Femme Fatale" (Betty Lou Beets, Ruth Snyder, Carolyn Warmus).

45. *Freeman's Journal*, August 15, 1934, 1.

46. *New York Times*, August 17, 1934, 2.

47. *Daily Star*, August 17, 1934, 2.

48. *Daily News*, August 21, 1934, 4.

49. *Ibid.*

50. *Daily News*, August 22, 1934, 10.

51. *Daily News*, August 22, 1934, 2.

52. As quoted in Eggleston, 81.

53. *Daily Mirror* (New York), August 19, 1934, 3.

54. *Daily Star*, August 21, 1934, 2.

55. *Daily Star*, August 22, 1934, 3.

56. *Freeman's Journal*, August 22, 1934, 1.

57. *Daily News*, August 23, 1934, 9.

58. *New York Times*, August 23, 1934, 36.

59. *Freeman's Journal*, August 29, 1934, 2.

60. *Daily Star*, August 24, 1934, 3.

61. *Ibid.*

62. *New York Times*, August 25, 1934, 3.

63. *Freeman's Journal*, August 29, 1934, 2.

64. *Daily News*, August 24, 1934, 4.

65. Kilgallen, Dorothy, 136.

66. *Daily Star*, August 27, 1934, 2.

67. *Daily Star*, August 28, 1934, 2.

68. *Daily Star*, August 29, 1934, 6.

69. *Daily News*, September 4, 1934, 4.

70. *Ibid.*

71. The rules for search warrant application were in effect even in 1934. Why the judge did not exclude the evidence is unclear. Rulings by Judge Heath during the trial clearly favored the prosecution and may be a reflection of the prevailing attitude toward criminal defendants during this era. His decision on the admissibility of the Crumhorn Mountain confession is difficult to reconcile. Even though police testified to bringing Wright's body to the scene and removing it from the coffin at the request

of Sheriff Mitchell, and although there was supporting testimony to that effect, the judge chose to accept it at face value. Curiously, during his charge to the jury on the admissibility of Coo's second confession, he told the jury that the only test of a valid confession was that "it was given voluntarily without the use of threats, duress, or fear." This was an obvious contradiction of his earlier ruling.

72. Brown, *They Died in the Chair*, 73.

73. *Daily Star*, August 18, 1934, 10.

74. *Freeman's Journal*, August 22, 1934, 1.

75. *Daily Star*, September 5, 1934, 3.

76. *Ibid.*

77. *New York Times*, September 6, 1934, 42.

78. D. Kilgallen, 142.

79. *Daily News*, September 7, 1934, 8.

80. *Daily News*, September 7, 1934, 3.

81. *Daily Star,* September 6, 1934, 1. Of the nine women executed in the State of New York from 1800 to 1934, six of those were executed for killing their husbands.

82. *New York Times*, September 7, 1934, 1.

83. *Ibid.*

84. *Daily Star*, September 6, 1934, 1.

85. Brown, *They Died in the Chair*, 86–87.

86. *Daily News*, September 7, 1934, 3.

87. *New York Times*, September 8, 1934, 30.

88. *Ibid.*

89. Sing Sing Prison Records, Prisoner Activity Log, #89508, September 7, 1934. (New York State Archives, Albany, NY).

90. *New York Times*, November 10, 1934, 4.

91. *New York Times*, March 5, 1935, 16.

92. *New York Times*, May 1, 1935, 14.

93. *New York Sun*, June 25, 1935, 15.

94. *New York Times*, June 20, 1935, 42.

95. *New York Post*, June 28, 1935, 3.

96. Robert G. Elliott, *Agent of Death: The Memoirs of an Executioner* (New York: E. P. Dutton, 1940), 168–169.

97. *New York Sun*, June 27, 1935, 15.

98. Lewis E. Lawes, *Life and Death in Sing Sing* (Doubleday, 1929), 155–157.

99. *New York Times*, June 23, 1935, 24.

100. *Daily News*, June 27, 1935, 3.

101. Brown, *They Died in the Chair*, 88.

102. Elliott, 216–217.

103. *Daily News*, June 27, 1935, 2.

104. *Daily News*, June 28, 1935, 3.

105. Zimmerman, 106.

106. A. Milton Learned, as quoted by Eggleston, 113.

107. Elliott, 218.

108. *New York Post*, June 28, 1935, 3.

109. *Daily News*, June 28, 1935, 3.

110. *New York Sun*, June 28, 1935, 4.

111. *New York Times*, June 28, 1935, 1.

112. *New York Sun*, June 28, 1935, 4.

113. D. Kilgallen, 149.

114. D. Kilgallen, 150.

115. Jay Robert Nash, *Look for the Woman* (New York: M. Evans and Company, 1981), 96.

CHAPTER 5

1. *Borgia* was a reference to Lucretia Borgia, a fourteenth-century Italian noblewoman whose family was notorious for its underhanded methods of achieving political power.

2. Nassau County Police Department, DD #401-Homicide #379, 3.

3. *Yonkers Herald*, July 11, 1923, 1.

4. Wenzel Brown, *They Died in the Chair* (Toronto: Popular Library), 93.

5. When Napoleon was banished to the island of St. Helena in the south Atlantic in 1815, he lived in a private mansion with a number of servants and a few loyal friends. Some years later, Napoleon became seriously ill and his health grew progressively worse. By 1821, he was dead. Doctors said that Napoleon, like his father before him, died from the effects of stomach cancer. Locks of his hair were preserved for posterity before he was buried in France. But when his body was later exhumed and found to be exceptionally well preserved, rumors of his murder began to grow. This is because arsenic was known to be an excellent preservative.

However, despite some intriguing circumstances, it is not feasible to accept intentional poisoning as a cause of Napoleon's death. Too many unanswered questions persist to arrive at this conclusion. From the outset, there is no way to be absolutely certain that hair said to be from the emperor's head was actually his. And even if it was, just the fact that the hair was to test positive does not mean the poison was intentionally administered. Former Chief Medical Examiner of New York Michael Baden once pointed out that a "person can be accidentally poisoned by arsenic through inhalation, absorption through the skin or mucous membranes, skin contact, and ingestion. People have died by breathing arsenic fumes, licking paintbrushes to make a fine point, or wearing inadequate clothing when applying arsenic-based products" (see Baden and Roach). From a legal perspective, there is no conclusive evidence, and there never has been, that Napoleon was murdered by arsenic poisoning.

6. *Daily News*, June 23, 1923, 3.

7. *Ibid.*

8. *Daily News*, June 23, 1923, 3.

9. *Ibid.*

10. *Daily News*, July 12, 1923, 3.

11. *Daily News*, July 14, 1923, 3.

12. Nassau County Police Department, DD #401-Homicide #379.

13. Brown, *They Died in the Chair,* 99.

14. Harold King, Commander of Detective Division of Nassau County Police Department, "The Creighton Case," 87.

15. Statement of Everett Appelgate, October 6, 1935.

16. King, 93.

17. Nassau County Police Department, DD #401-Homicide #379, 113.

18. Statement of Ruth Creighton, October 24, 1935.

19. *Ibid.*

20. *Ibid.*

21. King, 95.

22. King, 2.

23. King, 75.

24. *Ibid.*

25. As indicated in King, 1–5.

26. King, 78.

27. Brown, *They Died in the Chair,* 98.

28. Statement of Mary Frances Creighton, 1:50 a.m., October 9, 1935.

29. King, 87.

30. D. Kilgallen, 195.

31. Brown, *They Died in the Chair,* 100.

32. Statement of Mary Frances Creighton, 1:50 a.m., October 9, 1935.

33. The press wrote Everett's last name as "Applegate," although the correct spelling is actually "Appelgate," as he later noted in court. For the purpose of accuracy, the spelling in quotations of press accounts will appear throughout this text as it was originally written.

34. *Times,* October 9, 1935, 4.

35. *Times,* October 12, 1935, 2.

36. It is interesting to note that if Appelgate had been granted his own murder trial, he almost certainly would not have been convicted. A review of the case file shows that the strongest evidence against him was one statement of Mary Creighton. However, in other statements, Frances said he had nothing to do with the murder, therefore nullifying her original claim that he participated in the murder. Present New York Criminal Procedure Law does not allow a defendant to be convicted solely on the word of a coconspirator.

37. Nassau County Police Department, DD #401-Homicide #379, 302.

38. *Ibid.,* 297.

39. *Sun,* January 15, 1936, 6.

40. *Times,* January 17, 1936, 16.

41. *Herald Tribune,* January 21, 1936, 40.

42. *Sun,* January 21, 1936, 5.

43. Brown, *They Died in the Chair,* 107.

44. D. Kilgallen, from the trial court transcript published in her book, *Murder One.*

45. Brown, W., 108.

46. *Sun*, January 22, 1936, 3.
47. *Sun*, January 23, 1936, 5.
48. As published in the *New York Sun*, January 23, 1936, 3.
49. *Herald Tribune*, January 24, 1936, 18a.
50. *Daily News*, January 24, 1936, 3.
51. *Daily News*, January 24, 1936, 3.
52. Kilgallen, D., 221.
53. *Herald Tribune*, January 24, 1936, 2.
54. Brown, 111.
55. *Times*, January 24, 1936, 1.
56. *Sun*, January 24, 1936, 3.
57. *Ibid.*
58. D. Kilgallen, 228.
59. *Daily News*, January 25, 1936, 4.
60. D. Kilgallen, 229.
61. *Daily News*, January 25, 1936, 3.
62. *Ibid.*
63. *Times*, January 26, 1936, 1.
64. *Daily News*, January 25, 1936, 3.
65. *New York Post*, January 25, 1936, 3.
66. *Herald Tribune*, January 25, 1936, 1.
67. *Daily News*, January 25, 1936, 4.
68. January 25, 1936, 2.
69. *Sun*, January 25, 1936, 1.
70. *Post*, January 25, 1936, 1.
71. *Daily News*, January 25, 1936, 4.
72. *Post,* January 25, 1936, 3.
73. *Times*, January 26, 1936, 23.
74. *Post,* January 25, 1936, 3.
75. *Daily News*, January 25, 1936, 1.
76. *Times*, January 26, 1936, 2.
77. *Times*, July 8, 1936, 1.
78. It wasn't the first time that more than one person was executed for the actions of another. Pursuant to the "felony murder" law in New York State, any participant in a crime that causes the death of another can be charged with murder. This is what happened on January 9 that year, when four young men were executed for being accomplices to a crime. Only one of the suspects had shot and killed the victim, but all were convicted of Murder in the First Degree. This concept was carried to an extreme degree in the notorious Croton Lake Murder in 1911. In that case, six Italian immigrants committed a burglary in a Westchester County home where it was rumored a large amount of cash was hidden in a bedroom. One of the burglars, who acted independently from the other five, stabbed and killed an occupant on the second floor. After five trials, which were completed in two days, all defendants were convicted of the killing and sentenced to death. Despite worldwide pleas for mercy,

five of the men were electrocuted at Sing Sing on the night of August 12, 1912. The leader of the group was executed alone on July 8.

79. *Times*, July 14, 1936, 10.

80. *Herald Tribune*, July 16, 1936, 3.

81. Elliott, 206.

82. *Daily News*, July 17, 1936, 4.

83. *Sun*, July 17, 1936, 3.

84. *Herald Tribune*, July 17, 1936, 3.

85. *New York Post*, July 18, 1936, 5.

86. Elliott, 209.

87. Elliott, 210.

88. *Daily News*, July 17, 1936, 4.

89. *Ibid.*

90. *Daily News*, July 17, 1936, 4.

91. Elliott, 211.

CHAPTER 6

1. See Shipman, Chapter 9, "20th Century Black Defendants," 159.

2. On the morning of July 5, 1829, Cashiere and another condemned prisoner named Richard Johnson were taken from the city jail and whisked off to the East River docks where several thousand people had already gathered, "eager to witness the dying struggles of two of their fellow human beings" (Burrows and Wallace, 507). When the steamboat left the crowded dock, the massive crowd piled onto hundreds of canoes, skiffs, and boats that carried them over to Blackwell's Island, where the executions were to take place. Two of the vessels collided in the fast current and several people drowned. However, the executions went forward and Catherine Cashiere assumed her unenviable place in history as the only black female executed in New York during the nineteenth century.

3. Francel remained on the job for nearly fourteen years. He retired in 1953 and was replaced by a Columbia County Deputy Sheriff named Dow B. Hover. Like some of his predecessors, Hover took special care to prevent the media from learning his name or taking his photo. He habitually changed the license plate on his car whenever he drove to Sing Sing for an execution. His efforts were so successful that even in the small upstate town where he lived his entire life, no one knew that he was New York's official executioner.

4. *Niagara Falls Gazette*, December 9, 1943, 1.

5. *Ibid.*

6. *Gazette*, December 9, 1943, 6.

7. *Gazette*, December 11, 1943, 1.

8. *Buffalo Evening News*, December 11, 1943, 1.

9. Helen Fowler, letter to Acting Governor Hanley, November 16, 1944.

10. *Buffalo Evening News*, February 17, 1944, 31.

11. *Gazette*, December 17, 1943, 1.

12. Hearn, 218.

13. *Ibid.*

14. *Indictment*, January 6, 1944, Niagara County Court.

15. *Request for Separate Trial*, January 14, 1944, Niagara County Court.

16. *Ibid.*

17. Marsh, *People's Response*, January 17, 1944, Niagara County Court.

18. *Motion for Change of Venue*, January 24, 1944, Niagara County Court.

19. John Marsh, *Affidavit Opposing Motion of Defense*, January 25, 1944, Niagara County Court.

20. *Gazette*, February 5, 1944, 1.

21. Wenzell Brown, *They Died in the Chair*, 124.

22. *Gazette*, February 9, 1944, 18.

23. *Ibid.*

24. *Ibid.*

25. Brown, *They Died in the Chair*, 132.

26. *Buffalo Courier*, February 10, 1944, 22.

27. Brown, *They Died in the Chair*, 135.

28. *Buffalo Courier*, February 10, 1944, 22.

29. *Gazette*, February 11, 1944, 22.

30. Brown, *They Died in the Chair*, 141.

31. *Gazette*, February 11, 1944, 1.

32. *Ibid.*

33. *Motion for New Trial*, August 22, 1944, Niagara County Court.

34. Hinckley, 3.

35. *Buffalo Evening News*, February 12, 1944, 4.

36. *Times*, February 22, 1944, 25.

37. Lepke was born as Louis Bookhouse, the son of poor Jewish immigrants. He learned at a very early age that he could make money by stealing. He dropped out of school by the age of eleven to rob pushcart vendors along Canal Street and the Bowery. Using a sense of ruthlessness that knew no equal, Lepke soon had others working for him, and he took a cut of every theft. He organized a protection racket in which every pushcart operator had to pay him or suffer the consequences, which meant robbery, destruction, or murder. As his power grew, Lepke branched out into organized labor and soon learned to control the unions by intimidation and force. He single-handedly took over the influential cutter's union that was essential to the clothing industry in New York. From that base of power, Lepke built a criminal empire during the 1930s that rivaled and eventually surpassed that of Chicago's Alphonse Capone. It was reported that Lepke netted more than $50 million in one year alone, and all of it—the unions, the gambling saloons, and extortion schemes—was built on a river of blood, compliments of Murder Inc. This organization of paid hit men was responsible for hundreds of murders in New York City, Chicago, and Philadelphia. Staffed by sadistic, remorseless killers like Harry "Pittsburgh Phil" Strauss, "Happy" Malone, and Abe "Kid Twist" Reles, Murder Inc. was the enforcement arm of organized crime for decades, financed by Lepke's millions.

But more than anything else, the incredible rise to power of an impoverished, uneducated child of immigrants was a testament to the possibilities of what could be accomplished by those whose fierce ambition knew no bounds. For many young urban men of that generation, trapped in the cycle of poverty and despair, it was the only path to success.

38. *Times*, March 5, 1944, 1.
39. Earl Brydges and Louis E. Rotella, *Appeals of Helen Fowler*, August 22, 1944, 3.
40. *Ibid.*
41. *Ibid.*, 5.
42. Marsh, 2.
43. *Ibid.*
44. Hinckley, 4.
45. *Citizen Register*, November 16, 1944, 4.
46. Fowler letter, November 16, 1944.
47. *Certificate of Execution*, November 16, 1944, Condemned Files, State Archives, Albany, NY.
48. *Gazette*, November 17, 1944, 1.
49. *Times*, November 17, 1944, 13.
50. *Ibid.*
51. Brown, *They Died in the Chair*, 144.
52. Staba, 1.
53. Fowler letter dated November 16, 1944.

CHAPTER 7

1. *Daily News*, July 26, 1949, 36.
2. *Daily News*, July 26, 1949, 2X.
3. Wenzell Brown, *They Died in the Chair* (Toronto: Popular Library, 1958), 19.
4. *Daily News*, July 26, 1949, 36.
5. *Ibid.*
6. Brown, *They Died in the Chair*, 33.
7. *Daily News*, July 26, 1949, 4.
8. Brown, *They Died in the Chair*, 147.
9. Brown, *They Died in the Chair*, 50.
10. *Ibid.*, 77.
11. Buck, 17.
12. *Ibid.*
13. *Daily News*, July 26, 1949, 36.
14. *Times*, March 2, 1949, 36.
15. *Times*, March 2, 1949, 29.
16. *Daily News*, July 29, 1949, 2X.
17. *Times*, March 3, 1949, 28.
18. *Ibid.*
19. Kluger, 432.

20. *Times*, March 5, 1949, 28.
21. *Times*, March 9, 1949, 28.
22. *Ibid.*
23. *Times*, March 12, 1949, 26.
24. Brown, *They Died in the Chair*, 168.
25. *Daily News*, June 28, 1949, 3.
26. *Times*, June 28, 1949, 5.
27. *Ibid.*
28. *Daily News*, June 29, 1949, 3.
29. Although the Supreme Court decision in *Miranda v. Arizona* did not occur until 1966, police were well aware that constitutional rights had to be explained to suspects who were questioned in reference to criminal behavior. The procedure was understood by law enforcement professionals who had been advising suspects of these protections since the nineteenth century. Absent was any unified standard as to how and when these rights should be given. These standards were the issue addressed by the Earl Warren Supreme Court, which delivered a rather lengthy decision on five different cases that were decided as one under the *Miranda* title. As for Ernesto Miranda, the twenty-three-year-old rapist and kidnapper whose legal appeal changed the course of American justice, he was later stabbed and killed during a bar fight in Phoenix, Arizona, in 1976.
30. *Daily News*, June 30, 1949, X2
31. *Post,* July 8, 1949, 2.
32. *Daily News*, July 8, 1949, 3.
33. *Post*, July 12, 1949, 5.
34. *Herald Tribune*, July 13, 1949, 1.
35. *Daily News*, July 13, 1949, 10.
36. *Daily News*, July 22, 1949, 4.
37. *Daily News*, July 21, 1949, 8.
38. *Times*, July 14, 1949, 22.
39. *Daily News*, July 26, 1949, 36.
40. *Post*, July 27, 1949, 3.
41. *Ibid.*
42. *Daily News*, July 27, 1949, 3.
43. *Daily News*, July 28, 1949, 3.
44. *Ibid.*
45. *Post*, July 29, 1949, 3.
46. *Times*, July 28, 1949, 44.
47. *Daily News*, July 28, 1949, 3.
48. *Post*, July 29, 1949, 3.
49. *Daily News*, July 29, 1949, 4.
50. *Times*, July 29, 1949, 23.
51. *Post*, July 26, 1949, 3.
52. *Daily News*, July 30, 1949, 4.
53. *Daily News*, July 26, 1949, 36.

54. *Post*, August 10, 1949, 3.

55. *Times*, August 18, 1949, 22.

56. *Daily News*, August 18, 1949, 3.

57. *Post*, August 18, 1949, 1.

58. *Daily News*, August 19, 1949, 3.

59. *Times*, August 23, 1949, 24.

60. According to the prison visitor's log, Martha's two children never visited her during her entire stay on Death Row.

61. Beck letter, September 28, 1950.

62. Beck letter, September 22, 1950.

63. Fernandez letter, February 6, 1951.

64. September 28, 1950.

65. *People v. Fernandez* et al., July 11, 1950.

66. *Ibid.*

67. *Ibid.*

68. *Ibid.*

69. March 8, 1951, 2.

70. Beck, letter dated March 8, 1951.

71. *Citizen Register*, March 9, 1951, 3.

72. *Ibid.*

73. *Ibid.*

74. As quoted in Peary, 140.

75. *Herald Tribune*, March 9, 1951, 1.

CHAPTER 8

1. On the very night that the Rosenbergs were executed, 10,000 supporters gathered in mid-town Manhattan to show support. The controversy over their guilt or innocence continues to this day.

2. Streib, 2.

3. Timothy V. Kaufman-Osborn, "Gender and the Death Penalty."

4. Streib, 3.

5. *Daily News*, May 10, 1927, 3.

6. *Herald-Tribune*, May 11, 1927, 3.

7. *The Freeman's Journal*, September 19, 1934, 12.

8. Shipman, 77.

9. *People v. Fernandez*, 338.

10. Friedman, 420.

11. Myers, 371

12. See Chapter 10, "The Criminal Trial," in Gaines, Kaune, and Miller, *Criminal Justice in Action* (2000) for an excellent discussion on evidence, jury selection, and testimony during criminal trials.

13. Myers, 375.

14. Squire, 70–71.

15. Beck, letter of September 28, 1950.

16. *New York Times*, December 6, 1911, 5. All five defendants in those trials were found guilty and later executed at Sing Sing on the same day, August 12, 1912.

17. See Cheatwood, 165–181.

18. Squire, *Observations*, 7.

19. Siegel, 137.

20. Smith was only one of three to be executed that year in Oklahoma. Wanda Jean Allen became the first black woman executed since 1954 and Marilyn Kay Plantz was executed later that same year for the murder of her husband. All received lethal injection.

21. Brydges and Rotella, 2.

22. Shipman, 306.

Bibliography

BOOKS AND ARTICLES

"Act on Execution Picture." *New York Times,* February 22, 1928.

Baden, Michael, and Marion Roach. *Dead Reckoning: The New Science of Catching Killers.* New York: Simon and Schuster, 2001.

Beck, Martha. Letters from Death Row: September 1, 1950 to March 8, 1951. New York State Archives, Albany, NY.

Belton, John. *American Cinema/American Culture.* New York: McGraw-Hill, 1994.

Benedict, Helen. *Virgin or Vamp: How the Press Covers Sex Crimes.* New York: Oxford University Press, 1992.

Blumenthal, Ralph. *Miracle at Sing Sing: How One Man Transformed the Lives of America's Most Dangerous Prisoners.* New York: St. Martin's Press, 2004.

Britten, Loretta, and Paul Mathless, eds. *Our American Century: The Jazz Age, The 20s.* Alexandria, VA: Time-Life Books, 1998.

Brown, Wenzell. *They Died in the Chair.* Toronto: Popular Library, 1958.

———. *Introduction to Murder: The Unpublished Facts Behind the Notorious Lonely Hearts Killers Martha Beck and Raymond Fernandez.* New York: Greenberg, 1952.

Brydges, Earl, and Louis E. Rotella. Appeals of Helen Fowler, August 22, 1944. Niagara County Court, Lockport, NY.

Burrows, Edwin G, and Mike Wallace. *Gotham: A History of New York City to 1898.* New York: Oxford University Press, 1999.

Cain, James M. *The Postman Always Rings Twice: Double Indemnity, Mildred Pierce, and Selected Stories.* New York: Alfred A. Knopf, 2003.

"Calls Death Picture Fake." *New York Times,* January 14, 1928.

Cheatwood, Derral. "Capital Punishment and the Deterrence of Violent Crime in Comparable Counties." *Criminal Justice Review* (1993): 165–181.

Coo, Eva. Statement of June 18, 1934, Oneonta Police Department. From New York Historical Association, Cooperstown, NY.

Crime and Punishment: The Illustrated Crime Encyclopedia. Westport, CT: H. S. Stuttman, Inc., 1994.

Dolan, Frank. "Ruth and Judd Die in Chair." *New York Daily News.* January 13, 1928.

Drimmer, Frederick. *Until You Are Dead . . . The Book of Executions in America.* New York: Pinnacle Books, 1990.

Eggleston, Niles. *Eva Coo, Murderess.* Utica, NY: North County Books, 1997.

Elliott, Robert G. *Agent of Death: The Memoirs of an Executioner.* New York: E. P. Dutton & Co., Inc., 1940.

Fernandez, Ramon. Letters from Death Row: September 1, 1950, to March 8, 1951. New York State Archives, Albany, NY.

Fowler, Helen. Letter to Acting Governor J. Hanley. November 16, 1944. New York State Archives, Albany, NY.

Friedman, Lawrence M. *Crime and Punishment in American History.* New York: BasicBooks, 1993.

Gaines, Larry K., Michael Kaune, and Roger LeRoy Miller. *Criminal Justice in Action.* Belmont, CA: Wadsworth, 2000.

Gordon, Lois, and Alan Gordon. *American Chronicle: Year by Year Through the Twentieth Century.* New Haven, CT: Yale University Press, 1999.

Hearn, Daniel Allen. *Legal Executions in New York State, 1639–1963.* Jefferson, NC: McFarland and Co., 1997.

Hinckley, A. B. Motion for New Trial Decision, September 7, 1944. Niagara County Court, Lockport, NY.

Jones, Ann. *Women Who Kill.* Boston: Beacon Press, 1996.

Jones, Richard Glyn, ed. *Women Who Kill.* New York: Carroll & Graf Publishers, 2002.

Katz, Ephraim. *The Film Encyclopedia.* 3rd ed. New York: Harper Perennial, 1998.

Kaufman-Osborn, Timothy V. "Gender and the Death Penalty." *Signs* (Summer 1999): 1097–1102.

Kelleher, Michael D., and C. L. Kelleher. *Murder Most Rare: The Female Serial Killer.* New York: Dell Publishing, 1998.

Kilgallen, Dorothy. *Murder One.* New York: Random House, 1967.

Kilgallen, James L. "Mrs. Snyder, Gray Go to Deaths with Prayers on Lips." *Ossining Citizen Sentinel.* January 13, 1928.

King, Harold. "The Creighton Case," as told to Alan Hynd. Unpublished manuscript, 1936.

Kluger, Richard. *The Paper: The Life and Death of the New York Herald Tribune.* New York: Alfred A. Knopf, 1986.

Kobler, John. *The Trial of Ruth Snyder and Judd Gray.* New York: Doubleday, Doran & Company, Inc., 1938.

Kuhn, Irene. "Judd's Story Electrifies Court." *New York Daily Mirror.* May 5, 1927.

Lawes, Lewis E. *Life and Death in Sing Sing*. New York: Garden City Publishing Company, 1928.

————. *Twenty Thousand Years in Sing Sing*. New York: Ray Long & Richard Smith, 1932.

Lehman, Herbert H. *Public Papers of Herbert H. Lehman, Forty-Ninth Governor of the State of New York, 1933–1942*. New York: J. B. Lyon Co., 1942.

Leitch, Thomas. *Crime Films*. New York: Cambridge University Press, 2002.

Margolin, Leslie. *Murderess!* New York: Pinnacle Books, 1999.

Marsh, John S. Affidavit Against a New Trial, September 2, 1944. Niagara County Court, Lockport, NY.

Metzger, Th. *Blood and Volts: Edison, Tesla, and the Electric Chair*. New York: Autonomedia, 1996.

McLuhan, Marshall. *Understanding Media: The Extensions of Man*. Cambridge, MA: MIT Press, 1997.

"Mrs. Snyder Thought She Could Talk Gray Out of the Murder." *New York Times*, May 3, 1927.

Mumby, Jonathan. *Public Enemies, Public Heroes*. Chicago: University of Chicago Press, 1999.

Myers, David G. *Social Psychology*. New York: McGraw-Hill, 1996.

Nash, Jay Robert. *Look for the Woman*. New York: M. Evans and Company, 1981.

Nassau County Police Department, Case Reports: DD # 401 Homicide # 279, 1935.

O'Brian, Jack. "Mrs. Snyder and Gray Confess." *New York Daily News*, March 24, 1927.

Pearson, Patricia. *When She Was Bad: How and Why Women Get Away with Murder*. New York: Penguin Group, 1998.

Peary, Danny. *Cult Movies: The Classics, the Sleepers, the Weird, and the Wonderful*. New York: Dell Publishing Co., 1982.

People v. Fernandez et al., 301 NY 302, 93 N.E. 2d 859. Court of Appeals of New York, July 11, 1950.

Proper, Diana. "The Incomprehensible Crime of Leopold and Loeb: 'Just an Experiment.'" *Famous American Crimes and Trials;* Volume 3: 1913–1959. Westport, CT: Praeger, 2004.

Ramey, Jessie. "The Bloody Blonde and the Marble Woman: Gender and Power in the Case of Ruth Snyder." *Journal of Social History* (Spring 2004): 625–650.

Robinson, Grace. "Mrs. Snyder and Gray Indicted For Murder." *New York Daily News*, March 24, 1927.

Shadoian, Jack. *Dreams and Dead Ends: The American Gangster Film*. New York: Oxford University Press, 2003.

Shipman, Marlin. *The Penalty Is Death: U.S. Newspaper Coverage of Women's Executions*. Columbia, MO: University of Missouri Press, 2002.

Sing Sing Prison Records, Prisoner Activity Log, # 89508. September 7, 1934. New York State Archives, Albany, NY.

"Slayers Indicted; Snyder Case Trial Sought for April 4." *New York Times*, March 24, 1927.

Sloan, Bill. *I Watched a Wild Hog Eat My Baby! A Colorful History of the Tabloids and Their Cultural Impact.* Amherst, NY: Prometheus Books, 2001.

Squire, Amos O. *Observations Made at Electrocutions of 114 Men at Sing Sing Prison.* Transcript of seminar given to American Physicians Association. Boston: September 17, 1923.

————. *Sing Sing Doctor, Formerly Chief Physician of Sing Sing Prison, Now Medical Examiner of Westchester County.* Garden City, NY: Doubleday, Doran & Company, Inc., 1935.

Staba, David. "Falls Murder Case Presents Contrast to Northrup Verdict." *Niagara Falls Reporter.* December 4, 2001 (available at http://www.niagarafallsreporter.com/fowler.html).

Streib, Victor L. "Gendering the Death Penalty: Countering Sex Bias in a Masculine Sanctuary." *Ohio State Law Journal* (available at http://moritzlaw.osu.edu/lawjournal/issues/volume63/number1/streib.pdf).

"Wife Betrays Paramour as Murderer of Snyder and He Then Confesses." *New York Times,* March 22, 1927.

Zimmerman, Isidore, with Francis Bond. *Punishment without Crime.* New York: Clarkson N. Potter, Inc., 1964.

NEWSPAPERS

Albany Evening News
Buffalo Evening News
Buffalo Courier
Daily Star (Oneonta, NY)
Freeman's Journal (Cooperstown, NY)
New York Daily Mirror
New York Daily News
New York Herald Tribune
New York Post
New York Sun
New York Times
Niagara Falls Reporter
Niagara Gazette
Ossining Citizen Register
Ossining Citizen Sentinel
Poughkeepsie Eagle News
Record (Troy, NY)
Times-Union (Albany, NY)
Yonkers Herald

Index

About the Author

MARK GADO was a police detective in New York for over twenty-five years. His investigative work included murder, death cases, felony assaults, and sexual offenses, as well as hundreds of appearances in a courtroom setting. He was a federal agent with the DEA from 1999 to 2001 and currently writes on criminal justice issues and true crime for Court TV's *Crime Library*. He is the author of *Killer Priest* (Praeger, 2006) and a contributor to *Famous American Crimes and Trials* (Praeger, 2005).